Discourse, War and Terrorism

Discourse Approaches to Politics, Society and Culture

The series includes contributions that investigate political, social and cultural processes from a linguistic/discourse-analytic point of view. The aim is to publish monographs and edited volumes which combine language-based approaches with disciplines concerned essentially with human interaction — disciplines such as political science, international relations, social psychology, social anthropology, sociology, economics, and gender studies.

The book series complements the *Journal of Language and Politics*, edited by Ruth Wodak and Paul Chilton.

General editors

Ruth Wodak and Greg Myers
University of Lancaster

Editorial address: Ruth Wodak
Bowland College, Department of Linguistics and Modern English Language
University of Lancaster, Lancaster LA1 4YT, UK
r.wodak@lancaster.ac.uk and g.meyers@lancaster.ac.uk

Advisory board

Jan Blommaert
University of Ghent

Paul Chilton
University of East Anglia

Teun A. van Dijk
Universitat Pompeu Fabra, Barcelona

Mikhail V. Ilyin
Polis, Moscow

Andreas H. Jucker
University of Zurich

George Lakoff
University of California at Berkeley

J.R. Martin
University of Sydney

Luisa Martín Rojo
Universidad Autonoma de Madrid

Jacob L. Mey
University of Southern Denmark

Christina Schäffner
Aston University

Volume 24

Discourse, War and Terrorism
Edited by Adam Hodges and Chad Nilep

 **University of Hertfordshire**

College Lane, Hatfield, Herts AL10 9AB

Learning and Information Services

For renewal of Standard and One Week Loans,
please visit the website: **http://www.voyager.herts.ac.uk**

This item must be returned or the loan renewed by the due date.
The University reserves the right to recall items from loan at any time.
A fine will be charged for the late return of items.

Discourse, War and Terrorism

Edited by

Adam Hodges
Chad Nilep
University of Colorado

John Benjamins Publishing Company
Amsterdam/Philadelphia

™ The paper used in this publication meets the minimum requirements
of American National Standard for Information Sciences – Permanence
of Paper for Printed Library Materials, ANSI z39.48-1984.

Library of Congress Cataloging-in-Publication Data

Discourse, war and terrorism / edited by Adam Hodges and Chad Nilep.
        p.   cm. (Discourse Approaches to Politics, Society and Culture, ISSN
1569-9463 ; v. 24)
        "The book series complements the Journal of Language and Politics, edited
by Ruth Wodak and Paul Chilton."
Includes bibliographical references and indexes.
        1. September 11 Terrorist Attacks, 2001. 2. War on Terrorism, 2001-
        3. Critical discourse analysis. I. Hodges, Adam. II. Nilep, Chad. III. Journal
of language and politics.

        HV6432.7.D58 2007
909.83'1--dc22   2007003852
ISBN 978 90 272 2714 0 (Hb; alk. paper)

John Benjamins Publishing Co. · P.O. Box 36224 · 1020 ME Amsterdam · The Netherlands
John Benjamins North America · P.O. Box 27519 · Philadelphia PA 19118-0519 · USA

Table of contents

Acknowledgements

The impetus for this volume arose out of a panel organized for the annual meeting of the American Anthropological Association (AAA) in 2004. We would like to thank all of the original members of that panel, including the discussants, Paul Chilton and Monica Heller, for taking part in an exchange of ideas that formed the seed of this project. In an unusual turn of events, a last minute date and venue change for that meeting left the panelists with plane tickets to San Francisco but without a place to present their papers. We are grateful to Leanne Hinton, the Society for Linguistic Anthropology, and the Linguistics Department at the University of California-Berkeley for providing an alternative forum where we could discuss our work. We owe special thanks to Kira Hall for all of her diligent mentoring and encouragement over the years. We would also like to extend gratitude to our colleagues at the University of Colorado for providing a stimulating intellectual environment conducive to discussing, debating and developing ideas.

Author affiliations

Annette Becker, Johann Wolfgang Goethe University of Frankfurt am Main, Germany

Aomar Boum, Portland State University, USA

Patricia Dunmire, Kent State University, USA

Karmen Erjavec, University of Ljubljana, Slovenia

Adam Hodges, University of Colorado, USA

Annita Lazar, Lancaster University, UK; Nanyang Technological University, Singapore

Michelle M. Lazar, National University of Singapore

Katherine Lemons, University of California at Berkeley, USA

David Machin, University of Leicester, UK

Chad Nilep, University of Colorado, USA

Becky Schulthies, University of Arizona, USA

Matteo Stocchetti, Arcada University of Applied Sciences, Finland

Maija Stenvall, University of Helsinki, Finland

Greg Stoltz, University of Arizona, USA

Zala Volcic, University of Queensland, Australia

CHAPTER 1

Introduction

Discourse, war and terrorism

Adam Hodges and Chad Nilep

9/11 and the emergence of the "war on terror" discourse

The events of September 11, 2001 produced an abundance of reactions. The events of that day, as well as responses to them, have been discussed, debated, and critically considered by a range of scholars. Many specific treatments of 9/11 have emerged from the fields of political and cultural studies, where the critical lens has focused on the events, their history or consequences. James F. Hoge, Jr. and Gideon Rose (2001), for example, provide a collection of essays that explore the historical causes and political consequences of 9/11 in *How Did This Happen? Terrorism and the New War*. Other scholars have focused on the ends of al Qaeda and the 9/11 hijackers in an attempt to unravel Osama bin Laden's motivations for the attacks on the World Trade Center. Michael Doran (2001) argues that the underlying goal was not war with the United States, but rather to strengthen bin Laden's brand of radical Islam and to drive a wedge between Muslim citizens and pro-western governments in the Middle East. Doran suggests that the US response has only helped to inflame an Islamic civil war sought by bin Laden. In other treatments, scholars like Noam Chomsky (2001) have focused more directly on American foreign policy. In *9/11*, Chomsky attempts to provide a serious response to the question of "why" the events happened by taking into account America's past foreign policy. The contributors in Daniel J. Sherman and Terry Nardin's (2006) *Terror, Culture, Politics: Rethinking 9/11* examine not policy but cultural patterns – in art, literature, the media, law, etc. – that have shaped responses to 9/11. Other scholars have examined the role of neo-conservative ideology in the shaping of American reactions to 9/11. For example, Sut Jhally and Jeremy Earp (2004) document how the events of 9/11 were used by neo-conservative forces within the Bush administration to realize unrelated (but conveniently linked) foreign policy objectives – particularly, the war in Iraq. David Harvey (2005) explores the geopolitical and economic underpinnings of the neo-conservative ideology that underlies the Bush administration's vision for the world.

Among the various journal articles, collected volumes and monographs that deal with 9/11, some have turned an eye toward language. Richard Jackson (2005), for example, dissects the language used to manipulate public anxiety over the attacks as part of a broader discussion on ethical values and democratic participation. John Collins and Ross Glover (2002) provide "a user's guide" to the "war on terror" with a collection of essays that cover key terms such as "freedom", "justice" and "terrorism." In a more general examination of language and war, Mirjana N. Dedaić and Daniel N. Nelson's (2003) volume, *At War with Words*, examines both the language associated with war and the wars fought over language. In addition, journals such as *Discourse and Society* (Martin and Edwards 2004) and the *Journal of Language and Politics* (Chouliaraki 2005) have released special issues dealing with 9/11 and the Iraq War.

While much of the academic literature related to 9/11 has focused on the events themselves, this volume attempts to build upon those scholarly contributions noted above that have placed language under the critical lens. As such, we focus directly on the discourse generated in the aftermath of 9/11. As scholars working within the area of language and society have long recognized, discourse does more than merely reflect events that take place in the world; discourse interprets those events, formulates understandings, and constitutes their sociopolitical reality. The 9/11 Commission, the non-partisan body formed in the United States to investigate and write the official narrative of the events, states at the beginning of its Executive Summary, "At 8:46 on the morning of September 11, 2001, the United States became a nation transformed" (NC 2004: 1). Yet any transformation that has taken place – and one could certainly argue that various types of transformations have occurred – was affected through the use of language. Both the immediate reactions to events unfolding on that day, and understandings that have since come about are realized through discourse and human interaction. Language is used to create meanings; and the process of meaning making is inherently political in that it is imbued with relations of power that come together to maneuver, contest and negotiate the meanings at stake.

In response to events like those of 9/11, language formulates the questions and frames the responses. The initial question of "why?" is a cry for meaning to be made out of the devastation. Did it happen because "they hate our freedom,"[1] or was it "blowback"[2] for America's past imperial actions, an unintended consequence of the world's sole superpower wielding its hegemony in ways that have sewn disdain overseas? Language, entwined with power, frames and positions the response.

Following the initial "why" come a series of "who" and "what" questions. What was attacked on 9/11? We require an answer beyond the obvious physical buildings that were felled. Were the buildings symbols of "democracy" or "civilization"? Were they symbols of "military might" or "economic power"? The answers raise new understandings and new questions: Was it "an unprovoked attack on democracy," as President George W. Bush has proclaimed (e.g. 2006)? Or was it that "they attacked American foreign policy," as political scientist Chalmers Johnson (2001) has argued? And who are "they" anyway? Who is it that attacked "us"? In response to these questions, we want more than just a list of names; we want to know what the attackers represent and how we should react to them. This in turn requires us to decide who "we" are, since the negotiation of identities involves an intersubjective process of meaning making. Questions of personal, national, and other identities are deeply implicated. All of this is achieved through language use; and this is where we place the focus in this volume in an effort to understand the way that discourse shapes and is shaped by sociopolitical activity in response to 9/11, war and terrorism.

Out of the tragedy of 9/11 arose the rhetoric of the "war on terror," a lens through which US foreign policy and domestic politics have been refracted, bent and one might even say distorted for the better part of the Bush administration's tenure. The "war on terror" discourse constrains and shapes public discussion and debate within the US and around the world as social actors in Europe, Asia, the Middle East and elsewhere evoke its language to explain, react to, justify or understand a broad range of political, economic and social phenomena. The aim of the papers collected here is to explore the discursive production of identities, ideologies, and collective understandings in response to 9/11 within the United States and around the world. At issue are how enemies are defined and identified, how political leaders and citizens react, and how members of societies understand their position in the world in relation to terrorism.

Critical approaches to discourse in politics, society and culture

The contributors to this volume represent a consolidation of diverse sub-fields involved in the critical study of language, coming from backgrounds in sociocultural linguistics, as well as communication, media, cultural and political studies. A critical perspective and a focus on discourses of war and terrorism in light of 9/11 provide the central organizing principle shared among all the chapters.

By "critical", we mean to imply a broad understanding of critical scholarship. On a general level, such scholarship is characterized by careful analysis of empirical data. Moreover, it entails a certain amount of distance from the data in order to examine the issues from a wide, considered perspective. Yet critical scholarship does not pretend to operate from an Archimedean point outside the social world it studies. Critical scholarship recognizes that such a view from nowhere does not exist, and that analysts are also participants in the world under study. Our subject positions as scholars must therefore be taken into account. In addition, critical scholarship is motivated not only to study society for what it is, but for what it might become. In this way, critical scholarship desires to expose existing wrongs in society in an effort to shape a better world. Critical approaches, therefore, take a keen interest in understanding the workings of power in an effort to counter abuses of power.

The contributions to this volume derive from a diverse tradition of critical study across the social sciences. Scholars in a vast array of disciplines can be seen to draw generally on the tradition of critical theory (Horkheimer 1972). While its outlines are too broad to detail in a brief introduction, this "critical pool" also includes significant contributions from the fields of linguistic anthropology and sociolinguistics, among others.[3] Many of the chapters in this volume fall within the school known as Critical Discourse Analysis (CDA).[4] CDA is not so much a single theory or set of methods as an orientation to the study of *language in use* – that is, language embedded within its social context, or language "as a form of 'social practice'" (Fairclough and Wodak 1997: 258). CDA and its precursor, Critical Linguistics (CL) (Fowler et al. 1979), echo the Bakhtinian (1981, 1986) idea that language is never neutral. Language use – and the use of all social signs – emerges from sociocultural interaction, motivated by the struggles among different groups (cf. Maybin 2001: 65). The emphasis on discourse also reflects a broader focus on "all forms of meaningful semiotic human activity seen in connection with social, cultural, and historical patterns and developments of use" (Blommaert 2005: 3, cf. Martin and Wodak 2003: 4). This broad focus on semiotics is apparent in the analysis of war photography (Machin, chapter 7) in addition to the various forms of speech and text examined elsewhere in this volume.

While the contributions share a critical focus, their specific theoretical frameworks and methodologies vary considerably. In part, this stems from the diversity of approaches adopted by critical discourse analysts; in addition, it reflects an aim to bring together various critical tools in order to enhance our understanding of these theories and methods as complementary rather than competing. The volume attempts to strengthen an interdisciplinary approach to language and power that may lead to a more meaningful interpretation of social processes, such as the formation of identities and ideologies in political and media discourses in the aftermath of events like 9/11. Let us briefly highlight some of the key frameworks found in the chapters.

Theoretical frameworks

Much work done within Critical Linguistics and Critical Discourse Analysis has adopted the framework of Systemic Functional Linguistics (SFL), originally developed by M.A.K. Halliday (1985, inter alia). According to J.R. Martin and Ruth Wodak (2003), "Halliday's critical contribution has been to develop theory for building grammars of meaning which can then be used to track the materialization of social activity in discourse" (3). SFL theory centers on language function, and outlines three interdependent functions of language: the ideational, interpersonal and textual. These functions are concerned with the propositional content (i.e. referential meaning), the relationships among speakers, and the structure of the message, respectively. The unit of analysis in SFL is the text – itself a form of social action – and the lexico-grammar is modeled with the text in mind, taking into account the three levels of meaning represented by the three analytical functions described above (cf. Kress 1995, Halliday 1978). Annita Lazar and Michelle Lazar (chapter 3), David Machin (chapter 7), Annette Becker (chapter 9), and Maija Stenvall (chapter 11) each use SFL to varying degrees in their analyses. Both Becker and Stenvall adopt the Appraisal framework, an extension of SFL. The Appraisal framework provides a model for isolating the linguistic resources involved in the creation of evaluations, attitudes and emotions (Martin 1997).

From cognitive linguistics, the study of metaphor (Lakoff and Johnson 1980, Lakoff and Turner 1989) has provided valuable contributions to the analysis of political discourse (Chilton 1996, Chilton and Lakoff 1995). The contemporary theory of metaphor outlined by George Lakoff (1993) forwards the notion that metaphor is a cognitive phenomenon. Rather than an occasional figurative device, Lakoff shows us that language as a whole is largely metaphorical. Metaphors make use of a *source domain* as a basis of comparison for a *target domain*, and rely on semantic *frames* (Fillmore 1982, 1985), or areas of experience, that allow us to draw correspondences between source and target. The most common metaphor post-9/11, of course, is that of a "war on terror." Thus we hear ample rhetoric filled with lexical correspondences associated with a war frame for describing 9/11 and the struggle against terrorism more broadly (Lakoff 2001, Hodges 2004). Metaphors such as the "war on terror" allow us to draw upon previous areas of experience in order to understand new events and phenomena. Consequently, as Norman Fairclough (1989) notes, "Different metaphors imply different ways of dealing with things" (120). Matteo Stocchetti (chapter 12) makes use of these ideas in his discussion of the "crusade metaphor." In addition, Annita Lazar and Michelle Lazar examine metaphors in their analysis of rhetoric used by current and previous US administrations.

Multimodal analysis, pioneered by critical linguists (Kress and van Leeuwen 2001, inter alia), provides an approach to the analysis of social actors that examines how they are represented both linguistically (van Leeuwen 1996) and visually (van Leeuwen 2000, Machin and van Leeuwen 2005). David Machin adopts this approach in order to examine how soldiers, enemies and civilians are positioned for the viewer in photographs provided by commercial image banks for various media outlets.

Contributors to this volume also employ methods drawn from the field of linguistic anthropology. An important element of anthropological investigation – one shared by researchers in communication and media studies – is ethnography. Zala Volcic and Karmen Erjavec (chapter 10) employ ethnographic methods in their collection of interviews with young Serbian intellectuals to illustrate the way these intellectuals have appropriated the "war on terror" discourse to characterize their own position in the recent conflicts of their region.

Of importance for Becky Schulthies and Aomar Boum (chapter 8) are the Bakhtinian ideas of dialogism, heteroglossia and entexualization. In the dialogic emergence of culture (Tedlock and Mannheim 1995), discourse emerges in a particular socio-historical context where participants appropriate, challenge, and negotiate meanings (Bakhtin 1981: 428). This process of entexualization is central to Schulthies and Boum's analysis of the way programs on Al-Jazeera recontextualize Bush administration rhetoric. We also see this interdiscursivity (Fairclough 1992) at play in Zala Volcic and Karmen Erjavec's examination of the appropriation of the "war on terror" language by young Serbs.

As these processes unfold, we see the emergence of identities. Mary Bucholtz and Kira Hall's (2004) *tactics of intersubjectivity* provide a model taken up by Adam Hodges (chapter 4) to investigate the construction of sociopolitical identities. Bucholtz and Hall echo Pierre Bourdieu (1978, 1984; see also de Certeau 1984, inter alia) in the notion that social differences are discursively constructed rather than waiting to be found. We see this process of differentiation (Wodak 1996) in the construction of identities throughout the book. Zala Volcic and Karmen Erjavec bring a perspective from cultural and media studies to the study of identity as they explore binary positions in terms of Stuart Hall's (1989) "discourse of difference."

The study of narrative has been taken up by various researchers, many with a focus on personal narratives – that is, narratives told by individuals about personal experiences (e.g. Ochs and Capps 2001, Riessman 1993, Linde 1993). Adam Hodges extends narrative approaches (Bruner 1991, Labov 1972, Labov and Waletsky 1967) to the study of public political speech to offer a complementary perspective to work already done on political narrative within CDA (e.g. Martin and Wodak 2003, Wodak and van Dijk 2000).

The social theories of Michel Foucault have played an important role in the frameworks adopted by cultural and discourse analysts. Notably, Foucault's (1972) idea of a "discourse formation" is employed by Annita Lazar and Michelle Lazar in their exploration of the socio-historically contingent field of statements that make up what they call the "New World Order" discourse.

Finally, feminist theory is important to the critical approaches presented here. Katherine Lemons (chapter 5) engages especially with Lila Abu-Lughod's (2002) discussion of the situated nature of liberation, which calls for "recognizing and respecting differences" in the situated meanings of liberty, rather than "seeking to 'save' others" (783). Moreover, Lemons extends Leila Ahmed's (1992) discussion of discourses on the veil in colonial Egypt and other uses of feminist rhetoric as a tool of colonialist power. Contemporary discourses in the US and elsewhere, which propose to "save" Muslim women, erase individuals' own agency and leave them no position from which to speak (cf. Spivak 1988).

While qualitative analysis is the favored approach for nearly all of the contributors in this volume, Gregory Stoltz's (chapter 6) examination of how the term "Arab" is used in the American press is a notable exception. His chapter provides a glimpse of how quantitative methods can be integrated with CDA.

As evidenced in this sketch of the major frameworks and ideas used throughout the book, there is no single theory or methodology appropriate for the critical analysis of discourse. Rather, the variety of approaches offered in this volume provides a plethora of choices for researchers engaged in critical scholarship. As a result, we hope the perspectives in this volume will be of interest to students, teachers and researchers of language and politics from a variety of fields interested in media and political discourse. We now turn to a thematic overview of the individual chapters.

Overview of the chapters

Conceptually, the book begins with an examination of discourses that emanate from within the United States, including presidential speeches and media representations. From there, the book broadens into the international arena with a focus on various countries as well as international media outlets. Additionally, the themes found in these papers move from a specific focus on the American administration to more general discourses on 9/11, terrorism, and war, concluding with a critical inquiry into the politics of fear that underlies many of the discourses examined throughout the volume.

In "'Emerging Threats' and 'Coming Dangers': Claiming the Future for Preventive War," Patricia Dunmire examines ways that speakers lay claim to the future in political discourse. Her analysis of the National Security Strategy of the United

States, as well as speeches by President George W. Bush suggests that the US administration places itself in a privileged position in relation to knowledge of – and agency over – the future. This vision of the future has important consequences, as it helps to establish the administration's view of a (potential) future as true and inevitable, and paves the way for "preemptive war"[5] to preserve a naturalized view of global interests.

Annita Lazar and Michelle Lazar argue in "Enforcing Justice, Justifying Force: America's Justification of Violence in the New World Order" that the mode of world-making explored by Dunmire is not unique to the administration of George W. Bush. Their analysis of speeches by three US presidents – George H.W. Bush, William J. Clinton, and George W. Bush – suggests that a project of constructing a New World Order by mixing the language of policing and that of war has been an ongoing US project since the end of the Cold War.

In "The Narrative Construction of Identity: The Adequation of Saddam Hussein and Osama bin Laden in the 'War on Terror,'" Adam Hodges examines the role of presidential rhetoric in the imposition of sociopolitical identities on the world stage. In a series of speeches prior to and after the invasion of Iraq, George W. Bush constructs an enemy such that Saddam Hussein's Iraq and Osama bin Laden's al Qaeda network are sufficiently similar so that a strike against one is justified by its equivalence to a strike against the other. The resulting narrative legitimizes the administration's pre-9/11 policy of "regime change in Iraq" in relation to its conflict with al Qaeda to the extent that many Americans believe the two entities collaborated together prior to 9/11, a fact refuted in the 9/11 Commission Report.

In light of US media coverage of the Iraq War, Katherine Lemons, in "Discourses of Freedom: Gender and Religion in US Media Coverage of the War on Iraq," provides a close reading of several *New York Times* articles in order to highlight how the discursive economy of liberation engages in normative tropes that treat the female body as a mark of relative progress and Islam as a force of repression. She argues that what we see in these representations are normative assumptions with robust but reprehensible histories. The imposition of such assumptions about liberation and feminism omits the possibility of recognizing the legitimacy of different forms of liberty.

In a somewhat different fashion, Gregory Stoltz's reading of the *New York Times* and *Christian Science Monitor* – in "Arabs in the Morning Paper: A Case of Shifting Identity" – shows how, despite a single label, the definition of social groups can be seriously muddled. Stoltz argues that the shifting use of the label "Arab" as a regional, religious, ethnic or altogether different category contributes to the erasure (Irvine and Gal 2000) of the complex and multi-faceted nature of Arab identity and presents a confusing picture.

Media discourse also includes images, and the images of war play an important role in the representation of social actors. In "Visual Discourses of War: Multimodal Analysis of Photographs of the Iraq Occupation," David Machin shows that, even if the way the media speak and write about war during the past 150 years remains similar, the use of photographs has changed. In particular, the elements that are depicted – and the elements that are ignored – have shifted from war to war. Significantly, the use of commercial image banks and the tendency to treat photos not as documentary evidence but as elements in a visual layout help to conceal the realities of war, and allow talk of peacekeeping and maintaining order to go uncontested.

Moving to a discussion of media in the Middle East, Becky Schulthies and Aomar Boum's depiction of Al-Jazeera in "'Martyrs and Terrorists, Resistance and Insurgency': Contextualizing the Exchange of Terrorism Discourses on Al-Jazeera" describes the network's efforts to position itself in relation to both Western standards of objectivity and Arab audiences' expectations of engagement and perspective. In doing so, they explore language used in the network's programs to report, debate and respond to comments emanating from Washington. One result of the network's operations is to open up social space where multiple audiences appropriate and negotiate the meaning of events.

The impact of Bush administration policy after 9/11 – namely, its decision to invade Iraq without approval from the UN Security Council – has been the focus of sharp debate in Europe. In "Between 'Us' and 'Them': Two TV Interviews with German Chancellor Gerhard Schröder in the Run-up to the Iraq War," Annette Becker examines such debate from the perspective of domestic German politics. She describes the interactive elements at play when Gerhard Schröder faces media outlets with differing political orientations to discuss the then impending war in Iraq. The result is the creation of an "Us" versus "Them" dichotomy involving not Germany versus a foreign nation, but a dichotomy between rival factions within the German political landscape.

In Serbia, domestic sociopolitical actors have appropriated the "war on terror" discourse for their own purposes, according to Zala Volcic and Karmen Erjavec in "Discourse of War and Terrorism in Serbia: 'We Were Fighting the Terrorists already in Bosnia…'" Their collection and analysis of interviews conducted in Serbia illustrates a project of imagining and shaping contemporary war and politics, as well as geography and history. Young people construct an analogy in which Serbia is to Muslims in the Balkans as the United States is to terrorists like al Qaeda. This comparison resonates with US discourses conflating terrorists with "Militant Islamists" and casts Serbia as both a victim and anti-terrorist fighter of long standing.

International media, such as the major wire services, play a significant role in shaping emotional responses to terrorism. In "'Fear of Terror Attack Persists': Con-

structing Fear in Reports on Terrorism by International News Agencies," Maija Stenvall takes a textual approach towards the issue of fear in order to illuminate how reports in AP and Reuters construe emotions such as fear, worry and concern. The
result is that abstract fears become "actors" themselves in the response to terrorism.

Finally, fear is an issue that underlies many of the discourses of war and terrorism in the wake of 9/11. The volume concludes with a more philosophical discussion of the role of fear and violence in politics with Matteo Stocchetti's "The Politics of Fear: A Critical Inquiry into the Role of Violence in 21st Century Politics."
Through his inquiry into the narratives of fear, including a look at the underpinnings of the "crusade metaphor" and the perpetuation of a "clash of civilizations"
(Huntington 1993) mentality, his discussion attempts to overcome the "paralysis
of criticism" (Marcuse 2002) that often grips society when an enemy is dehuman-
ized beyond the point of rational thought.

Limitations and contributions of discourse studies

As Matteo Stocchetti suggests, sanity and humanistic values often become casualties in the discourses of war and terrorism, but do critical discourse studies offer
any contribution to the resistance of those casualties? Much academic debate takes
place both among practitioners and detractors of CDA about the true value of
discourse analysis within the bigger picture of social struggle. For example, Paul
Chilton (2005) ponders "whether CDA has any credible efficacy on its own terms,
as an instrument of social justice" (21). In other words, does it really provide any
tangible benefits outside of the potential academic contributions it may make to
the study of culture, language and social practice? Another critique of discourse
analytic approaches even questions the value of their potential academic contributions and maintains that one cannot fully understand cultural and political processes without detailed and extended ethnography.[6] Let us take a moment to address these concerns and acknowledge the limitations of discourse analysis before
concluding with a discussion of the role it can play within the social sciences.

The importance of ethnography as an accompaniment to discourse analysis
should not be discounted or underestimated. Indeed, ethnography can play a vital
role in turning textual analyses into fuller explanations of social phenomena (see,
for example, van Leeuwen 2005). Discourse analysis can analyze presidential
speeches and examine the language circulated among the media, but what are the
reactions of an undecided voter in Ohio before the 2004 US presidential election?
What does a soccer mom shopping at Wal-Mart really think about 9/11? What effect – if any – do the pronouncements of a member of parliament in Berlin have
on a college student in Munich? These are all questions that discourse analysis

cannot answer alone and require ethnography to illuminate. Moreover, since analysts tend to live (and practice discourse) in urban, Western settings, the talk and practices of people in highly dissimilar settings may be even more opaque from the point of view of discourse analysis. To fully understand language in society, additional social analytic methods such as ethnography need to be taken into account.[7] Discourse analysis – including the textual focus of many contributions in this volume – remains but one piece in a larger academic puzzle.

Nevertheless, the focus on discourse taken by papers in this volume does have a role to play in academic explorations of war and terrorism. Insofar as traditional ethnography uses language as a transparent medium to describe meanings often presumed to be stable, the emphasis remains on the events and "not the stories informants create about them" (Rosenwald and Ochberg 1992: 2, Riessman 1993: 4). Discourse analysis, by contrast, shifts the focus towards the stories, the language, and the texts that create the meanings. As a result, one begins to notice the instability of those meanings and the role language plays in their construction.

In his philosophy of language and meaning, Charles Taylor (1985) stresses the constitutive dimension of language, which goes beyond the mere denotation of pre-existing phenomena. Language expresses, creates a public space and then places items into that space. It sets up relations among individuals and establishes shared meanings. In effect, "relations of power and property themselves are not possible without language; they are essentially realized in language" (271).

Where philosophy provides grand theories, and ethnography provides descriptions that can only be gleaned through extended participant observation, discourse analysis provides a focus on the use of language – that is, the precise workings of language too easily overlooked or dismissed as a transparent medium of human interaction. If language is constitutive of social reality – a notion inherent in the discursive turn in the social sciences – then how does the linguistic process involved in the constitution of that reality unfold? How does language stake out, justify and defend positions? How does language define, shape and identify events and individuals? How does language come together in discourse to construct ideologies, beliefs and understandings? In many ways, these questions require a focus on discourse that only close textual analysis can provide. The aim of the volume is to illuminate some of these processes in the critical study of politics, society and culture in the wake of 9/11.

In that case, where do academic explanations of the discourses of war and terrorism leave us with regard to the casualties of sanity and humanistic values pointed out above? Perhaps there is little value beyond any potential contributions to academic theories. But if language plays an integral role in the process of justifying war and violence, in spreading fear and dehumanizing enemies; then it seems inevitable that it should also hold the capacity to address the complexities of events like 9/11 and construct the ethos to engage in communicative practices capable of checking abuses of power (cf. Foucault 1977: 298). We do not intend to imply that this volume accomplishes these feats, but change is always an ongoing process comprised of many seemingly inconsequential steps. Moreover, the desire to be a part of this process of positive social change remains an important motivation as expressed by many within CDA (cf. Chilton 2005: 21).

Conclusion

In order to understand the relationship between discourse and war (including the strategy of terrorism), let us consider Carl von Clausewitz's (1976) maxim that war is simply politics by other means. One may imagine a continuum of political strategy, with war and diplomacy occupying opposite ends. Diplomacy represents the art of communication employed in the service of peaceful cohabitation. As diplomacy's opposite, war represents the breakdown of communication, resulting in physical violence. It is important to note, however, that both ends of this continuum rely crucially on uses of language. The practice of diplomacy relies on dialogue and tireless negotiation in an effort to reach shared understandings among rival groups. War, too, relies on discourse – communication within the group to divide interests and dehumanize the Other as a prelude to violence.

As Paul Chilton (2004) points out, Aristotle's notion that humans are "political animals" rests upon our unique capacity for language, or "the power of speech" (4–5). The capacity for language therefore undergirds human engagement in politics at both ends of the continuum sketched out above; language is a prerequisite for both war and diplomacy. Michael Billig (2003), drawing on Henri Tajfel (1981), provides an extended discussion of the consequences of this idea, which contradicts early beliefs in psychology that associated war with an innate primitive instinct and language with higher thought (McDougall 1920). Billig (2003) writes,

> The apparent irrationality of war is not the product of irrational psychological drives, but is the outcome of the seemingly rational human propensity to make sense of the social world. [...] When Bush and the majority of the American people advocated the bombing of Afghanistan after September 11, 2001, they were not responding to a release of innate, instinctual urges. Their collective response was based upon understandings of the social world, which involved a heightened sense of "us" and "them" (xi–xii).

It therefore follows that – in constructing understandings of the social world – language not only holds the capacity for dehumanizing the Other and justifying seemingly irrational actions, but of bridging towards mutual understandings and recognizing the Other as not wholly unlike ourselves. The "tough on security" image[8] embraced by politicians that privileges the use of war over the use of diplomacy in international affairs is merely a powerful narrative constructed, at base, through language. What language creates, language can dislodge and build anew. Only language can create new narratives and images that embrace the diplomatic end of the spectrum as a mark of political strength. In a nuclear age where the power of language to lead us into war and sanitize[9] its destruction presents indescribable consequences for ourselves and the planet, shifting the balance of language use towards the diplomatic end of that continuum of politics remains a vital necessity.

Discourses since 9/11 have constructed the reality and provided the frameworks through which the world now views and discusses war and terrorism. Dissecting these discourses may be one piece in the construction of new ones that bring the casualties of sanity and humanistic values back to life. The primary social function of scholars, after all, is "to influence discourse" (Graham et al 2004: 216). While discourse analysts are no more important than others in this regard, discourse studies can play an incisive role in understanding the workings of the discursive process at play in politics, society and culture.

Notes

1.   The iterations of this rhetoric in George W. Bush's speeches are ubiquitous. For example, in a March 19, 2002 speech at a Republican Party dinner in Saint Louis, he explains: "They hate our freedom. They hate our freedom to worship. They hate our freedom to vote. They hate our freedom of the press. They hate our freedom to say what you want to say. They can't stand what we stand for" (Bush 2002).

2.   In an article in *The Nation* a month after 9/11, Chalmers Johnson (2001) describes "blowback" as follows: "'Blowback' is a CIA term first used in March 1954 in a recently declassified report on the 1953 operation to overthrow the government of Mohammed Mossadegh in Iran. It is a metaphor for the unintended consequences of the US government's international activities that have been kept secret from the American people." Johnson (2004) further fleshes out this concept.

3.   For a discussion of this "landscape of critical approaches", see Blommaert (2005: 5–13).

4.   For a historical overview of CDA, see Wodak (2001), Wodak and de Cillia (2006).

5.   Noam Chomsky (2003) points out that the Bush administration's policy of "preemptive" war is in actuality a policy of *preventive* war, as it allows for "the use of military force to eliminate an invented or imagined threat."

6.   We are grateful for review comments that challenged us to deeply consider this critique.

7.   For an example of how extended ethnography can further our understanding of the linguistic construction of culture, see Lindquist (2002).

8.   For a discussion on the language of "peace, security and terrorism", see van Dijk (2005: 82–86).

9.   Carol Cohn (1987) illuminates the way "technostrategic language" can rationalize otherwise seemingly irrational behavior, namely, the complete destruction of entire cities and civilian populations with nuclear weapons.

References

Abu-Lughod, L. 2002. "Do Muslim Women Really Need Saving? Anthropological Reflections on Cultural Relativism and Its Others." *American Anthropologist* 104(3): 783–790.

Ahmed, L. 1992. *Women and Gender in Islam.* New Haven: Yale University Press.

Bakhtin, M. 1981. *The Dialogic Imagination: Four Essays.* Michael Holquist (ed.), Caryl Emerson and Michael Holquist (trans.) Austin: University of Texas Press.

Bakhtin, Mikhail. 1986. *Speech Genres and Other Late Essays,* Vern W. McGee (trans.), Caryl Emerson and Michael Holquist (eds.) Austin: University of Austin Press.

Billig, M. 2003. "Preface: Language as forms of death." In *At War With Words,* M.N. Dedaić and D.N. Nelson (eds.), vi–xvii. New York: Mouton de Gruyter.

Blommaert, J. 2005. *Discourse: A Critical Introduction.* Cambridge: Cambridge University Press.

Bourdieu, P. 1978. *Outline of a Theory of Practice.* R. Nice (trans.). Cambridge: Cambridge University Press.

Bourdieu, P. 1984. *Distinction: A Social Critique of the Judgment of Taste.* Cambridge, MA: Harvard University Press.

Bruner, J. 19991. "The Narrative Construction of Reality." *Critical Inquiry* 18: 1–24.

Bucholtz, M. and Hall, K. 2004. "Language and identity." In *A Companion to Linguistic Anthropology,* A. Duranti (ed.). Malden, MA: Blackwell.

Bush, G.W. 2002, March 19. Speech at a Republican Party Dinner in Saint Louis, Missouri. Available at http://www.whitehouse.gov/news/releases/2002/03/20020319-5.html.

Bush, G.W. 2006, July 28. Press Conference in the East Room of the White House. Available at http://www.whitehouse.gov/news/releases/2006/07/20060728-1.html.

Chilton, P. 1996. *Security Metaphors.* New York: Peter Lang.

Chilton, P. 2004. *Analysing Political Discourse.* London: Routledge.

Chilton, P. 2005. "Missing links in mainstream CDA: Modules, blends and the critical instinct." In *A New Agenda in (Critical) Discourse Analysis,* R. Wodak and P. Chilton (eds.), 19–51. Amsterdam: John Benjamins.

Chilton, P. and Lakoff, G. 1995. "Foreign policy by metaphor." In *Language and Peace,* C. Schäffner and A. Wenden (eds.), 37–60. Aldershot: Dartmouth.

Chomsky, N. 2001. *9/11.* New York: Seven Stories Press.

Chomsky, N. 2003, August 11. "Preventive war: 'The supreme crime.'" *Z Magazine.* Available: www.zmag.org/content/showarticle.cfm?ItemID=4030.

Chouliaraki, L. (ed.) 2005. Special Issue: The Soft Power of War: Legitimacy and Community in Iraq War Discourses. *Journal of Language and Politics* 4(1).

Cohn, C. 1987. "Sex and death in the rational world of defense intellectuals." *Signs* 12(4): 687–718.

Collins, J. and Glover, R. (eds.) 2002. *Collateral Language: A User's Guide to America's New War.* New York: New York University Press.

De Certeau, M. 1984. *The Practice of Everyday Life*, S. Rendall (trans.). Berkeley: University of California Press.

Dedaić, M.N. and Nelson, D.N. (eds.) 2003. *At War With Words*. New York: Mouton de Gruyter.

Doran, M.S. 2001. "Somebody else's civil war." In *How Did This Happen? Terrorism and the New War*, J. Hoge and G. Rose (eds.), 31–52. Oxford: Public Affairs.

Fairclough, N. 1989. *Language and Power*. London: Longman.

Fairclough, N. 1992. *Discourse and Social Change*. Cambridge: Polity Press.

Fairclough, N. and Wodak, R. 1997. "Critical discourse analysis." In *Discourse as Social Interaction. Discourse Studies: A Multidisciplinary Introduction* (volume 2), T.A. van Dijk (ed.), 258–284. London: Sage.

Fillmore, C.J. 1982. "Frame semantics." In *Linguistics in the Morning Calm*, 111–137. Seoul, South Korea: Hanshin Publishing.

Fillmore, C.J. 1985. "Frames and the Semantics of Understanding." *Quaderni di Semantica*, 6(2): 222–254.

Foucault, M. 1972. *The Archaeology of Knowledge*. London: Tavistock.

Foucault, M. 1977. "The ethics of concern for self as a practice of freedom." In *Michel Foucault: Ethics, Subjectivity and Truth*, P. Rabinow (ed.), 281–301. New York: The New Press.

Fowler, R., Hodge, R., Kress, G.R. and Trew, T. 1979. *Language and Control*. London: Routledge.

Graham, P., Keenan, T. and Dowd, A. 2004. "A call to arms at the end of history: A discourse-historical analysis of George W. Bush's declaration of war on terror." *Discourse and Society* 15(2–3): 199–221.

Hall, S. 1989. *Ideologie, Kultur, Medien: Neue Rechte, Rassismus*. Hamburg: Argument.

Halliday, M.A.K. 1978. *Language as Social Semiotic*. London: Edward Arnold.

Halliday, M.A.K. 1985. *An Introduction to Functional Grammar*. London: Edward Arnold.

Harvey, D. 2003. *The New Imperialism*. Oxford: Oxford University Press.

Hodges, A. 2004. "Framing terror: Ideological struggle underlying the characterization of terrorism." Paper presented at Crossroads 2004: Fifth International Conference of the Association for Cultural Studies, University of Illinois at Urbana-Champaign, June 25–28.

Hoge, J. and Rose, G. (eds.) 2001. *How Did This Happen? Terrorism and the New War*. Oxford: Public Affairs.

Horkheimer, M. 1972. *Critical Theory: Selected Essays* M.J. O'Connell (trans). New York: Herder and Herder.

Huntington, S.P. 1993. "The Clash of Civilizations." *Foreign Affairs*, 72 (3): 22–28.

Irvine, J.T. and Gal, S. 2000. "Language ideology and linguistic differentiation." In *Regimes of Language: Ideologies, Polities, and Identities*, P. Kroskrity (ed.), 35–83.

Jackson, R. 2005. *Writing the War on Terrorism: Language, Politics, and Counter-Terrorism*. Manchester, UK: Manchester University Press.

Jhally, S. and Earp. J. 2004. *Hijacking Catastrophe: 9/11, Fear and the Selling of American Empire*. Northampton, MA: Olive Branch Press.

Johnson, C.A. 2001, October 15. "Blowback." *The Nation*. Available at http://www.thenation.com/doc/20011015/johnson.

Johnson, C.A. 2004. *Blowback: The Costs and Consequences of American Empire*. New York: Metropolitan / Owl Books.

Kress, G. 1995. "The social production of language: History and structures of domination." In *Discourse in Society: Systemic Functional Perspectives*, P.H. Fries & M. Gregory (eds.), 115–140. Norwood, NJ: Ablex.

Kress, G. and van Leeuwen, T. 2001. *Multimodal Discourse: The Modes and Media of Contemporary Communication*. London: Arnold.

Labov, W. 1972. "The transformation of experience in narrative syntax." In *Language in the Inner City: Studies in the Black English Vernacular*, W. Labov (ed.), 354–396. Philadelphia: University of Pennsylvania Press.

Labov, W. and Waletsky, J. 1967. "Narrative analysis: Oral versions of personal experience." In *Essays on the Verbal and Visual Arts*, J. Helm (ed.), 12–44. Seattle: University of Washington Press.

Lakoff, G., and Johnson, M. 1980. *Metaphors We Live By*. Chicago: University of Chicago Press.

Lakoff, G, and Turner, M. 1989. *More Than Cool Reason: A Field Guide to Poetic Metaphor*. Chicago: University of Chicago Press.

Lakoff, G. 1993. The Contemporary Theory of Metaphor. In *Metaphor and Thought* (second edition), A. Ortony (ed.), 202–251. Cambridge: Cambridge University Press.

Lakoff, G. 2001, September 16. "Metaphors of Terror." In *The Days After*. Chicago: University of Chicago Press. Available: http://www.press.uchicago.edu/News/911lakoff.html.

Linde, C. 1993. *Life Stories: The Creation of Coherence*. New York: Oxford University Press.

Lindquist, J. 2002. *A Place to Stand: Politics and Persuasion in a Working-Class Bar*. Oxford: Oxford University Press.

Machin, D. and Van Leeuwen, T. 2005. "Computer games as political discourse: The case of Black Hawk Down." *Journal of Language and Politics* 4 (1): 119–141.

Marcuse, H. 2002 [1964]. *One-Dimensional Man. Studies in the Ideology of Advanced Industrial Society*. London: Routledge.

Martin, J.R. 1997. "Analysing genre: Functional parameters." In *Genre and Institutions: Social Processes in the Workplace and School*, F. Christie and J.R. Martin (eds.), 3–39. London: Cassell.

Martin, J.R. and Edwards, J. (eds.) 2004. Special Issue: Interpreting Tragedy: The Language of 11 September 2001. *Discourse and Society* 15(2–3).

Martin, J.R. and Wodak, R. 2003. "Introduction." In *Re/reading the Past*, J.R. Martin and R. Wodak (eds.), 1–16. Amsterdam: John Benjamins.

Martin, J.R. and Wodak, R. (eds.) 2003. *Re/reading the Past*. Amsterdam: John Benjamins.

Maybin, J. 2001. "Language, struggle and voice: The Bakhtin/Volosinov writings." In *Discourse Theory and Practice: A Reader*, M. Wetherell, S. Taylor and S.J. Yates (eds.), 64–71. London: Sage.

McDougall, W. 1920. *The Group Mind*. Cambridge: Cambridge University Press.

National Commission on Terrorist Attacks upon the United States. 2004. *Executive Summary of the 9/11 Commission Report*. Available at http://www.gpoaccess.gov/911/pdf/execsummary.pdf.

NC – see National Commission on Terrorist Attacks upon the United States.

Ochs, E. and Capps, L. 2001. *Living Narrative: Creating Lives in Everyday Storytelling*. Cambridge, MA: Harvard University Press.

Riessman, C.K. 1993. *Narrative Analysis*. London: Sage Publications.

Rosenwald, G.C. and Ochberg, R.L. 1992. "Introduction: Life stories, cultural politics, and self-understanding." In *Storied Lives: The Cultural Politics of Self-Understanding*, G.C. Rosenwald and R.L. Ochenberg (eds.), 1–18. New Haven: Yale University Press.

Sherman, D.J. and Nardin, T. (eds.) 2006. *Terror, Culture, Politics: Rethinking 9/11*. Bloomington: Indiana University Press.

Spivak, G. 1988. "Can the Subaltern Speak?" In *Marxism and the Interpretation of Culture*, C. Nelson and L. Grossberg (eds), 271–313. Urbana: University of Illinois Press.

Tajfel, H. 1981. *Human Groups and Social Categories*. Cambridge: Cambridge University Press.

Taylor, C. 1985. *Human Agency and Language: Philosophical Papers 1*. Cambridge: Cambridge University Press.

Tedlock, D. and Mannheim, B. 1995. *The Dialogic Emergence of Culture*. Chicago: University of Illinois Press.

Van Dijk, T.A. 2005. "War Rhetoric of a Little Ally: Political implicatures and Aznar's legitimization of the war in Iraq." *Journal of Language and Politics* 4(1): 65–91.

Van Leeuwen, T. 1996. "The representation of social actors." In *Texts and Practices - Readings in Critical Discourse Analysis*, C. Caldas-Coulthard and M. Coulthard (eds.), 32–71. London: Routledge.

Van Leeuwen, T. 2000. "Visual racism." In *The Semiotics of Racism – Approaches in Critical Discourse Analysis*, M. Reisigl and R. Wodak (eds.), 333–350. Vienna: Passagen Verlag.

Van Leeuwen, T. 2005. "Three models of interdisciplinarity." In *A New Agenda in (Critical) Discourse Analysis*, R. Wodak and P. Chilton (eds.), 3–18. Amsterdam: John Benjamins.

Von Clausewitz, C. 1976. *On War*. M. Howard and P. Paret (eds.) Princeton: Princeton University Press.

Wodak, R. 1996. "The Genesis of Racist Discourse in Austria." In *Texts and Practices: Readings in Critical Discourse Analysis,* C.R. Caldas-Coulthard and M. Coulthard (eds.), 107–128. London: Routledge.

Wodak, R. 2001. "What CDA is about – a summary of its history, important concepts and its developments." In *Methods of Critical Discourse Analysis*, R. Wodak and M. Meyer (eds.), 1–14. London: Sage.

Wodak, R. and de Cillia, R. 2006. "Politics and language: Overview." In *Encyclopedia of Language and Linguistics* (second edition), K. Brown (ed.), 707–719. London: Elsevier.

Wodak, R. and van Dijk, T.A. (eds.). 2000. *Racism at the Top: Parliamentary Discourses on Ethnic Issues in Six European States*. Klagenfurt, Austria: Drava Verlag.

CHAPTER 2

"Emerging threats" and "coming dangers"

Claiming the future for preventive war

Patricia L. Dunmire

Overview

An important task for critical discourse analysis is to demonstrate the linguistic and discursive means through which the future is claimed and appropriated by dominant groups and institutions. As Hebdige (1993) explains, exploiting the "actively performative" functions of communication requires that analysts examine "the various ways in which different futures are imagined" (275). Analytic attention, therefore, needs to focus on how "particular discursive strategies open up or close down particular lines of possibility; how they invite or inhibit particular identifications for particular social fractions at particular moments" (275). Following Hebdige, this paper posits that as the domain of the potential and possible, the future represents an ideologically significant site in which dominant political actors and institutions can exert political power and control. As such, I examine the discursive and linguistic means by which these actors and institutions constrain the way the future can be imagined, articulated, and realized. My analysis focuses on representations of the future embedded within and projected through particular instances of political discourse, namely the National Security Strategy of the United States (NSS) and two speeches President Bush delivered concerning war in Iraq.

The NSS is a particularly important site in which and through which the Bush administration stakes its claim on the future. First, it presents a "blueprint" for U.S. relations with the rest of the world as it outlines military and economic policies designed to assure U.S. global dominance for the near and long term future. As the document states, the U. S. "must build and maintain our defenses beyond challenge" and "must dissuade future military competition" (United States National Security Council 2002: 25). Second, the NSS redefines the "doctrine of preemption," an internationally recognized right to use military force against an "imminent threat," in such a way as to significantly lower the threshold for military action. Although the administration's approach to "preemption" is not new in practice, it has never been explicitly incorporated into the national security strate-gies of previous administrations (Burns and Ansin 2004; Kirk 2003).[1] As I will show, this redefinition positions the administration in a particular way regarding knowledge and agency with respect to the future.

It is also important to consider how the concepts presented in the NSS are concretized and implemented within the context of specific foreign policy situa-tions and how they are presented to the public. The Bush administration's war in Iraq is the first manifestation of its national security strategy. As such, I examine two pre-war speeches delivered by President Bush to the American public: his speech in Cincinnati on October 7, 2002 (the one-year anniversary of the war in Afghanistan) and his speech to the nation on March 17, 2003 (two days prior to the start of the war). The relationship between the NSS and these speeches is one of reciprocal articulation and realization as the speeches represent a public articu-lation and concrete realization of the concepts and policies outlined in the NSS document. Moreover, we can understand these texts as comprising distinct yet interrelated sites for legitimating the Bush Administration's policy of preemptive war. As van Dijk (1998a) explains, legitimation is a crucial social function of ideol-ogy which often manifests as "a complex, ongoing discourse practice involving a set of interrelated discourses" (255). Examining the NSS, a policy document, and the public speeches can reveal the various linguistic means by which legitimation is enacted and how it functions rhetorically in the post-9/11 context.

In *Re/reading the Past: Critical and Functional Perspectives on Time and Value*, Martin and Wodak (2002) argue for the timeliness of their volume by noting the significance of discourses about the past within post-World War II and post-colo-nial contexts. The significance of these discourses derives from their role in "proc-esses of reconciliation, debates on war crimes, and restitution" (1). The key ques-tion to ask in the post-colonial period, Martin contends, is "Whose history? Who speaks of the past and in what terms?" (Martin 2002: 19). A similar case can be made concerning the post-Cold War context and discourses about the future. That is, just as the post-World War II, post-colonial era provides particular motivations for examining how the past is negotiated and made meaningful, the post-Cold War era should motivate critical attention to the ways in which the future is con-strued and whose interests those construals serve. Indeed, the end of the Cold War has seen the proliferation of what Lazar and Lazar (2004) term the "New World Order discourse" (see also, Lazar and Lazar, Chapter 3). The authors explain that this discourse has come into being because of "the determination of the United States to retain its superpower status" and "the emergence and articulation of 'new' threats" (225). A key feature of this discourse is its concern with the future and the need to "shape" the future in particular ways. In his statement inaugurating the concept of a "new world order" and, with it, a new discourse, President George H.W. Bush declared at the outset of the 1991 Persian Gulf War that "This is an historic moment... we have before us the opportunity to forge for ourselves and for **future generations** a new world order" (G.H.W. Bush 1991). The President's Defense Secretary, Dick Cheney, echoed and operationalized this sentiment in *A Defense Strategy for the 1990s: The Regional Defense Strategy*, insisting that "We must not squander the position of security we achieved at great sacrifice through the Cold War, **nor eliminate our ability to shape an uncertain future in ways favorable to us**" (Cheney 1993). Ten years later the Project for the New American Century, noting that "America's grand strategy" should be to extend its strategic position "as far into the future as possible," asked, "Does America have the resolve to **shape a new century in ways favorable to American principles and interests?**" (Project for the New American Century 2000). Borrowing from Martin, it seems clear that the key questions for understanding the post-Cold War era should include "Whose future? Who speaks about the future and in what terms?"

Politics and ideology of the future

The function of political discourse to project and shape conceptions and visions of the future has long been recognized by political and cultural scholars and critics. In his treatise on classical rhetoric, Aristotle designates the future as the temporal domain of deliberative rhetoric, "political speaking urges us either to do or not to do something [...] [It] is concerned with the future: it is about things to be done hereafter [...]" (1954: 32). In Aristotle's scheme, deliberative rhetoric focuses on future actions that "we have it in our power to set going" and aims to establish the "expediency" or "harmfulness" of a proposed course of action (35).

Murray Edelman (1971, 1988) echoes Aristotle's view regarding the deontic modality of political discourse – that it is concerned with what might, should or must be done in the future. Edelman also contends, however, that political discourse is further characterized by epistemic modality as it asserts what will *be* at some future moment. That is, in making proposals about future actions and policies, political actors also make claims, assertions, and declarations concerning the future "realities" that give rise to and are implicated in those actions. He sees this as a rhetorical act through which political actors make "rhetorical evocations of a remote time unlikely to arrive." These evocations, in turn, have material effects by legitimating more immediate proposals and policies which serve the partisan's political goals and interests (1988: 18). Edelman (1971) further explains that governmental institutions are uniquely positioned to prescribe projections of the future for the public because "only government can evoke fairly confident expectations of future welfare and deprivation" and can create "the perceived worlds that in turn shape perceptions and interpretations of current events and therefore the behavior with which people respond to them" (7). Indeed, creating representations of "what people can be led to expect of the future" is an especially potent means by which political actors shape the political cognitions and behavior of large numbers of people (7–8). According to Edelman, such expectations generally concern social status and "security from perceived threats" (8). By projecting representations of such expectations of the future, political actors are able to influence people's interpretation and perception of "ambiguous current facts" in ways that typically serve the political actor's goals (8). As such, Edelman contends that an adequate explanation of political behavior must focus on "creation and change in common meanings through symbolic apprehension in groups of peoples' interests, pressures, **threats,** and **possibilities** (2; emphasis added).

Edelman's assessment of contemporary political discourse is reminiscent of what Foucault (1984) terms the "true discourses" that held sway in Greece during the 6th century B.C. Foucault explains that the political and material significance of these discourses derived from their function to prophesize the future. In so doing, such a discourse "not only announced what was going to happen but helped to make it happen, carrying men's minds along with it and thus weaving itself into the fabric of destiny" (112). Similarly, Silverstein (2003) notes that by invoking particular "futurities" in his Gettysburg Address, President Lincoln encouraged the audience to support his policies by assuring them that they could effect political and social change by "being dedicated to joining Lincoln in the 'we' who will bring about actual futurities" (61).

Clearly, the future orientation of political discourse has ideological implications for the political actors who produce it and for those who try to resist it and the actions and realities it potentially entails. Grosz (1999) argues that the "indeterminacy" and "unforeseeability" of the future challenges political ideals of stability and control. She further contends that Foucault's conception of power can be understood as "that which functions... to dampen and suppress" the potentiality and possibility inherent in the future (16). Analyses have demonstrated the linguistic means by which particular political discourses exert this power by projecting deterministic representations that render particular future scenarios as known and inevitable – as future reality. Fairclough (2000) argues, for example, that the power of discourses favoring globalization derives from the fact that they render globalization as an inevitable, natural phenomenon developing outside human deliberation, design, or resistance. Dunmire (1997) demonstrates how a hypothetical event, an Iraqi invasion of Saudi Arabia, was linguistically construed as an inevitable future event and how that future 'reality', in turn, was used to justify U.S. military action against Iraq during the 1991 Persian Gulf War. Such determinism undermines the potentiality of the future by annihilating "any future uncontained in the present or past" (Grosz 1999: 4). Indeed, to render the future as known, Grosz contends, is to "deny it as future, to place it as given, as past" (6). For Levitas (1993), the ideological function of dominant representations of the future resides in the impact they have on political resistance and activism. She contends that such discourse potentially "paralyzes political action" by undermining the future as the conceptual space for imagining and working for political change (257).

Analysis

The following analysis is informed by work within critical discourse analysis (CDA) and systemic functional linguistics (SFL). I understand discourse to be an important means by which social actors exert power and control. Within this view, discourse analysis is a method for understanding the differential relations of power that are embedded within and mediated through discourses and, relatedly, the ways discourses function to exert social and political control (Fairclough 1989, 1995; Caldas-Coulthard and Coulthard 1996). Moreover, I adopt an SFL conception of text as product and process and as a form of social action (Kress 1995; Halliday 1978). As product and process, a text doubly articulates the struggle and contestation that underlies and is articulated through it. As product, a text "encodes the state-of-play in the social-linguistic system;" as process it participates in and has an effect on that system (Kress 1995: 121). This effect is realized to the extent that social subjects are implicated in its representation of "reality" and in the social relations it embeds and projects.

I also draw on Scollon and Scollon's (2000; see also de Saint-Georges 2003; Scollon 2001) work on "anticipatory discourses." Arguing that discourse analysis has tended to favor "a kind of past-oriented analysis," the authors contend that critical discourse analysis needs to examine the ways in which social agents position themselves, or are positioned by others, with respect to knowledge and agency of the future. Positions concerning knowledge of the future range from the "oracular," which holds that the future can be known and/or is known, to the "probabilistic," which holds that the future is neither fixed nor entirely free, to the "agnostic," which holds that the future cannot be known. Positions concerning agency in the future range from "fatalistic," according to which nothing can be done to alter or affect the future, to the "agentive," according to which social actors are seen as highly effective agents who can bring about effects on future events.

My analysis begins by examining the construction of knowledge and agency in the NSS. I then consider the linguistic nature and rhetorical function of those representations in President Bush's speeches concerning war in Iraq.

Preempting the future: knowledge and agency in the National Security Strategy

Throughout the NSS document the two principle agents, the U.S. and "our ene-mies," are represented as highly agentive with respect to the future. For example, the document declares that the U.S,

(1) will defend this just peace against threats from terrorists and tyrants

(2) will preserve the peace by building good relations among the great powers

(3) will extend the peace by encouraging free and open societies on every conti-nent (United States National Security Council: 1)

Our enemies are also capable of profoundly affecting the future,

(4) Shadowy networks of individuals can bring great chaos and suffering to our shores for less than it costs to purchase a single tank (United States National Security Council 1).

(5) Our enemies have openly declared that they are seeking weapons of mass de-struction and evidence indicates that they are doing so with great determina-tion (United States National Security Council 2).

(6) These states are determined to acquire weapons of mass destruction to be used as threats or offensively to achieve the aggressive designs of these re-gimes (United States National Security Council 12).

What we get through these statements is a depiction of the U.S. acting to affect the future of global society. Our adversaries are also highly agentive as they plan to cause catastrophic events throughout the free world. Such "promises" and "threats" about the future typify much of political discourse (van Dijk 1998b: 27).

Although both principles are represented as capable of affecting the future, they are positioned differently relative to one another. Our enemies are positioned as agents of deliberate choice as they pursue their "ambitions" and "aggressive de-signs." Indeed, the document declares that "the nature and motives of these new adversaries, their determination to obtain destructive powers... and the greater likelihood that they will use weapons of mass destruction, make today's security environment more complex and dangerous" (United States National Security Council 12). In this statement, the aggressive agency of our enemies to do specific things in the future – "to obtain destructive weapons" – is represented as deter-mining the present moment – "today's security environment." According to Lazar and Lazar (2004) such overlexicalization of "the enemy" as a calculating, deliberate actor in Bush's discourse functions as a device for "out-casting", a macrostructure based upon the "dichotomization and mutual antagonism of out-groups ('them') and in-groups ('us')" (227; cf. chapter 3).[2] The enemy's agency is tempered somewhat, however, as it depends on the complicity of the U.S. and its allies. That is, the U.S. and its allies are potentially implicated in any future actions taken by the enemy should they fail to prevent them. These contrasting positions of enemy action and U. S. "preemption" are articulated through a transition in modality, from an epistemic modality of certainty and reality, in which the future actions of the enemy are presupposed, to a deontic modality of obligation and necessity,

(7) **Given the goals** of rogue states and terrorists, the U. S. **can no longer solely rely** on a reactive posture as we have in the past. The inability to deter a potential attacker, the immediacy of today's threats, and the magnitude of potential harm that **could be caused** by our adversaries' choice of weapons, **do not permit** that option. We **cannot let** our enemies strike first (13).

(8) The U. S. and countries cooperating with us **must not allow** terrorists to develop new home bases (1).

(9) The U. S. **will not allow** these efforts to succeed (2).

As the NSS states, "History will judge harshly those who saw this coming danger but failed to act" (2). The future actions of the U.S. are marked almost exclusively through the modal auxiliaries of "will" and "must," denoting the certain and obligatory nature of U.S. agency. As such, although the U.S. is positioned as highly agentive in these statements, it is an agency of necessity and obligation rather than choice as its actions are required to preempt "coming dangers" and the future reality they entail. Lakoff (2001) makes a similar point in his analysis of the metaphorical function of "evil" in Bush's discourse concerning the war on terrorism. He explains that by framing the war on terrorism as a fight against evil, the discourse obligates the "morally strong" (i.e. the United States) to take a stand against evil, "Evil is inherent, an essential trait, that **determines** how you will act in the world" (4; emphasis added). Within this framework, morality lies in showing overwhelming strength in the face of evil because inaction "will induce evildoers to perform more evil deeds because they'll think they can get away with it" (4).

Important to the representation of agency is the NSS's construal of the future reality that compels "preemptive" action by the U.S. Although the document makes several assertions concerning the future actions of the enemy, these actions are most often represented through the nominalization "threat" rather than through verbal forms. In fact, the future actions of our enemies are rendered as presuppositions over twice as often as they are rendered as assertions. This transformation process can be seen in excerpt 10,

(10) Now shadowy networks of individuals **can bring** great chaos and suffering to our shores for less than it costs to purchase a single tank. Terrorists **are organized to penetrate** open societies and **to turn** the power of modern technolo-

gies against us. To defeat **this threat** we **must make use** of every tool in our arsenal... (1–2).

Nominalization is a process of transformation through which verbs, which represent "reality" in terms of processes and actions, are reclassified as nouns, which represent "reality" in terms of objects and entities, that is, as "reified processes." Through the process of nominalization the future potentiality of "can bring" and "are organized to penetrate... and to turn" is objectified as an extant entity, "threat." Moreover, this process establishes the future actions of the enemy as presupposed, background information. In this passage, the nominalization results, reasonably enough, from the development and progression of the text as the verbal forms in the first two sentences are transformed into the nominalization "threat," which serves as the theme in the third sentence. With "threat" in the thematic position, the future actions projected through the verbal forms become presupposed as the text moves away from making assertions about future Iraqi actions and toward assertions of what the U.S. should do in light of this threat. Givón (1989) explains that the extensive use of nominalizations places propositions within the "presuppositional epistemic modality" (133, 137), thereby rendering them as background, assumed information. According to Latour (1987) such constructions encode statements within a "positive modality" which moves the text "downstream," away from the details and conditions of its production, "making it solid enough to render some other consequences necessary" (23). Finally, Fleischman (1982) explains that such representations construe future events as an assumed part of future reality rather than as a contingency. And it is this presupposed future action that legitimates "preemptive" U.S. military action.

This "tropos of threat" can be understood as functioning interpersonally as a legitimating discourse within the post-9/11 context as it rhetorically "justifies 'official' action in terms of rights and duties" (Reisigl 2006: 598; van Dijk 1998a).[3] Van Dijk conceives of legitimation as a crucial social function of ideology that is typically used in institutional contexts. Acts of legitimation within political settings tend to occur when an actor expects "principled opposition" to particular policies or actions; they are deemed "imperative" when the legitimacy of the state is at stake (256). At such times, legitimation discourses function rhetorically to justify the actions and values of the in-group while delegitimating those of the out-group (257). The specific tropos of threat functions to create a feeling of insecurity within the in-group, while simultaneously vilifying the out-group (Reisigl 2006). Moreover, van Dijk (2005) explains that within post-9/11 discourses the topic of terrorism threat is becoming a standard argument that does not require evidentiary backing. As such, it is used in a variety of arguments as a means of justifying a range of activities, including going to war (85).

The use of threat to legitimate the preemption policy in the NSS functions in much the same way as does "globalization" in policy discussions within the European Union concerning employment issues. Wodak (2000) conceives of globalization as a discursive construction of the state of affairs that serves particular rhetorical functions in arguments concerning employment policies. From the employers' point of view, globalization is rendered as an inevitable, natural, and decontextualized phenomenon that is presupposed in economic contexts and ideas (74). As a presupposition, the employers use "globalization" to sanction specific policies and actions that will ensure the success of the European Union within the competitive environment globalization entails.

Tropes such as "threat" also function ideationally to "invent" particular political realities (Reisigl 2006: 598). In this regard, the use of "threat" has two important consequences for the NSS text as product and process and for the political context within which it functions. As a nominalization, threat conflates present and future as it simultaneously "describes" the present moment and projects deontic and epistemic futures that can evolve from that present. Because it indicates an action to be taken at some point in the future, the verb "to threaten" is inherently future-oriented. Take, for example, the hypothetical statement "Saddam Hussein has threatened to provide weapons of mass destruction to al Qaeda." While the act of making a threat occurs at the moment of the utterance, the "threat" asserts a specific action or consequence that could come about at some future moment. In short, threat "has future action as one of its felicity conditions" (Chilton 2003: 100). Interestingly, there are no statements in the NSS indicating that Saddam Hussein, or any other of "our enemies," has made a threat against the U.S. The document contains three statements[4] which use the verbal form of *threaten*, only one of which indicates that the U.S. is in the present state of being threatened:

(11)   America **is now threatened** less by conquering states than by failing ones (6).

The other two statements locate the act of threatening in the future, as an unrealized action that the U.S. "will prevent" and "must stop" from being realized,

(12)   To achieve these goals, the U.S. **will:... prevent** our enemies **from threatening** us, our allies, and our friends with weapons of mass destruction (6–7).

(13)   We **must be prepared to stop** rogue states and their terrorist clients **before they are able to threaten** or use weapons of mass destruction against the U.S. or our allies and friends (21).

Through the extensive use of nominalization the NSS mystifies the temporality of "threatening" in such a way as to make it a component of the present context which compels U.S. military action. That is, the nominalized form highlights the presentness of "threaten" and suppresses its future as-yet-to-be-realized dimension, thereby rendering the threat as imminent. When lexicalized as verbs, processes and actions are located in specific temporal moments and are coded as to degree of likelihood, certainty, volition, and so forth. Nominalizations, however, do not receive explicit temporal or modal coding and, as such, appear to reference existing, acontextual entities. As a nominalization, then, "threat" is represented as an objectified entity that exists at the present moment.

Kress (1995) and Fairclough (2005) explain that nominalizations can take on the roles, functions, and characteristics of nouns. For example, Fairclough notes how the nominal "globalization" assumes agentive capacity in Tony Blair's discourse through statements such as "globalization has transformed our economies and our working practices" (45). What we see here is how, through nominalized representations, abstract, inanimate processes and actions can take on the function and character of a noun in the transitivity structure of a text. These reified processes and actions are endowed with agentivity: they can do things to participants and objects. At the same time, however, nominalization obscures agency by positioning reified processes, rather than animate agents, as the doers of action. Consider, for example, the following excerpts,

(14)   Our immediate focus will be... defending the United States... by identifying and destroying the **threat before it reaches our borders** (7).

(15)   Forming coalitions of the willing and cooperative security arrangements are key to confronting **these emerging transnational threats** (10).

(16)   ... America will act against **such emerging threats before they are fully formed** (1).

(17)   The United States will not use force in all cases to **preempt emerging threats**... (14).

(18)   We will build better... intelligence capabilities to provide... information on **threats, wherever they may emerge** (14).

In these excerpts we see the abstraction "threat" engaged in actions and processes. We do not, however, see Saddam Hussein, al Qaeda, or North Korea taking specific actions that pose or indicate a threat to the U.S. or its allies. In fact, the NSS contains very few references to specific nations, organizations, or individuals that it classifies as enemies of the U.S. Of the 189 total references to "our enemies," specific nations or groups are named only eleven times.[5] The most common term is "terrorists," and the variants "terror" and "terrorism," which occur 79 times (41%). Threat, however, is the second most common label as it accounts for 60 (32%) of the total references to the enemy of the U.S. and the object of U.S. actions. This paucity of specifically named enemies is, to some extent, an artifact of the genre. As a policy document, the

NSS outlines general guidelines and principles and, as such, operates in a more abstract register than, say, a speech delivered to a particular audience that makes an argument for a specific military action. Interestingly, several studies of speeches and statements by Bush Administration officials concerning the 9/11 terrorist attacks and the war in Iraq reveal a similar reliance on abstract terms and an absence of specifically named enemies and adversaries. In this context, the tropos of threat functions as what Graham et al (2004) term a "plastic abstraction", a rhetorically potent device for representing the "evil Other" in Bush's call to arms rhetoric (213). Through terms such as "evil-doers", "enemies of civilization", and "the embittered few", this rhetoric provides an "elastic definition" of the enemies of the U.S. which allows for the inclusion of a range of specific actors in the post-9/11 security environment (213; see also Collins and Glover 2002).

What we get with the nominalized constructions in the NSS is an "elision" or "displacement of agency" as agentivity no longer resides with animate agents taking specific actions at specific times and places (Kress 1995). Rather, it resides with abstract, reified processes acting in unspecified, ambiguous material and temporal contexts. In short, nominalization results in a (re)classification process that redirects transitivity structures away from characterizing "reality" in terms of actions taken by animate actors against specified participants and toward inanimate agents and nondirected actions (Kress 1995).

As the preceding analysis demonstrates, U.S. agency is premised on the need to prevent a particular future reality from coming to fruition. As such, agency and knowledge regarding the future are inextricably linked in the NSS as "preemptive" military action is grounded in a particular kind of expertise concerning knowledge of the future. The following discussion examines the nature of this knowledge and its evidential basis.

Knowing the future: redefining preemption

As mentioned earlier, The Bush administration's national security strategy is remarkable for its redefinition of the "doctrine of preemption." This change in policy centers on redefining the concept of "imminent threat." The NSS contends that in a post-9/11 world, a reactive military posture is unlikely to be effective against "emerging transnational threats" (10). Consequently, the U.S. must be able to defend itself by "identifying and destroying" these threats "before they reach our borders" (7). The NSS explains that the concept of preemptive action is not new; nations can act preemptively "against forces that present an imminent danger of attack" (13). Within the international legal community, an imminent threat is most often indicated by "a visible mobilization of armies, navies, and air forces preparing to attack" (13). The Bush administration contends, however, that the

U.S. "must adapt the concept of imminent threat to the capabilities and objectives of today's adversaries" (14). Within the post-9/11 security environment the concept of "imminent threat" must be understood to include "emerging threats" that are not yet "fully formed" (2). Such a reconceptualization will allow for "anticipatory action" against these threats "even if uncertainty remains as to the time and place of an enemy's attack" (14). The U.S. cannot – indeed will not – "remain idle while dangers gather" (14).

As the preceding excerpts reveal, the NSS articulates a notable change in the official U.S. policy regarding the use of military force. U.S. military posture can no longer be a defensive one focused on *preempting* co-present hostile actions and material circumstances. Rather, the post-9/11 security environment necessitates a *preventive* posture that anticipates potential future actions of nascent transnational threats emerging from and within under-specified temporal and material contexts. According to Dennis Ross, former Director of Policy Planning for the State Department, the more accurate term for the Bush policy is "prevention," not preemption. While the latter concerns military action against a co-present military force, "prevention" significantly "lowers the threshold to military action" and focuses on long-term nascent threats and on acting in advance to prevent those threats from materializing (Kirk 2003). Chomsky (2003) likewise emphasizes that this new policy should be understood as preventive as it allows for "the use of military force to eliminate an invented or imagined threat" (2).

Through its articulation of a preventive, anticipatory posture for the U.S. military, the NSS positions the Bush administration in a particular way with respect to knowledge of the future. That is, in its reconceptualization of "imminent threat," the policy sanctions a new type of expertise concerning knowledge of the future and, thereby, stakes a claim on the future. Knowledge of future actions and events no longer requires evidential grounding in the "visible mobilization" of military forces "preparing to attack." Rather, the security strategy sanctions knowledge of the future that lacks such an evidential basis and that derives, instead, from "emerging threats" that are not yet "fully formed." Indeed, "knowledge of the future" need not be based in fully developed material circumstances at all as the U.S. will act "preemptively" against its enemies "even if uncertainty remains as to the time and place" of attack. Newhouse (2003) points out, however, that this preventive-based strategy requires the "sustained and timely collection of intelligence that is rarely available" (13). Similarly, Keyes (2005) explains that a preventive strategy eliminates "crucial criteria" needed for determining that anticipatory military action is just and legitimate. The NSS, nevertheless, legitimizes and validates the ability of the administration to "read" and "know" the future and to speak from an oracular position even when the material signs that might provide clues to the future do not exist or are not fully realized.

Through its representation of agency and its objectification of future reality, the NSS mystifies the processes, history, and motivations underlying the Bush administration's doctrine of "preemption." This policy is not represented as the outcome of individual, deliberate choices motivated by the politics, ideology, or goals of the administration. Rather, it is presented as a necessary response to external imperatives, forces and impending future realities, a response that derives from an oracular vision of the future. The significance of such a representation is that it obscures the agency and history of the administration's policy. By retaining the language of preemption, the administration obfuscates the ideological and material significance of the change it has made to U.S. military policy.[6] That is, its doctrine is presented as a natural extension of, rather than a radical departure from, the traditional conception of preemption that is recognized by the international community.[7] According to Fairclough (2005) this construction of a new discourse through the "articulation of elements of existing discourses" is a key moment in the dialectics of discourse and social change (43). Moreover, the document conceals the concerted efforts of people within and/or closely associated with the Bush administration, who, well before September 11, 2001 sought to change the posture of the military from preemption to prevention.

According to Chalmers Johnson, the terrorist attacks of September 11, 2001 did not provide the impetus for the administration's redefinition of the preemption policy; rather, they provided the "opportunity" for a private agenda for U.S. foreign policy to become public policy (Burns and Ansin 2004). Similarly, Lazar & Lazar (2004) view the Bush Doctrine as a "discourse-in-the-making" that has been under development since the end of the Cold War (224). In this context, the events of September 11 are to be understood as a particular moment in "the fuller working out of this discourse logic" (224). The policy can be traced back to 1992 to the "Wolfowitz Doctrine," a paper in which Paul Wolfowitz promoted the policy of "striking first to defend America and to project its values" (Kirk 2003). Kirk notes that when laid side-by-side the NSS and the Wolfowitz Doctrine reveal "huge areas of similarity." Wolfowitz's policy of "preemption" appeared again eight years later in a publication of the Project for a New American Century in September 2000, *Rebuilding America's Defenses: Strategy, Forces, and Resources for New Century* (Project for the New American Century 2000). The authors of this document include Dick Cheney, Donald Rumsfeld, Paul Wolfowitz, Jeb Bush, and Lewis Libby. Rahal Mahajan describes the document as a "more honest version of the NSS" as it addresses the issue of how the U.S. can take advantage of the post-cold war "unipolar moment" (Burns and Ansin 2004). The answer provided by the authors is a "blueprint for maintaining global U.S. pre-eminence, precluding the rise of a great power rival, and shaping the international security order in line with American principles and interests." This "American grand strategy" must be advanced "as far into the future as possible" (Project for the

New American Century 2000). The authors note, however, that the process for implementing this strategy is "likely to be a long one, absent some catastrophic and catalyzing event – like a new Pearl Harbor" (51).

Realizing the future: preventive war in Iraq

On March 19, 2003 the Bush administration put its doctrine of prevention into action by initiating war in Iraq. The relationship between the NSS and the Iraq War is one of reciprocal legitimation: the NSS provided the justification for going to war and the war provides evidence of the administration's very real commitment to the doctrine (Burns and Ansin 2004). In his prewar speeches, the President presents a public articulation of the doctrine as he makes his case to the nation for war in Iraq. As such, analysis of these texts can shed light on the role the speeches play within the context of political, conceptual, and linguistic change articulated in the NSS. The following analysis examines the representations of agency and knowledge with respect to the future in the Cincinnati speech and March 17 speech.

Depictions of U.S. and Iraqi agency in both the Cincinnati and March 17 speeches are similar to those in the NSS document. The U.S. is represented as a highly effective and active agent whose actions are compelled by external forces and exigencies. In the Cincinnati speech President Bush declares that, "Understanding the threats of our time, knowing the designs... of the Iraqi regime, we have... an urgent duty to prevent the worst from happening" (G.W. Bush 2002). Through the March 17 speech the public is told that "The United States and other nations did nothing to deserve or invite this threat, but we will do everything to defeat it" (G.W. Bush 2003). Indeed, the beginning of military conflict is explicitly represented as the result of Iraqi action, "Should Saddam Hussein choose confrontation, the American people can know that every measure has been taken to avoid war" and "Their refusal to do so [leave Iraq within 48 hours] will result in military conflict, commenced at a time of our choosing" (G.W. Bush 2003). (See also van Dijk (2005) for a similar analysis of representations of Iraqi agency.)

The Cincinnati speech represents Iraq/Saddam Hussein as a deliberate agent but one whose future actions depend on the inaction of the U.S. and its allies, as excerpt 19 shows.

(19)   If the Iraqi regime **is able** to produce, buy, or steal an amount of highly enriched uranium..., it **could have** a nuclear weapon in less than a year. And **if we allow that to happen**, a terrible line would be crossed. Saddam Hussein **would be** in a position to blackmail anyone who opposes his aggression. He **would be** in a position to dominate the Middle East. He **would be** in a posi-

tion to threaten America. And Saddam Hussein **would be** in a position to pass nuclear secrets to terrorists (G.W. Bush 2002).

Similarly, in March President Bush declares that:

(20) **In one year or five years** the power of Iraq to inflict harm on all free nations **would be** multiplied several times over. With these capabilities, Saddam Hussein and his terrorist allies **could choose** the moment of deadly conflict when they are the strongest (G.W. Bush 2003).

In both speeches, these assertions of future Iraqi action are transformed into the nominalization "threat." As in the NSS, "threat" plays an important role in the lexical composition and transitivity structure of the speeches and their construal of future reality. Moreover, "threat" functions as a particular type of linguistic process that has implications for the political context within which the speeches arise and within which they function.

As in the NSS, we see "threat" rendered as an agentive entity in the prewar speeches,

(21) **The threat comes from** Iraq.

(22) We resolved then and we are resolved today to **confront every threat from any source that could bring** sudden terror and suffering to America.

(23) While there are many dangers in the world, **the threat from Iraq stands alone because it gathers** the most serious dangers of our age in one place.

(24) Knowing these realities, America must not ignore **the threat gathering** against us.

(25) Today in Iraq we see **a threat whose outlines are more clearly defined and whose consequences** are far more deadly.

(26) We choose to meet **that threat now where it arises before it can appear** suddenly in our skies and cities.

Such intertextual connections should not be understood simply as similarities in content, however. They also indicate what Kress refers to as the "complex processes of (re)production of social and linguistic forms, and, in that, the role of institutions and of subjects as both social and linguistic agents" (1995: 123–124). As such, it is important to consider how the Cincinnati and March 17 speeches function as instantiations of and mechanisms for the Bush administration's redefinition of conditions of military engagement. According to Kress (1995), the significance of newly produced transitivity forms such as "threat" derives from the ideological work they do. He explains that "particular coding orientations have particular social origins, and that the (new) coding orientation, in its turn reproduces a particular social reality and produces subjects who come to regard that reality as unproblematically given" (127). In the present context, the tropos of threat in the President's speeches to the public supports and advances the political and conceptual change articulated in the NSS. Specifically, "threat" provides the lexical and syntactic structure needed for the public to "see" and talk about the reality of the future as the administration does: as comprising active, emerging threats that are gathering against us and that compel us to act preventively in order to stave off the "future of fear" that will result if America "remains idle" (G.W. Bush 2002). According to Kaufer and Butler (1996), as an "interactive performative", the issuance of a threat serves a more immediate and specific rhetorical function by constructing a particular relationship between a speaker and an audience with respect to future events and present behavior (248–249). They explain that in making a threat a speaker presents events that project negative future consequences. These threats may take the form, as they do in Bush's speeches, of a speaker threatening an audience with an opponent's future world. This vision of the future, in turn, obligates the audience to take or support actions that will prevent the speaker's opponent from getting "rein on the future" (249; see also Edelman 1971: 109–111). Above, we see the public being threatened with a future world in which Saddam Hussein and "WMD-armed adversaries" are in control. Wodak (2000) identified a similar use of the tropos of threat in her study of policy documents and debates concerning employment policies in the European Union. In that context, the threat takes the form of a future world in which critics of globalization prevail, a world in which the European Union "loses ground in the worldwide competition and condemns itself to decline" (90).

As explained earlier, the NSS sanctions preventive military action by positioning Bush administration officials as experts who can "read" and "know" the future. This expertise manifests in the speeches primarily through systematic variations in their modal coding. The Cincinnati speech is marked by evidential contrasts in its presentation of alternative visions of the future and by a contrast between the modal coding of the declarations of the Iraqi threat and the coding of the evidentiary statements from which those declarations derive. The March 17 speech similarly presents alternative future scenarios of U.S. action and the futures that could result from those actions, although less explicitly and extensively than the Cincinnati speech. In addition, the March 17 speech contrasts the future actions of Iraq that the U.S. is acting to prevent with the future actions of Iraq that could result from a military strike by the U.S. As the following analysis demonstrates, the alternative futures projected through both speeches are construed in such a way as to privilege the Bush administration's plans and view of the future and to marginalize the others. I begin with the Cincinnati speech and then discuss the March 17 speech.

The Cincinnati speech presents two competing visions of the future, both of which comprise deontic and epistemic futures. Through this juxtaposition of contrasting futures the administration projects its representation of the opposing viewpoints concerning war with Iraq (Dedaić 2006). In the future privileged by the Bush administration, the U.S. engages in decisive military action against Iraq which ensures a future of freedom and democracy and a "world without fear." The oppositional future is characterized as one of inaction – of "waiting" and "hoping" – which leads to the use of weapons of mass destruction and a "future of fear." Lazuka (2006) identified similar types of statements in her analysis of Bush's discourse concerning the attacks of 9/11 and the war in Iraq. These "predictives" present a "consolatory vision" to an audience and project future events that the audience will desire and benefit from. The rhetorical goal of such statements is to garner the audience's support for actions to be taken in the near term, while also "raising their spirits in the face of future threats" (31).

The presentation of these privileged and oppositional futures is remarkable for its systematic and contrastive use of evidential markers. The oppositional future is consistently projected through mental and verbal process clauses of the outsider-citizen which encode that future within a modality of "hope," "belief," "wonder," "worry," and "argument." Moreover, these statements are marked with modal auxiliaries that encode this information as potential and possible; as such, they take a probabilistic stance toward the future. The privileged future, however, is articulated through an oracular stance as it is presented through the "absolute modality" of "is" and "will be," a modality that derives from evidence, history, and reason. We can see these evidential contrasts in each of the following excerpts in which the first sentence projects the oppositional future and the second projects the privileged future (G.W. Bush 2002),

(27) **Some have argued** that confronting the threat from Iraq **could** detract from the war against terror. To the contrary, confronting the threat posed by Iraqi **is crucial to winning** the war on terror.

(28) **Some people believe** that we **can** address this danger by **simply resuming the old approach** to inspections and by applying diplomatic and economic pressure. Yet this **is precisely** what the world **has tried to do since 1991**.

(29) **America hopes** the regime will make that choice. Unfortunately, at least so far, we **have little reason** to expect it.

(30) **Some worry** that a change of leadership in Iraq could create instability and make the situation worse. The situation **could hardly get worse** for world security and for the people of Iraq.

Wodak (2000) identified a similar rhetorical move in the policy debates concerning the European Union economy. She explains that a key part of the argument embedded in the "topics list" involved explicating the "beliefs and fears which are related to globalization in the minds of 'people'" (87). These irrational concerns were systematically juxtaposed with the rational thoughts of the "experts" (104). Contrasts in evidentiality in the President's speeches can also be seen in the rhetorical use of question/answer pairs which juxtapose the competing projections of the future. The questions, which are attributed at the beginning of the speech to "many Americans," project the oppositional future and the answers project the privileged future,

(31)   First **I'm asked** why Iraq is different from other countries and regions that also have terrible weapons. While **there are** many dangers in the world, the threat from **Iraq stands alone** because it **gathers** the most serious dangers of our age in one place.

(32)   **Some ask** how urgent this danger is to America. The danger **is already significant** and it only **grows worse with time**.

In these excerpts, we see the oppositional future projected through the verbal process clause of "asking," which codes that future as equivocal and as deriving from a lack of knowledge. The answers, however, are not projected through either verbal or mental process ("I think," "my administration believes") clauses; they are presented as unmediated statements about the future that are grounded in reality.

The Cincinnati speech also reveals a marked contrast between the declarations about the nature of the threat posed by Iraq and their supporting evidentiary statements. For example, the President declares that "The danger is already significant and it only grows worse with time." As the following excerpts show, this unmediated and unequivocal statement is a transformation of interpretations of data from underspecified sources and conjectures about present and future Iraqi actions.

(33)   **The inspectors**, however, concluded that Iraq **had likely produced two to four times** that amount.

(34)   Iraq possesses ballistic missiles with a **likely range** of hundreds of miles, far enough to strike Saudi Arabia, Israel, Turkey and other nations in a region where more than 135,000 American civilians and service members work and live.

(35)   **We've also discovered through intelligence** that Iraq has **a growing fleet** of manned and unmanned aerial vehicles that **could be** used to disperse chemical or biological weapons across broad areas.

(36)   All that **might be** required are small containers and one terrorist or Iraqi intelligence operative to deliver it.

In sum, these excerpts show that evidentiary statements explicitly marked as to source and degree of certainty were transformed into an unmarked declaration about the present situation and its progression into the future. Gellner and Pincus

(2003) found similar contradictions between the modality of claims being made by the administration and that of the evidence underlying them in a range of statements and speeches by the Bush administration. They have documented the way in which administration officials systematically transformed hedged and speculative data into unequivocal, definitive statements about the nature and extent of Iraq's nuclear weapons program. The authors describe a pattern in both public and private statements made by administration officials that depicted Iraq's weapons program as "more active, more certain, and more imminent in its threat" than the data actually supported. They further note that the administration regularly "withheld evidence" that didn't conform to its position and "seldom corrected misstatements or acknowledged loss of confidence" in data they had previously cited as credible. (See Miller (2004) for a similar assessment.)

The March 17 speech juxtaposes two future scenarios similar to those presented in the Cincinnati speech. The privileged future in which the U.S. takes military action against Iraq, thereby ensuring a future of peace and freedom, is contrasted with the oppositional future in which the U.S. fails to act, thereby enabling Iraq to realize its aggressive designs. Interestingly, both of these futures center on the issue of agency, specifically on who gets to choose what the future will be. Within the privileged future the choice lies with the United States as President Bush states that "the future we choose" is one in which "the greatest power of freedom is to overcome hatred and violence, and turn the creative gifts of men and women to the pursuits of peace." In the oppositional future the choice rests with Saddam Hussein and his "terrorist allies," who "could choose the moment of deadly conflict when they are strongest." President Bush denies them that choice, however, by declaring that "we choose to meet that threat now where it arises before it can appear suddenly in our skies and cities."

While the privileged future projected through the Cincinnati speech focused only on the positive outcomes of U.S. military action, the March 17 speech also projects future actions that Iraq "might" take in reaction to U.S. military action,

(37) In **desperation** he and terrorist groups **might try to conduct** terrorist operations against the American people and our friends. These attacks are not **inevitable**. They are, however, **possible**.

(38) **Should** enemies strike our country they **would be attempting to shift** our attention with panic and weaken our morale with fear. In this they **would fail**. **No act of theirs can alter** the course or shake the resolve of this country.

(39) **If** our enemies dare to strike us, they and all who have aided them **will face** fearful consequences.

Lazuka (2006) terms such statements "suppositives", the purpose of which is to present the audience with particular information about the nature of the enemy and how the enemy's actions could affect them. Such "fear appeals" prepare the audience for an upcoming conflict by intensifying the negative associations the audience has regarding the enemy (321). These appeals, however, must be articulated in such a way that arouses the audience's negative feelings toward the enemy while not hampering its support for taking action against that enemy. In the preceding statements this balance is struck through modal qualification and elaboration. In excerpt 37, Iraqi retaliation is characterized as an act of "desperation" which is qualified by "might", the only occurrence of "might" as a modal auxiliary in the entire speech. The relatively low degree of certainty attributed to this future action is reinforced by the second and third sentences which characterize Iraqi retaliation as a "possibility" rather than an "inevitability." In addition to modal auxiliaries, excerpts 38 and 39 are modalized by being constructed as conditional statements; that is, they follow an "if/then" structure. Palmer (1986) explains that the function of conditionals is not to assert that an event could, might, or will occur. Rather, conditionals merely project hypothetical scenarios concerning future conditions and contingencies and assert the dependence of one proposition upon another (see also Dancygier 1998 and Sweetser 1990). As such, Iraqi retaliation is presented here not as a probable or even possible future action, but rather as a hypothetic scenario. Moreover, in both these statements, the hypothetical Iraqi action is elaborated in interesting ways. In excerpt 38, the goal of the enemies' strike is represented in terms of its psychological, rather than physical or material, goals and consequences. We are told, quite emphatically, however, that this goal will never be realized. In excerpt 39, the elaboration focuses on the "fearful consequences" our enemies "will face" rather than the effect these actions will have on the American people or U.S. troops.

These mitigating tactics contrast sharply with the modal coding of the future Iraqi actions that will result if the U.S. does not act.

(40) Using chemical, biological or, one day, nuclear weapons, obtained with the help of Iraq, the terrorists **could fulfill** their stated ambitions and kills [sic] thousands or hundreds of thousands of innocent people in our country or any other.

(41) In one year or five years the power of Iraq to inflict harm on all free nations **would be** multiplied many times over.

(42) With these capabilities, Saddam Hussein and his terrorist allies **could choose** the moment of deadly conflict when they are the strongest.

Variation in the certainty of these different future scenarios functions, potentially, to shore up support for and belief in the declared cause and outcomes of "preemptive" U.S. action while, simultaneously, tempering concerns about the consequences of that action.

Conclusion

Through its national security strategy, the Bush administration projects a future in which the U.S. will "extend the benefits of freedom across the globe" (2). Indeed, this is the future promised to the Iraqi people:

> [T]he first and greatest benefit **will come** to the Iraqi men, women, and children. The oppression of the Kurds, of Assyrians, Turkomans, Shi'a, Sunnis and others **will be lifted**. The long captivity of Iraq **will end** and an era of new hope **will begin**.... By our resolve **we will give** strength to others. By our courage **we will give** hope to others. And by our action **we will secure** peace and lead the world to a better day (G.W. Bush 2002).

Over four years since the beginning of "Operation Iraqi Freedom," this future has yet to be realized. Indeed, in a BBC interview Donald Rumsfeld admitted that as of June 2005 Iraq was no safer than it was in May 2003 when major combat operations ended (United States Department of Defense 2005). The Bush administration has, nevertheless, staked a claim on the future. It has done so, in part, by transforming politically motivated policies and goals into an objectified world of "coming dangers" and "emerging threats" that "must be defeated."

Taken together the NSS and Iraq war speeches play a significant, consequential role in the discursive process of establishing the Bush vision of the future as the "word" (Hodge and Kress 1988). The power of this vision derives, in part, from discursive processes which strip away its "transformational history, of the process via which it came into existence" (147). And it is this process of transforming individualized interests into "reified" and "universal" interests that helps ensure the ideological success of the discourse (Menz 2002: 142). In sum, the process of mystification that elevates politically interested and motivated assertions about the future into the "word" is well underway in the Bush administration's discourse of "preemptive" war. The modality of potentiality, uncertainty, and speculation is left behind in the details as alternative positions, interpretations, and visions are "trimmed and reworked into their place within the 'word'" (Hodge and Kress 1988: 148). An important task for discourse analysts, it seems to me, is to reclaim the agency and potentialities the future offers for social and political transformation. In short, we need to reclaim the future "as a virtual space – blank, colourless, shapeless, a space to be made over, a space where everything is still to be won" (Hebdige 1993: 278).

Notes

1.   The U.S. has justified preemptive military action by making misleading, sometimes false claims of imminent threats faced by the U.S. and/or its allies (e.g. The Gulf of Tonkin incident, Grenada, the sinking of the Maine in the Spanish-American war, alleged Iraqi plans to invade Saudi Arabia in 1990 (see Dunmire, 1997)). Moreover, the concept of preemption dates back to Daniel Webster's tenure as Secretary of State under William Henry Harrison (Keyes 2005).

2.   Such positive self presentation and negative other presentation is a global semantic strategy prevalent in post-9/11 discourses (van Dijk 2005: 68; see also Chilton 2003; Lazuka 2006; Leudar, Marsland and Nekvapil 2004; Graham, Keenan and Dowd 2004), as well as other conflict-oriented discourses (van Dijk 1992).

3.   See also Lazuka (2006) for an analysis of legitimation devices used in President Bush's post-9/11 statements and speeches.

4.   Actually, there are four statements which use the verbal form. However, one of these statements is a section heading which repeats statement #12, which appears in the body of the document.

5.   The named groups and nations are al Qaeda, the Taliban, Afghanistan, North Korea, Iran, and Iraq. With the exception of Afghanistan, which is mentioned six times, each of the others is mentioned only once. Other terms used include "WMD-armed adversaries," "new deadly challenges," "the embittered few," "enemies of civilization," and "evil, stealth, deceit, and murder." Lazuka (2006) noted a similar phenomenon in the use of pronominals "us" and "them" in Bush's speeches. She notes that references to "them", i.e. "the enemy", do not name specific people or countries, while references to "us" do specify individuals, nations, and groups (322). See also Graham and Luke (2005: 16) and Lazar and Lazar (2004: 226, 239).

6.   See a January 27, 2004 press briefing in which Scott McClellan rejects a reporter's suggestion that the administration's policy should be referred to as a policy of prevention rather than a policy of preemption (available at www.whitehouse.gov/news/releases/2004/01/20040127.6 htmlwww.whitehouse.gov/news/releases/2004/01/20040127-.6.html.)

7.   I am grateful to the editors of this volume for bringing this point, as well as the press conference cited above, to my attention.

References

Aristotle. 1954. *The Rhetoric and Poetics of Aristotle*. W. Rhys Roberts (trans). New York: Modern Library.

Burns, M. & Ansin, G. (producers). 2004. *Preventive Warriors*. Michael Burns Films.

Bush, G.H.W.1991, January 16. "Address to the Nation Announcing Allied Military Action in the Persian Gulf." Available: bushlibrary.tamu.edu/research/papers/1991/91011602.html.

Bush, G.W. 2002, October 7. "President Bush outlines Iraqi threat." Available: www.whitehouse.gov/news/releases/2002/10/20021007-8.html.

Bush, G.W. 2003, March 17. "President says Saddam Hussein must leave Iraq within 48 hours." Available: www.whitehouse.gov/news/releases/2003/03/20030317-7.html.

Caldas-Coulthard, C. and Coulthard, M. 1996. *Texts and Practices: Readings in Critical Discourse Analysis*. London: Routledge.

Cheney, R. 1993. "Defense Strategy for the 1990s: The Regional Defense Strategy." Available: www.informationclearinghouse.info/pdf/naarpr_Defense.pdf.

Chilton, P. 2003. "Deixis and distance: President Clinton's justification of intervention in Kosovo." In *At War with Words*, M. Dedaic & D. Nelson (eds.), 95–126. New York: Mouton de Gruyter.

Chomsky, N. 2003. "Preventive war 'The supreme crime.'" *Z Magazine*. Available: www.zmag.org/content/showarticle.cfm?ItemID=4030.

Collins, J. and Glover, R. 2002. *Collateral Language: A User's Guide to America's New War*. New York : New York University Press.

Dancygier, B. 1998. *Conditionals and Prediction: Time, Knowledge, and Causation in Conditional Construction*. Cambridge: Cambridge University Press.

Dedaić, M. 2006. "Political speech and persuasive argumentation." In *Encyclopedia of Language and Linguistics* (2nd ed.), Keith Brown (ed.), 700–706. Boston: Elsevier.

De Saint-Georges, I. 2003. "Anticipatory Discourses: Producing Futures of Action in Vocational Work Programs for Long-Term Unemployed." Doctoral Dissertation, Georgetown University, Washington, D.C.

Dunmire, P. 1997. "Naturalizing the future in factual discourse: A critical linguistic analysis of a projected event." *Written Communication* 14(2): 221–263.

Edelman, M. 1971. *Politics as Symbolic Action: Mass Arousal and Quiescence*. Chicago: Markham.

Edelman, M. 1988. *Constructing the Political Spectacle*. Chicago: Chicago University Press.

Fairclough, N. 1989. *Language and Power*. London: Longman.

Fairclough, N. 1995. *Critical Discourse Analysis*. London: Longman.

Fairclough, N. 2000. "Representations of change in neo-liberal discourse." Available: www.cddc.vt.edu/host/lnc/Lncarchive.html.

Fairclough, N. 2005. "Blair's contribution to elaborating a new 'doctrine of international community.'" *Journal of Language and Politics* 4 (1): 41–63.

Fleischman, S. 1982. *The Future in Thought and Language*. Cambridge: Cambridge University Press.

Foucault, M. 1984. "The order of discourse." In *Language and Politics*, M. Shapiro (ed.), 108–138. New York: New York University Press.

Gellner, B. & Pincus, W. 2003, August 12. "Depictions of threat outgrew supporting evidence." Available: www.washingtonpost.com.

Givón, T. 1989. *Mind, Code, Context: Essays in Pragmatics*. Hillsdale, N. J.: Lawrence Erlbaum.

Graham, P. and Luke, A. 2005. "The language of neofeudal corporatism and the war on Iraq." *Journal of Language and Politics* 4(1): 11–39.

Graham, P., Keenan, T., and Dowd, A. 2004. "A call to arms at the end of history: a discourse-historical analysis of George W. Bush's declaration of war on terror." *Discourse and Society* 15(2–3): 199–221.

Grosz, E. 1999. "Becoming . . . an introduction." In *Becomings: Explorations in Time, Memory, and Futures*, E. Grosz (ed), 1–11. Ithaca: Cornell University Press.

Halliday, M.A.K. 1978. *Language as Social Semiotic*. London: Edward Arnold.

Hebdige, D. 1993. "Training some thoughts on the future." In *Mapping the Futures: Local Cultures, Global Change*, J. Bird, B. Curtis, T. Putnam, G. Robertson, and L. Tickner (eds.), 270–279. London: Routledge.

Hodge, B. and Kress, G. 1988. *Social Semiotics* (2nd ed.). Ithaca: Cornell.

Kaufer, D. S. and Butler, B. 1996. *Rhetoric and the Arts of Design*. Mahwah, N.J.: Lawrence Erlbaum.

Keyes, C. 2005. "Defining just preemption." JSCOPE 2005. Available: www.usafa.af.mil/jscope/JSCOPE05/Keyes05.html.

Kirk, M. (producer). 2003. *The War Behind Closed Doors*. The WGBH Educational Foundation.

Kress, G. 1995. "The social production of language: History and structures of domination." In *Discourse in Society: Systemic Functional Perspectives*, P.H. Fries & M. Gregory (eds), 115–140. Norwood, NJ: Ablex.

Lakoff, G. 2001, September 16. "Metaphors of terror." *The Days After*. Available: www.press.uchicago.edu/News/911lakoff.html.

Latour, B. 1987. *Science in Action: How to Follow Scientists and Engineers Through Society*. Cambridge: Harvard University Press.

Lazar, A. and Lazar, M. M. 2004. "The discourse of the new world order: 'out-casting' the double face of threat." *Discourse and Society* 15(2–3): 223–242.

Lazuka, A. 2006. "Communicative intention in George W. Bush's presidential speeches and statements from 11 September 2001 to 11 September 2003." *Discourse and Society* 17(3): 299–330.

Leudar, I., Marsland, V., and Nekvpil, J. 2004. "On membership categorization: 'Us' and 'them' and 'doing violence' in political discourse." *Discourse and Society* 15(2–3): 243–266.

Levitas, R. 1993. "The future of thinking about the future." In *Mapping the Futures: Local Cultures, Global Change*, J. Bird, B. Curtis, T. Putnam, G. Roberston, and L. Tickner (eds.), 257–266. London: Routledge.

Martin, J.R. 2002. "Making history: Grammar for interpretation." In *Re/reading the Past: Critical and Function Perspectives on Time and Value*, J.R. Martin and R. Wodak (eds.), 19–60. Amsterdam/Philadelphia: John Benjamins.

Martin, J.R. and Wodak, R. (eds.). 2002. *Re/reading the Past: Critical and Function Perspectives on Time and Value*. Amsterdam/Philadelphia: John Benjamins.

Menz, F. 2002. "The language of the past: On the reconstruction of a collective history through individual stories." In *Re/reading the Past: Critical and Function Perspectives on Time and Value*, J.R. Martin and R. Wodak (eds), 139–175. Amsterdam/Philadelphia: John Benjamins.

Miller, D. (ed.). 2004. *Tell Me Lies: Propaganda and Media Distortion in the Attack on Iraq*. London: Pluto Press.

Newhouse, J. 2003. *Imperial America: The Bush Assault on the World Order*. New York: Alfred A. Knopf.

Palmer, F. 1986. *Mood and Modality*. Cambridge: Cambridge University Press.

Project for the New American Century. 2000. "Rebuilding America's Defenses: Strategy, Forces and Resources for a New Century." Available: www.newamericancentury.org/RebuildingAmericasDefenses.pdf.

Reisigl, M. 2006. "Rhetorical tropes in political discourse." In *Encyclopedia of Language and Linguistics* (2nd ed.), Keith Brown (ed.). Boston: Elsevier.

Scollon, S. 2001. "Habitus, consciousness, agency and the problem of intention: How we carry and are carried by political discourses." Folio Linguistica XXXV: 97–129.

Scollon, S. and Scollon, R. 2000. "The construction of agency and action in anticipatory discourse: Positioning ourselves against neo-liberalism." Paper presented at the III Conference for Sociocultural Research, Campinas, Sao Paulo, Brazil.

Silverstein, M. 2003. *Talking Politics: The Substance of Style from Abe to "W."* Chicago: Prickly Paradigm Press.

Sweetser, E. 1990. *From Etymology to Pragmatics: Metaphorical and Cultural Aspects of Semantic Structure.* Cambridge: Cambridge University Press.

United States Department of Defense. 2005, June 13. "Secretary Rumsfeld Interview with Sir David Frost, BBC News." Available: www.defenselink.mil/transcripts/2005/tr20050615-secdef3043.html.

United States National Security Council. 2002. *The National Security Strategy of the United States of America.* Available: www.whitehouse.gov/nsc/nss.html.

Van Dijk, T. 1992. "Discourse and the denial of racism." *Discourse and Society* 3(1): 87–118.

Van Dijk, T. 1998a. *Ideology: An Interdisciplinary Approach.* London: Sage.

Van Dijk, T. 1998b. "What is political discourse?" In *Political Linguistics*, J. Blommaert (ed.), 11–52. Amsterdam/Philadelphia: John Benjamins.

Van Dijk, T. 2005. "War rhetoric of a little ally: Political implicatures and Aznar's legitimation of the war on Iraq." *Journal of Language and Politics* 4(1): 65–91.

Wodak, R. 2000. "From conflict to consensus? The co-construction of a policy paper." In *European Union Discourses on Un/employment: An Interdisciplinary Approach to Employment Policy-Making and Organizational Change*, P. Muntigl, G. Weiss, and R. Wodak (eds.), 73–114. Amsterdam/Philadelphia: John Benjamins.

CHAPTER 3

Enforcing justice, justifying force

America's justification of violence in the New World Order

Annita Lazar and Michelle M. Lazar

"Out of these troubled times ... a new world order can emerge: a new era – freer from the threat of terror, stronger in the pursuit of justice, and more secure in the quest for peace." – George H.W. Bush, September 11, 1990

Introduction

This chapter is concerned with America's articulation of the pursuit of justice in securing the New World Order. It follows from our earlier work in which we outlined the emergence of the "discourse of the New World Order" in the post-Cold War era, and discussed in detail its constitution in terms of the formulation of 'new threats' during this period (Lazar and Lazar 2004). The New World Order is a 'discourse formation' (Foucault 1972) in that it comprises a socio-historically contingent field of related statements, which produces and normatively structures knowledge of contemporary international relations and America's role within it. We have argued that the 'New World Order' has been a discourse-in-formation in the post-Cold War period, notably from President George H.W. Bush's inaugural statement in 1990 to President George W. Bush's administration.[1] In a world no longer divided along strategic bipolar lines with the demise of the 'Soviet threat', the New World Order discourse refers to America's articulation of its unipolar global hegemony in the face of a world otherwise gravitating towards multipolar centers of power. Even though America possessed unrivalled military power at the time of the Soviet debacle, Europe and Japan posed industrial and economic competition.[2]

A foundational element of the New World Order discourse, which we have earlier identified, is the establishment of an American-led moral order (Lazar and Lazar 2004). It is an order that is built up vis-à-vis the enunciation of the aberrant

'Other' or 'threat' which at the same time justifies the identification, division and excision of that threat (Foucault 1967). In the post-Cold War era, the 'threat of terror' has been identified as the new enemy, comprising Saddam Hussein and Osama bin Laden and his associates[3] (with the list expanding in the present Bush administration to include still others). Our analysis of the 'twin terrors' has shown that based upon the dual principles that "They are all the same," and "They are different from Us" (cf. Said 1978), Saddam Hussein and Osama bin Laden have been conflated as a related class of threat, and in similar ways multiply condemned from a variety of fields by a discursive strategy we call 'out-casting.' Outcasting is a process of border control by which individuals and/or groups are systematically marked and set aside as outcasts of a social order. Unlike the more general term 'Othering', 'outcasting' is intended to capture the historical variability of currently casting previous allies as political pariahs, i.e. ejecting them from their place within the international community.[4] Used in both senses as noun and verb, outcasting is a macro-strategy encompassing a range of inter-related micro-strategies: 'criminalization', 'enemization', 'evilification' and 'orientalization.' In terms of the law, Saddam Hussein and Osama bin Laden are cast as criminals ('criminalization') – for example, they are "murderers" (G.W. Bush 2001e) and "killers" (G.W. Bush 2002a; Clinton 1998a); politically, they are enemies of freedom and democracy ('enemization') – for example, they "hate our freedoms" (G.W. Bush 2001e); in spiritual terms, "they are evil" (G.W. Bush 2002a) ('evilification'); and historico-culturally, they are moral degenerates ('orientalization') – for example, they are "barbaric" (G.W. Bush 2001f) and "merciless" (G.W. Bush 2002b). The over-negativization represents 'them' as a hypersignified Other, who threatens the moral values of the New World Order on all fronts.

Entailed by America's definition of the moral order, the present chapter focuses on America's policing and defending of the New World Order against the named threats. The strategies of outcasting specifically evoke a frame of conflict, which makes counter-violence by America and its allies justifiable, indeed necessary; from the four strategies of outcasting emerges a composite picture of the Other as a culturally bellicose people, attacking 'our' values of freedom and liberty, relishing in death and destruction, and as the personification of evil battling the good. The use of force, therefore, becomes morally justified on all and every front in order to ensure peace and security of the order. Two implications arise from this. First, because action is possible in principle on multiple fronts, the Other can be defeated one way or another. In modern international relations, however, it is acceptable to explicitly pursue the Other based on criminality and warfare rather than on civilizational difference or as vanquishing evil. The result is an overt mix of police and war frames in America's pursuit of justice in the New World Order, commensurate with criminalization and enemization. Yet because orientalization and evilification, as mentioned, also powerfully evoke frames of aggression and struggle, civilizational and spiritual tropes are drawn into, and indeed reify, the rhetoric of justification, without themselves seeming to be the primary cause for America's political (counter) violence. Second, the ready threat of military force by America, in particular, has become a prominent feature of the New World Order. By this we mean that the current political order has become increasingly characterized both by talk about the potential for and righteousness of military action; as well as, importantly, the actual use of military force against threats. As Chomsky (1991) explained, with the disappearance of the Soviet deterrent, America has become freer in the use of force – shifting problems to the arena of forceful confrontation, in which America maintains near monopoly of military might. It is important to recognize, therefore, the linkage between discursive and military acts of power.

In what follows, we provide an analysis of America's justifications for the use of force in the construal of policing and defending the New World Order. As a discourse-in-formation, this involves analysis of an intertextual archive of speeches and written statements of the three post-Cold War American leaders across time and specific historical events, and their respective administrations. The archive for the present study comprises President George W. Bush's speeches in the aftermath of 9/11 including the attack and occupation of Iraq since 2003; President Bill Clinton's speeches in the context of American military action in Afghanistan and Sudan, and Iraq in 1998; and President G.H.W. Bush's statements in the context of the 1990–1991 Gulf War. The intertextual analysis of the discourse is based on identification of particular themes with regards to policing and defending action that emerged from the data. We will organize our discussion based on these discursive themes below, and show how these themes are manifested through clusters of lexico-grammatical (Halliday 1985) and rhetorical strategies including the use of metaphors, frames, speech acts and argument structures (including justification strategies) (Fairclough 1989; Lakoff 1991; van Dijk 1995; Benke and Wodak 2003).

Policing the New World Order

Policing is one means of securing the New World Order. In this section, we observe the following themes constitutive of the discourse on policing: reference to the law; construction of the 'criminal' as transgressor of the law; and America's role as global policeman. There is also textual evidence to suggest that in spite of the fact that America's justifications for actions against the enemies is based on the rule of law, America itself, at times, appears not to be bound by legal conduct, and is above the law.

The rule of law

Central to policing in the New World Order discourse is the disciplining of the international polity through the maintenance of 'law and order.' The invocation of law is foundational in the new world order as originally espoused in G.H.W. Bush's vision (see below) as well as subsequently continued in the discourse formation.

(1)   Today, that new world is struggling to be born ... a world where *the rule of law* supplants the rule of the jungle (G.H.W. Bush 1990b).

(2)   *Iraq's brutality, aggression and violation of international law* cannot be allowed to succeed... (G.H.W. Bush 1991b)

(3)   *The long arm of American law* has reached out around the world and brought to trial those guilty of attacks in New York, in Virginia and in the Pacific (Clinton 1998a).

(4)   The search is underway for those who are behind these evil acts. I have directed *the full resources of our intelligence and law enforcement communities* to find those responsible... (G.W. Bush 2001a)

The appeal of the field of law – both domestic and international – rests on the assumption of clear and objective rules, principles and procedures. In these examples, references to the law in the topic or subject positions (plus their embeddedness in the noun phrases as postmodifiers instead of as 'heads', which makes scrutiny harder), show how the basis of this appeal is presupposed as self-evident, and thus not requiring elaboration. Reference to the law alone is sufficient grounds for the legitimation of action. The invocation of the rule of law, however, is based upon relations of power, dominance and control.

Foucault (1977) has argued that the penal system, although a seemingly more humane system than war, is nonetheless a form of domination, albeit via a different mode, practiced as a 'discourse of right.' It is exercised through processes of normalization, whereby subjects are bound to one another in a social contract of prescribed behavioral norms. We can say the social contract exists for various levels of actors – at the sub-state, state, and trans-state/global levels.

In the New World Order discourse, the prescribed behavioral norms connote civilizational superiority. Note particularly the contrast between the "rule of the jungle" and the "rule of law" in example (1). Hayward (1994: 237) comments that for Americans, the expression the "rule of the jungle," with associations of the primitive, alludes particularly to Africa and Asia. If this is so, then the implication is that a world order based upon the rule of the law refers to 'our' province; that of the 'civilized.' The relation between the two, moreover, is not merely one of dissimilarity but, as the verb *supplants* suggests, one of ascendancy.

Constructing the criminal other

The 'criminal' is a transgressor of the behavioral norms laid down by law. Criminalization of Osama bin Laden and Saddam Hussein has been discursively produced in a number of ways, which we discussed in Lazar and Lazar 2004. To summarize, the casting of the Other as 'criminal' is accomplished through rhetorical strategies which represent the transgressive acts as well as the transgressor's perverse state of mind: overlexicalization and listing of criminal acts, characterization of victims, concretization of criminal acts, and highlighting the intentionality and perverseness of actors.

Overlexicalization and listing of criminal acts

(5) Saddam Hussein systematically raped, pillaged and plundered [...] maimed and murdered (G.H.W. Bush 1991a)

(6) terrorists would unleash blackmail and genocide and chaos (G.W. Bush 2002b)

Characterization of victims

  as vulnerable
(7) a small and helpless neighbor [Kuwait] (G.H.W. Bush 1991c) [in the context of the US-led liberation of Kuwait]

  as ordinary
(8) the victims were in airplanes or in their offices. Secretaries, business men and women, military and federal workers. Moms and dads. Friends and neighbors (G.W. Bush 2001e) [in the context of 9/11]

  as innocent
(9) the murder of innocents (G.W. Bush 2002b [referring to 9/11]; Clinton 1998a [referring to the 'terrorist' bombing of US embassies in Kenya and Tanzania])

Concretization of the acts in graphic, horrific terms

(10) Iraq's occupation of Kuwait has been a nightmare ... homes, buildings and factories have been looted. Babies have been torn from incubators; children shot in front of their parents (G.H.W. Bush 1990c).

(11) Iraq ... a regime that has already used poison gas to murder thousands of its own citizens, leaving bodies of mothers huddled over their dead children (G. W. Bush 2002a)

Highlighting the intentionality and perverseness of their actions

(12)   their mission is murder (Clinton 1998a)

(13)   our enemies send other people's children on missions of suicide and murder. They embrace tyranny and death as a cause and a creed (G.W. Bush 2002a).

Criminalization, furthermore, is accentuated by elements of orientalization and 'evilification':

(14)   *Iraq's brutality, aggression and violation of international law* cannot be allowed to succeed... (G.H.W. Bush 1991b)

(15)   The search is underway for those who are behind these *evil* acts. I have directed *the full resources of our intelligence and law enforcement communities* to find those responsible... (G.W. Bush 2001a)

(16)   We're going to find those *evil*doers, those *barbaric* people who attacked our country (G.W. Bush 2001d).

(17)   We fight to protect the innocent so that *the lawless and merciless will not inherit the Earth* (G.W. Bush 2001f).

In these examples, orientalist and religious classificatory schemes are in operation: in (15) and (16) via premodifiers or classifiers "evil" and "barbaric"; and in (14) and (17) through co-ordination that links the field of law with orientalist and religious tropes, respectively. In the case of (14), the co-ordinate structure produces a list whereby "brutality" and "aggression", which suggest lapses of civility or morality, are linked with illegality. In the case of (17), the field of law is incorporated and thereby recontextualized within religious discourse, i.e. the "lawless" in conjunction with the "merciless" constitutes the (grammatical) subject that "will not inherit the Earth." Interestingly, though, the religious discourse referenced here is not a direct quotation from the Bible, but creatively spliced together from two different verses from the Beatitudes –"Blessed are the meek, for they shall inherit the earth" (Matthew 5:5) and "Blessed are the merciful, for they shall obtain mercy" (Matthew 5:7) (American Standard Version) – and negated, for prescriptive effect. On the one hand, it could be argued that the double-articulation (the inflection of criminality with elements of the supernatural and/or the uncivilized) in these examples potentially places the Other outside the remit of 'our' modern and secular penal system. Yet, on the other hand, the orientalist and religious descriptors contribute directly to the construction of the criminal as they categorize the indefensible nature of the criminal acts, thus adding moral gravity to the offenses. Indeed, given the hypersignification of the Other as a multi-dimensional outcast (as earlier discussed), the double-articulation of criminal acts in the discourse is hardly either surprising or unexpected.

Although in the New World Order discourse on the whole, Saddam Hussein and Osama bin Laden are cast as the main criminals, President George W. Bush's administration includes several other actors as potential criminals because of their association with the outlaws. In the examples given below, the wider circle of potential criminals refers to Actors – ranging from the less specific "those" and "the people" to the more specific "the government" – whose actions benefit the offenders (Goals), i.e. harboring, hiding, housing and feeding them. In pragmatics terms, these utterances all express the speech act of warning, which is felicitous based on knowledge of Anglo-Saxon law that treats perpetrators and abettors of crime as equally culpable and deserving of punishment.

(18) I gave fair warning to *the government that harbors them* in Afghanistan. The Taliban made a choice to continue hiding terrorists, and now they are paying a price (G.W. Bush 2001h).

(19) We will make no distinction between the terrorists who committed these acts and *those who harbor them* (G.W. Bush 2001a).

(20) We're going to hold *the people who house them* accountable. *The people who think they can provide safe havens*[5] will be held accountable. *The people who feed them* will be held accountable (G.W. Bush 2001d).

America as global policeman

Just as the discourse of right is premised upon the legitimate requirement of obedience and conformity to the social order, it invests authority structures with the legitimate right to pursue and punish offenders. America assumes the role of global policeman, or marshal tasked with seeking out the offenders. "Search", "find", and "hunt" in (21) to (23) below constitute the semantic field of a massive manhunt for elusive perpetrators.

(21) *The search* is under way for those who are behind these evil acts. I have directed the full resources of our intelligence and law enforcement communities *to find* those responsible [...] (G.W. Bush 2001a).

(22) We're going *to find* those evildoers (G.W. Bush 2001d).

(23) We *hunt*[6] an enemy that hides in shadows and caves (G.W. Bush 2001g).

The search is undertaken in the pursuit of 'justice' – a notion that once again (like 'the law') is presented as if its meaning was self-evident and singular. The invocation of the concept of justice, because of its strong sense of righteousness, enables America to garner support both domestically and internationally for its police (and military) action.

(24) whether we bring our enemies to *justice* or bring *justice* to our enemies, *justice* will be done (G.W. Bush 2001e)

(25) we will […] bring terrorists to *justice* (G.W. Bush 2002a)

(26) you will not escape *the justice* of this nation (G.W. Bush 2002a)

However, references to liability and punishment, as seen below in the emergent semantic field, points to only one kind of justice in the New World Order discourse, namely, retributive justice, and not also distributive and restorative forms of justice.

(27) Iraq's brutality, aggression and violation of international law *cannot be allowed to succeed* (G.H.W. Bush 1991b).

(28) the world can therefore seize this opportunity to fulfill the long-held promise of a new world order – where brutality *will go unrewarded* and aggression will meet collective resistance (G.H.W. Bush 1991a).

(29) We're going to find those evildoers, those barbaric people who attacked our country, and we're going to hold them *accountable* (G.W. Bush 2001d).

Horwitz (1990: 24) has argued that penal systems are moralistic forms of social control. Not only are offenders punished for their moral wrong-doing, but the justification for punishment also lies in its moral correctness. Hence, in (27) and (28) the use of the negative – "cannot be allowed to succeed" and "will go unrewarded" – suggests that the actions are morally unacceptable and must be denied any equivocation of meaning. Indeed, retribution for the moral violation is the only solution. Note below the metaphor of retribution in the phrase 'to pay a price' which operates on a payback principle needed to right a wrong in the restoration of the moral balance. The payback is the consequence in the cause-consequence argument structure set out in (30) and (31), i.e. *because X, the consequence Y*.[7] By authorizing and legitimating the commission of violence (upon violence) then, law enforcement, like war, is a coercive system that institutionalizes violence (Foucault 1977).

(30) …we're delivering a powerful message to Saddam. *If you act recklessly, you will pay a heavy price* (Clinton 1998b).

(31) I gave warning to the government that harbors them in Afghanistan. *The Taliban made a choice to continue hiding terrorists, and now they are paying a price* (G.W. Bush 2001h).

The exercise of power in 'bringing to justice' the criminals are both intensive and extensive. While the goal of punishment is foremost, the tenacity in policing arguably also acts as deterrence. Such tenacity at the same time bolsters America's self-presentation as a committed, thorough and effective global law enforcer. The intensity of power is evident from the formulation of lists of adjectives denoting constant policing:

(32)   Our military action is also designed to clear the way for *sustained, comprehensive and relentless* operations to drive them out and bring them to justice (G. W. Bush 2001f).

(33)   Our nation will continue to be *steadfast and patient and persistent* in the pursuit of two great objectives. First, we will shut down terrorist camps, disrupt terrorist plans and bring terrorists to justice. Second [...] (G.W. Bush 2002a)

The exercise and effects of disciplinary power are also far-reaching. Drawing on Bentham's 'panoptican' (see Foucault 1977) – a potentially wide-reaching and all-seeing surveillance system – we could argue that a similar mechanism is at work in examples (34) and (35) below. Here, the spatial circumstantials of extent (*around the world; 7000 miles away; across oceans and continents*) and location (*on mountain tops and in caves*) show the reach of power to be everywhere, signaling too that America quite literally is a 'global' policeman. Furthermore, the efficacy of such power relations rests on the curious mix of generalizability of reach (most of the spatial circumstantials denote indefiniteness) as well as specificity (the definite measurement of extent: *7000 miles away* as opposed to 'thousands of miles away') and concreteness (the metaphor of *the long arm of American law* makes the reach almost palpable).

(34)   The long arm of American law has reached out *around the world* and brought to trial those guilty of attacks in New York, in Virginia and in the Pacific (Clinton 1998a).

(35)   The men and women of our armed forces have delivered a message now clear to every enemy of the United States: *even 7000 miles away, across oceans and continents, on mountain tops and in caves*, you will not escape the justice of this nation (G.W. Bush 2002a).

America as above the law

Although modern policing is about the enforcement of law and order, it appears that in the New World Order discourse the twin notions 'law and order' cannot be assumed always to be collocates. Indeed, they sometimes come apart in the discourse, revealing that keeping order out of moral outrage may supersede principles of legality. Conventionally, while retribution underlies the disciplinary technology of punishment, within the frame of the legal system, retribution is to be accomplished without prejudice and in observance of due process. Yet in the aftermath of the 9/11 attacks on America, President G.W. Bush's speeches and actions betrayed traces of outright vengeance and lack of impartiality in the pursuit of justice, and in some instances is also suggestive that America is above the law. Consider the following examples:

(36)   Our grief has turned to anger, and anger to resolution. Whether we bring our enemies to justice, or bring justice to our enemies, justice will be done (G.W. Bush 2001e).

(37)   I will not forget this wound to our country or those who inflicted it. I will not yield; I will not rest; I will not relent in waging this struggle for freedom and security for the American people (G.W. Bush 2001e).

(38)   America will not forget the lives that were taken and the justice their death requires (G.W. Bush 2002b).

In (36) to (38), motivations of revenge surface in several ways. First, through the language of emotion: the expressive modality of the words 'grief' and 'anger', and the transmutation from 'grief' to 'anger' to 'resolution', which entails that America's 'resolution' is based upon passion rather than reason. Note too the metaphors of pain and injury ('wound' and 'inflicted') that connote an emotional response. Second, explicit statements of personal resolve suggest the lack of impartiality. The personal is evident in the choice of the grammatical subjects below: 'our grief', 'I' and 'America' (where in the latter case, the state-as-person metaphor, as suggested by Lakoff (1991), is at work). The 'inflicted'/'wound' metaphor also is suggestive of personal physical injury on one's body (in this case, the body politic of America). The personal is tied to America's doggedness, expressed explicitly in the word 'resolution' and in speech acts of resolution: "America will not forget," "I will not forget," and "I will not relent." Given the specific circumstances of the 9/11 attacks on America, expressions of emotion and personal resolve are understandable, even expected. However, this has significant implications for America's role as disinterested global law enforcer. If we consider the conventional police script or narrative as comprising an innocent victim, a treacherous villain and a police hero (Lakoff 1991), in this case America is both the victim and the police hero, which begs the question of America's impartiality. The resolve uttered in these instances, therefore, is not simply a reflection of dedicated police duty, but signifies personal score-keeping. This comes across more clearly in the third way revenge is made manifest in the discourse, namely, through the reason-result argument structure employed, where the pursuit of justice ('result') is tied to personal grievances ('reason').

Present in the discourse are also resonances of the notion of 'frontier justice', which sets America above the law, particularly in regard to the observance of due process. It is justice at all cost; an assassination order. The clearest allusion to 'frontier justice' or 'Western' justice is President Bush's statement in the days following the 9/11 attacks: "*I want justice. And there's an old poster out West [...] I recall, that said 'Wanted. Dead or Alive'*" (G.W. Bush 2001d). This is a historical reference to a form of policing practiced during the settling of the 'Wild West', when solitary sheriffs or in some cases individual ranchers took justice into their own hands and executed outlaws, without a fair trial. Hayward (1994) notes that the criminal, usually not brought to court, was gunned down publicly in the streets (as happens in the 'Western' movie genre) or hunted and killed in his hideout. The reiteration of the verbal phrase 'to hunt down' (below) in Bush's speeches resonates with this idea.

(39)   the United States will *hunt down* and punish those responsible for these cowardly acts (G.W. Bush 2001a)

(40)   I have called our military into action *to hunt down* the members of the al-Qaeda organization who murdered innocent Americans (G.W. Bush 2001h).

(41)   Our government has a responsibility *to hunt down* our enemies, and we will (G.W. Bush 2001h).

(42)   We are deliberately and systematically *hunting down* these murderers (G.W. Bush 2001h).

With one man acting as judge, jury and executioner, 'Wild West justice', as noted by McCarthy (2002: 129), was "inherently and undeniably cruel" in terms of the "brutality with which those 'judged' guilty were treated."[8] The hunting metaphor, for instance, suggests the dehumanization of the criminal as an animal, to be thus treated as such. In the context of the New World Order discourse, animalization of the criminal is doubly layered with orientalist significations for, as discussed elsewhere (Lazar and Lazar 2004, 2005), the dehumanization of the Other is a common orientalist trope.

America's punitive action against Afghanistan in 2001 is a case in point, where frontier justice is exercised on another sovereign nation. Bypassing the legal requirement for credible evidence, America started bombing Afghanistan within a month of the 9/11 attacks, when there was no hard proof at the time of al-Qaeda's and Afghanistan's culpability. Jack Bussell, a board member of the Maine Veterans for Peace, in fact noted, "If you remember, the Taliban offered to turn bin Laden over to us if we furnished proof, and this has been reissued and both times it has been rejected. The first thing we do is reach for our guns. This is frontier justice" (Bruce 2001: 18).

Defending the New World Order

Whereas enforcement of justice is primarily the domain of police work, justification of force is the linchpin of defense work. Defense, construed in the discourse specifically in terms of military action, constitutes another technology of power to secure order coercively in the New World Order. In this section, we examine two discursive themes: how the frame of 'war' is invoked vis-à-vis 'peace', and how the legitimation of America's use of force is based upon an appeal to 'just causes'.

Shifting frames of war and peace

Military defense is premised upon the frame of war:

(43)   A second *invasion*, or at the very least, *military intimidation* [by Saddam Hussein on Kuwait] appeared imminent (G.H.W. Bush 1990c).

(44)   A few months ago, and again this week, bin Laden publicly vowed to wage a *terrorist war against America* (Clinton 1998a).

(45)   The deliberate and deadly *attacks* which were carried out yesterday *against our country* were more than acts of terror. They were *acts of war* (G.W. Bush 2001b).

(46)   I said that this was the first *act of war on America*, in the twenty-first century, and I was right, particularly having seen the scene [in New York] (G.W. Bush 2001c).

(47)   enemies *attacked our country* (G.W. Bush 2001c).

The war frame is triggered by the semantic field of combat: *attacks, invasion, military intimidation* and *war*. With the exception of the first example, which involved aggression by one state against another (i.e. a war in the conventional military sense), in the rest of the examples the aggression by a non-state actor detracts from the conventional understanding of war. Yet Clinton's and G.W. Bush's naming of the type of aggression as 'war' squarely places the interpretive frame as this kind of event, rather than as criminal acts. America and others in this 'war' have been the targets of attack by enemies.

The war frame[9] is necessary in order to make intelligible and legitimate America's use of counter-force. In the process, the frame itself is adjusted to accommodate America's higher moral calling in the New World Order for taking up arms against the enemy, namely, in the quest for peace. Peace is a value that collocates with justice (e.g. "justice and peace" (G.W. Bush 2001a); "a just and lasting peace" (G.H.W. Bush 1991a) and freedom (e.g. "freedom and peace" (G.W. Bush 2005b)). In what follows, we observe rhetorical shifts in the relations between war and peace, such that the war frame flexibly comprises these, on the one hand, as antithetical values and, on the other, as quite indistinguishable in that they share a similar semantic space. In the first instance, 'war' and 'peace' are set up through contrastive relations as opposites; they are locked in an irreconcilable polar struggle with America and "the world" on the side of "peace":

(48)   While the world talked peace and withdrawal, Saddam Hussein dug in and moved massive forces into Kuwait (G.H.W. Bush 1991c).

(49)   I prefer to think of peace, not war (G.H.W. Bush 1991c).

(50)   I want to reiterate that the United States wants peace, not conflict (Clinton 1998a).

The oppositional war/peace logic, however, is not absolute. Also present in the discourse is the close relationship between war and peace – specifically, that the ultimate pursuit of peace entails war. In the clausal structures (51)-(55), we find that, paradoxically, peace is the triumphant outcome of non-peaceful rather than peaceful actions/interventions. Through various structures of argument, the imbrication of peace and war is represented: war provides the occasion and is guarantor of peace, just as peace is the reason and purpose for war.

Purpose/reason for war is peace

(51)   [Americans fighting in the Gulf] bravely struggle, to earn for America, for the world, and for the future, a just and lasting peace (G.H.W. Bush 1991a).

(52)   We fight […] for the peace in the world (G.W. Bush 2002c).

War as occasion for peace

(53)   We have a great opportunity during this time of war to lead the world toward the values that will bring lasting peace (G.W. Bush 2002a).

War as sole guarantor of peace

(54)   I want to reiterate that the United States wants peace, not conflict. But in this day, no campaign for peace can succeed without determination to fight terrorism (Clinton 1998a).

(55)   In the long run […] the best way to make sure our children can live in peace is to take the battle to the enemy and to stop them (G.W. Bush 2001h).

Finally, also evident in the discourse is a double-speak that makes indistinguishable distinctions between war and peace. Speaking of American-led military attacks on Iraq in 1991, G.H.W. Bush made the following comment:

(56)   We are the only nation on this Earth that could assemble *the forces of peace* (G.H.W. Bush 1991a).

Later in the same speech, he made a similar (collocational) reference:

(57)   *The forces of freedom* are together and united (G.H.W. Bush 1991a).

In the context, the "forces of peace/freedom" refer unmistakably to military forces or forces of war.[10] Yet, through the strategy of re-lexicalization, war is replaced by peace, which offers a euphemistic way of talking about war as a necessary precursor to peace, as discussed above. However, this is no ordinary euphemism that recontextualizes meaning in a more palatable way (cf. for example 'to die'/'to pass away' and 'euthanasia'/'mercy killing'). Instead, this involves a radical re-semanticization that draws on its antonym (recall that elsewhere in the discourse, war and peace are opposites; see examples 48–50) to refer to the same action. Note, though, that the radical re-semanticization – here, strikingly Orwellian – applies only when 'we' use military force:[11] WAR is PEACE when it's something 'we' do, but WAR is WAR when it's something 'they' do.

'Just cause' and (self-)defense

According to the theory of 'just war', if a war is to be fought, it must be for a 'just cause' (see Rawls 1973; Vaux 1992; Walzer 1992; and Elstain 1994). American reflexivity on this notion is evident below in the explicit, peremptory declarations that name its cause as 'just' (and as synonymously 'right' and 'moral'). Appropriation of this notion provides moral and political leverage in mobilizing troops for combat and rallying general support. As the enemy is a globalized threat, support is required not only domestically, but in terms of the formation of an international coalition.

(58)   Any cost in lives, any cost, is beyond our power to measure. But the cost of closing our eyes to aggression is beyond mankind's power to imagine. This we do know: *our cause is just, our cause is moral, our cause is right* (G.H.W. Bush 1991a).

(59)   Fellow citizens, we'll meet violence with patient justice – assured of *the rightness of our cause* (G.W. Bush 2001e).

(60)   To all the men and women in our military, every soldier, sailor, every airman […], I say this: Your mission is defined. The objectives are clear. *Your goal is just* (G.W. Bush 2001f).

(61)   We have come together to mark a terrible day, to reaffirm *a just and vital cause* (G.W. Bush 2002b).

Defense against the enemy provides explication of why America's use of counterforce is just(ified) and necessary. In discussing America's defensive campaign, we might ask, who/what is in need of defense, and why? In relation to the 'who/what' question, the central object of defense unsurprisingly is America, expressed through self-referential noun phrases such as "*our* national security" (Clinton 1998a); "*our* citizens" (Clinton 1998a); "Americans" (G.W. Bush 2001e); and "*our* country" (G.W. Bush 2002a).

Beyond the 'national self', America also performs its role as a global power by showing that its responsibilities and influences extend beyond the local. Through textual strategies of listing and coordination, others are aligned with it, constituting a larger 'global self' that America defends:

(62) The mission of our troops is wholly defensive. [...] They will not initiate hostilities but they will defend themselves, the Kingdom of Saudi Arabia and other friends in the Persian Gulf (G.H.W. Bush 1990a).

(63) [American troops in the Gulf] volunteered to provide for this nation's [Kuwait's] defense, and now they bravely struggle to earn for America, for the world, and for future generations, a just and lasting peace (G.H.W. Bush 1991a).

(64) [American armed forces'] purpose is to protect the national interest of the United States, and indeed the interests of people throughout the Middle East and around the world (Clinton 1998b).

Dealing with the 'why' part of the question (i.e. why the need for defense) reveals three 'just causes' for America's national/global defensive campaign, which accord with just-war ethics: protection of civilian life, self-preservation or self-defense, and restoration of human rights. First, the protection of civilian populations includes not only America's own but also other innocent civilians. Note the specific American referents in (65) and (66) and the more general/universal referents in (67) and (68). Both classes of referent are represented as Goals or Beneficiaries of America's military efforts.

(65) we must take extraordinary steps *to protect the safety of our citizens* (Clinton 1998a)

(66) we will take defensive measures against terrorism *to protect Americans* (G.W. Bush 2001e)

(67) Now, with remarkable technological advances like the Patriot missile, we can *defend against ballistic missile attacks aimed at innocent civilians* (G.H.W. Bush 1991a).

(68) We fight *to protect the innocent* so that the lawless and merciless will not inherit the Earth (G.W. Bush 2001f).

Second, America must protect a threatened polity – see the lexical reiterations "challenged" (69), "at stake" (72), and "threatened" (71), (73). Unlike the case above ('innocents'/civilians) where the referent is relatively concrete, in the examples below the referent in need of defense is an abstraction: "national security"[12]/ "survival"/ "vital interests". This abstract conception is politically significant, for to securitize something (i.e. to use the term "security") is to invoke the frame of self-defense and accord it top priority or urgent status. It is clear from the examples below that America's national security concern is key. The word "very" in "our very national security" (69) used as an adjective instead of its conventional grammatical function as an intensifier of an adjective indicates the extent of the national security importance. Similarly, the pricelessness of security is conveyed through the economic metaphor of cost (70).

(69)   But there have been and will be times when law enforcement and diplomacy are simply not enough when *our very national security is challenged* ... (Clinton 1998a)

(70)   My budget includes the largest increase in defense spending in two decades, because *while the price of freedom and security is high, it is never too high*. Whatever it costs to defend our country, we will pay (G.W. Bush 29 January 2002a).

America's security concerns, however, are inextricably tied to the security of certain others, such as Kuwait and more generally the Middle East, which extends America's scope of defense to other nations and regions, thereby globalizing its security concerns. The noun phrases "energy security" (72), "our vital interests" (73) and "the security of the world" (which includes America) (74) in varying degrees of explicitness reveal America's economic self-interests. In this context, any military action by America against Iraq is construed a self-defense.

(71)   Iraq can never again be in a position to *threaten the survival of its neighbors or our vital interests* (G.H.W. Bush 1990b).

(72)   *our national security is at stake [...]. Energy security is national security* and we must be prepared to act accordingly (Clinton 1998b).

(73)   The hard fact is that so long as Saddam remains in power, *he threatens the well-being of his people, the peace of his region, the security of the world* (Clinton 1998b).

The third just cause for using military force is the benevolent rescue of the oppressed and the restoration of human rights. In the transitivity structures below America represents itself as a hero/savior, who liberates people from tyranny[13]; note the lexical choices 'save', 'free', 'liberate' and 'extend blessings' (the last, with obvious religious overtones). The liberating mission is encompassed in the military operations – explicitly stated as "part of that [just and vital] cause" or represented in a checklist of objectives.[14] (Note, too, the telling names given to Bush's military campaigns: 'Operation Enduring Freedom' (in Afghanistan) and 'Operation Iraqi Freedom'). The linear order of the objectives on the checklist, though, is worth comment: on the one hand, it seems to reflect a temporal sequencing of events i.e. only after ridding the threat does it become possible to liberate the oppressed. On the other hand, the appearance of liberation as the last item on the lists arguably also belies the order of priority. In fact, rather than a targeted priority in itself, rescue and liberation of others can be interpreted as 'collateral benefits' of military self-defense.

(74) We fight not to impose our will, but to defend ourselves and *extend the blessings of freedom* (G.W. Bush 2001f).

(75) In four short months, our nation has comforted the victims, began to rebuild New York and Pentagon, […] captured, arrested and rid the thousands of terrorists, destroyed Afghanistan's training camps, *saved a people from starvation and freed a country from brutal oppression* (G.W. Bush 2002a).

(76) We have come together to mark a terrible day, to reaffirm a just and vital cause […] Part of that cause was to *liberate the Afghan people from terrorist occupation*, and we did so. Next week, the schools reopen in Afghanistan. They will be opened to all, and many young girls will go to schools for the first time in their young lives (G.W. Bush 2002b).

(77) Within weeks, commands went forth from this place [the Pentagon] that would clear terrorist camps and caves and *liberate a nation* (G.W. Bush 2002c).

Underlying the benevolent outcome of liberation is a political pragmatism of American self-interest. As the causal relations in the statements (78) and (79) show, America's own security is contingent upon that of others – a point earlier made. In fact, one dimension of self-preservation has become increasingly and overtly associated with the spread of freedom, liberty and democracy so that others who imbibe 'our' values will no longer pose a threat to 'us'. This might be called a strategy of benevolent pre-emption, which is premised upon the Kantian belief that democracies do not go to war with each other (see Lazar and Lazar, forthcoming).

(78) Listen to Hollywood Huddleston, marine lance corporal. He says: "Let's free these people so we can go home and be free again" (G.H.W. Bush 1991c).

(79) The experience of recent years has taught us an important lesson: The survival of liberty in our land increasingly depends on the success of liberty in other lands. Because of our actions, freedom is taking root in Iraq, and the American people are more secure (G.W. Bush 2005a).

Conclusion

This paper has aimed to show America's justifications in policing and defending the New World Order. While violence perpetrated by the enemy is decried and negativized as immoral and unjustified, America's violence is positively presented as a moral and just cause in the pursuit of a just peace. In presenting the enemy and its cause negatively, on the one hand, and America and its cause positively, on the other hand, America's use of force through policing and defending is justified as actionable violence against an unruly enemy.

Police and defense operations are important technologies of power in securing the American-led New World Order – technologies that are exercised as much through actions as they are through language. The co-deployment of the two frames enable a wide interpretative repertoire for enforcing justice and justifying force: America's actions can simultaneously be read as self-defense (note the broad sense of the 'self' in 'self-defense'), a just war (i.e. why the recourse to war is morally the right thing to do under extenuating circumstances), retributive justice (to punish the wrong-doer and to restore the status quo between perpetrator and victim),[15] and even frontier justice (a rudimentary form of self-preservation). In sum, what emerges then from this paper is that the viability of the New World Order requires not only representing the enemy categorically as an 'outcast', but also in punishing and defeating the enemy for the challenge they pose to the norms and values of that order.

Internationalizing America's war has also required a more expansive notion of a just cause (or rather, just causes), as well as an extension beyond the national self to represent a global community of nations. These serve to bolster its moral cause and raise its moral authority as a global leader. At the same time, it serves to secure its own national interests in (selectively) defending others and legitimating its military interventions abroad.

Notes

1.   Although the term 'New World Order' had been used by others (such as Cecil Rhodes) in earlier times, our concern is with the specific articulation of this concept as initiated by President G.H.W. Bush in 1990, dictated by the changing geopolitical realities since the late 20th century.

2.   For a fuller discussion of the politico-historical context of the discourse of the New World Order, see Lazar and Lazar (2004).

3.   During the administration of G.H.W. Bush, Saddam Hussein was the named threat, whereas in the Clinton administration Osama bin Laden gradually filled the major role. Since September 11, 2001, Osama bin Laden has continued to be a leading threat, subsequently extended to also re-include Saddam Hussein.

4.   'Outcasting' also suggests a further process of 're-casting', whereby once exorcized, it is possible for pariah states (e.g. Afghanistan and Iraq) to be readmitted into the international community of nations (see Lazar and Lazar, forthcoming).

5.   Note that although the notion of "safe haven" could elsewhere be used to refer to refugees and the homeless, here President G.W. Bush uses this to link the criminal with those who aid and abet, i.e. in this case referring to those who give refuge to criminals.

6.   One is reminded here of a manhunt or a fugitive. This also evokes the hunting frame referred to in (39) to (42). This metaphor is particularly resonant with the common images of bin Laden living /hiding out in the mountains, and the description of Hussein's hide-out as a 'rat hole.'

7.   As we have witnessed in the historical events concerning Afghanistan and Saddam Hussein's Iraq, the nature of the payback has been punishment by force.

8.   It is ironic that "cruel[ty]" and "brutality", which are orientalist traits of the Other, here describe America's own actions.

9.   See also Chilton (2002: 186).

10.   Clinton too used the expression "forces of peace" as a general reference on one occasion (at an American University commencement ceremony) and when speaking specifically about the deadlock in Northern Ireland on another – the texts, respectively, follow: (1) "I hope very much that you will use this moment to deal with the big challenges and the big opportunities that are still out there for us: [...] to build a world where the *forces of peace* and prosperity and humanity are stronger than the old demons of war and disease and poverty" (Clinton 2000); (2) "if it can be resolved, I think it will give great impetus to the *forces of peace* throughout the world" (Clinton 1999). In these instances, "forces of peace" relies on a militaristic metaphor, but in the absence of a literal reference to military combat – as in the case of G.H.W. Bush on Iraq – the radical re-semanticization is mitigated.

11.   Dubbing the MX Missile (a nuclear weapon of mass destruction) "The Peacekeeper" during the Reagan years was a similar case of 'radical re-semanticization.'

12.   In Political Science/Security Studies, national security is an ambiguous and amorphous concept that often encompasses a range of core values (see Wolfers 1962). Safeguarding national survival and national vital interests, however defined, are those that come under the rubric of national security.

13.   For a detailed discussion on how America is aligned with positive values of "freedom," "liberation" and "democracy" and how the Other is portrayed negatively as devoid of these values, see Lazar and Lazar (2004). America's benevolent attempts at spreading democracy to others as part of its project of neo-liberal internationalism is taken up at some length in Lazar and Lazar (forthcoming).

14.   In terms of transitivity analysis, the acts of saving and liberating in (75) and (77) are represented as 'Goals', the "blessings of freedom" in (74), in Hallidayan terms, is 'Range.'

15.   The reversal of victim-perpetrator is also generally a common discursive strategy. For the application of this strategy in another context, see for example, Benke and Wodak (2003).

References

Benke, G. and Wodak, R. 2003. "The discursive construction of individual memories: How Austrian 'Wehrmacht' soldiers remember WWII." In *Re/reading the Past: Critical and Functional Perspectives of Time and Value*, J. Martin and R. Wodak (eds.), 115–138. Amsterdam: John Benjamins.

Bruce, N. 2001, October. "Should we give peace a chance?" *The Portland Phoenix*, 18–25.

Bush, G.H.W. 1990a, August 9. "Excerpts from Bush's statement on US defense of Saudis." *New York Times*.

Bush, G.H.W. 1990b, September 11. "Transcript of President's address to joint session of Congress." *New York Times*.

Bush, G.H.W. 1990c, November 26. "Why are we in the Gulf." *Newsweek*.

Bush, G.H.W. 1991a, January 29. "State of the Union speech." United States Information Service (USIS).

Bush, G.H.W. 1991b [1990]. "President Bush's news conference at the White House." In *The Gulf War Reader: History, Documents and Opinions*, M.L. Sifry and C. Cerf (eds.), 228–229. New York: Random House.

Bush, G.H.W. 1991c. "Liberation of Kuwait has begun." In *The Gulf War Reader: History, Documents and Opinions*, M.L. Sifry and C. Cerf (eds.), 311–314. New York: Random House.

Bush, G.W. 2001a, September 11. "Transcript of President Bush's remarks to the nation." *Associated Press*.

Bush, G.W. 2001b, September 13. "Bush's remarks to cabinet and advisers." *New York Times*.

Bush, G.W. 2001c, September 15. "President, in New York, offers resolute vows atop the rubble." *New York Times*.

Bush, G.W. 2001d, September 17. "Transcript of President Bush's speech from the Islamic Center." *Washington Post*.

Bush, G.W. 2001e, September 21. "Text of George Bush's speech." *Guardian Unlimited*.

Bush, G.W. 2001f, October 8. "Announcement that US and British forces have begun attacking Afghanistan." Available: http://www.news.com.au.

Bush, G.W. 2001g, November 6. Remarks by the President to the Warsaw Conference on Combating Terrorism. Washington, D.C.

Bush, G.W. 2001h, November 8. "Transcript of Bush Speech in Atlanta." *CNN.com*. Available: http://archives.cnn.com/2001/US/11/08/rec.bush.transcript.

Bush, G.W. 2002a, January 29. "Full text: State of the Union Address." *BBC News Online*. Available: http://news.bbc.co.uk/1/hi/world/americas/1790537.stm.

Bush, G.W. 2002b, March 11. "Bush: 'America Will Not Forget'" *CNN.com*. Available: http://www.cnn.com/2002/US/03/11/gen.bush.speech/index.html.

Bush, G.W. 2002c, September 11. "President Bush's remarks at Pentagon ceremony." *CNN.com*. Available: http://archives.cnn.cm/2002/US/09/ar911.bush.pentagon.

Bush, G.W. 2005a, March 19. President's Radio Address. Washington, D.C.

Bush, G.W. 2005b, August 22. President Honors Veterans of Foreign Wars at National Convention. Washington, D.C.

Chilton, P. 2002. "Do something! Conceptualising responses to the attacks of 11 September 2001." *Journal of Language and Politics* 1(1): 181–195.

Chomsky, N. 1991. *Deterring Democracy.* London: Verso.

Clinton, W.J. 1998a, August 26. "Clinton's statement in full." *BBC News Online.* Available: http://news.bbc.co.uk/1/hi/world/americas/155412.stm.

Clinton, W.J. 1998b, December 16. "Clinton announces Iraq strikes: Full Text." *BBC News Online.* Available: http://news.bbc.co.uk/2/hi/events/crisis_in_the_gulf/texts_and_transcripts/236858.stm.

Clinton, W.J. 1999, July 21. Press Conference by the President. Washington, D.C.

Clinton, W.J. 2000, June 10. Remarks by President William Jefferson Clinton, 12th Carleton College Commencement Exercises. White House Press Office.

Elstain, J.B. 1994. *Just War Theory.* New York: New York University Press.

Fairclough, N. 1989. *Language and Power.* London: Longman.

Foucault, M. 1967. *Madness and Civilization: A History of Insanity in the Age of Reason.* London: Tavistock.

Foucault, M. 1972. *The Archaeology of Knowledge.* London: Tavistock.

Foucault, M. 1977. *Discipline and Punish: The Birth of the Prison.* London: Allen Lane.

Halliday, M.A.K. 1985. *Introduction to Functional Grammar.* London: Edward Arnold.

Hayward, M. 1994. "The Making of the New World Order: The Role of the Media." In *The Gulf War and the New World Order,* T. Ismael and J. Ismael (eds.), 224–241. Gainsville: University Press of Florida.

Horwitz, A.V. 1990. *The Logic of Social Control.* New York: Plenum Press.

Lakoff, G. 1991. "Metaphor and war: The metaphor system used to justify war in the Gulf." *Viet Nam Generation Journal and Newsletter* 3(3).

Lazar, A. and Lazar, M.M. 2004. "The discourse of the New World Order: 'Out-casting' the double face of threat." *Discourse and Society* 15(2–3): 223–242.

Lazar, A. and Lazar, M.M. 2005. "The politics of 'othering' in the New World Order." Malaysia International Conference on Languages, Literatures, and Cultures: Critical Perspectives on Theory and Practice in the New World Order. Malaysia: Universiti Putra Malaysia.

Lazar, A. and Lazar, M.M. Forthcoming. "Global governance: American neo-liberal hegemony in the post-Cold War era." *Journal of Language and Politics.*

McCarthy, E. 2002. "Justice." In *Collateral Language: A User's Guide to America's New War,* J. Collins and R. Glover (eds.), 125–137. New York: New York University Press.

Rawls, J. 1973. *A Theory of Justice.* Oxford: Oxford University Press.

Said, E. 1978. *Orientalism.* London: Penguin.

Van Dijk, T.A. 1995. "Ideological Discourse Analysis." *New Courant* 4: 135–6.

Vaux, K. 1992. *Ethics and the Gulf War: Religion, Rhetoric, and Righteousness.* Boulder, Colorado: Westview Press.

Walzer, M. 1992. *Just and Unjust Wars: A Moral Argument with Historical Illustrations* (Second Edition). New York: Basic Books.

Wolfers, A. 1962. *Discord and Collaboration: Essays on International Politics.* Baltimore: John Hopkins Press.

CHAPTER 4

The narrative construction of identity

The adequation of Saddam Hussein and Osama bin Laden in the "war on terror"[1]

Adam Hodges

> *"I have not seen a smoking-gun, concrete evidence about the connection."*
> *– Secretary of State Colin Powell (quoted in Marquis 2004)*

Introduction

The question of an Iraq-al Qaeda connection has generated intense interest before and after the March 2003 invasion of Iraq by the United States. The notion of a collaborative relationship between the disparate nation-state of Iraq led by Saddam Hussein and Osama bin Laden's al Qaeda network was given little credence in Europe and among some domestic critics of the Bush administration prior to the war. In the months and years since the beginning of the war, mainstream political opponents in the US have also attempted to highlight a lack of evidence in administration claims of a relationship. In addition, experts including the non-partisan 9/11 Commission have refuted the idea of a collaborative relationship between the two (NC 2004: 83).[2] Nevertheless, the Bush administration's perspective – i.e. that prior to the war, Iraq and al Qaeda were involved in a relationship significant enough to treat the two as a cohesive enemy in the putative "war on terror" – gained significant traction among the American public during the buildup for war, and continued to receive widespread acceptance even in light of subsequent challenges.

On April 22, 2004, The Program on International Policy Attitudes (PIPA) at the University of Maryland released a study that showed "a majority of Americans (57%) continue to believe that before the war Iraq was providing substantial support to al Qaeda, including 20% who believe that Iraq was directly involved in the September 11 attacks" (PIPA 2004a). Such public belief remained consistent since the February 2003 buildup to the invasion of Iraq. Similarly, a Pew Research Center poll conducted at the beginning of October 2002 showed that two-thirds of Americans believed "Saddam Hussein helped the terrorists in the September 11th attacks" (Pew 2002). Polls of public attitudes, such as those conducted by PIPA and the Pew Research Center, provide an interesting snapshot of social beliefs and understandings. In short, these particular studies illustrate a widespread acceptance of a perspective on sociopolitical reality in line with Bush administration rhetoric.[3]

At issue in this chapter is the power of narrative to shape sociopolitical reality. Against the backdrop of Bush administration claims about an Iraq-al Qaeda connection and their acceptance among a large portion of the American public, how is such a linkage discursively constructed and accepted?

The narrative construction of sociopolitical reality

While the power of rhetoric in political speech as a persuasive tool has been recognized since the days of Aristotle, the discursive turn in the social sciences has provided crucial import to the role of language in social practice. Contemporary research at the intersection of discourse and society recognizes that language does more than merely represent a pre-existing social world; more significantly, language, commonly through narrative, plays a primary role in the constitution of that social reality. As Bruner (1991) notes, "we organize our experience and our memory of human happenings mainly in the form of narrative – stories, excuses, myths, reasons for doing and not doing, and so on" (4). Likewise, against the backdrop of modern democracies, political leaders address the public to, yes, inform, debate and persuade[4], but more pointedly, to organize the collective experience of the nations they lead through the narratives they tell.

The dramatic events of September 11, 2001 left a nation looking for ways to describe and make sense of what happened – to organize the experience and the complex issues surrounding it. The nation had to find a way to conceptualize what took place, and narratives provide a means to do just that – "narratives," as Riessman (1993) notes, "structure perceptual experience" (2). Moreover, narratives are important in establishing identities of individuals and groups that populate that experience.

The discursive linkage of Iraq and al Qaeda at issue in this analysis is prominently featured in a series of presidential speeches, starting with the October 2002 speech in Cincinnati that launched the push for war in Iraq. Additional speeches used in the analysis include the May 1 speech aboard the USS Abraham Lincoln off the coast of San Diego where the President declared the end of major combat operations in Iraq, and the September 2003 address to the nation from the White House. Each of these speeches contains a section of narrative I am here terming the Bush War on Terror Narrative (henceforth, the BWOTN).

The BWOTN, now ubiquitous in administration rhetoric in various forms, recounts American involvement in a global "war on terror" that starts with the *precipitating event* (Labov and Waletsky 1967) of the terrorist acts of September 11, 2001. Each telling of the narrative in the four speeches analyzed consists of the following components:

1. Introduction of the theme: a global "war on terror"
2. Naming of the precipitating event: September 11, 2001
3. Mentioning of the first "battle": Afghanistan
4. Discussion of the lengthy, ongoing nature of the war to be fought on many global fronts (often naming various "fronts" in addition to Afghanistan and Iraq)
5. Talk of the "battle" of Iraq (forecast in the speech prior to war and recounted in speeches after its start)
6. Recap of the precipitating event and commitment to continue the war

Most of the data in the analysis come from the first of the four speeches: the October 7, 2002 address in Cincinnati, Ohio. This is a key speech that lays out the initial justification for war against Iraq vis-à-vis the events of 9/11, and effectively begins the *adequation* (Bucholtz and Hall 2004) of Iraq and al Qaeda that becomes entrenched in subsequent rhetoric.

The adequation of disparate enemies

Bucholtz and Hall's (2004) model, the *tactics of intersubjectivity*, provides a means for investigating how "social identities come to be created through language" (370). Moving beyond essentialist notions that take the two poles of identity – sameness and difference – as static, objective states, the framework dissects the components involved in the process of identity work to further an understanding of identity as a dynamic phenomenon emergent in social interaction.

The emergent aspect of identity formation – that identity is a social achievement – is evident in times of war, where the sharp difference between Us and Them is drawn with vivid lines. The tactic of *distinction* sets up the binary opposition with the enemy Other that the nation fights. Differences between Us and Them are highlighted, while similarities are set aside or ignored. Conversely, the tactic of *adequation* creates "socially recognized sameness" within the national community. "In this relation, potentially salient differences are set aside in favor of perceived or asserted similarities that are taken to be more situationally relevant" (Bucholtz and Hall 2004: 383). Differences within the polity are ignored and commonalities are brought to the forefront to form a united stance.

Ideology plays an important role in identity work. The basic elements of sameness and difference combine with ideologies and practices to achieve adequation or distinction. Irvine and Gal's (2000) term, erasure, underscores the role ideology plays in erasing differences in the process of adequation. Erasure "renders some persons or activities...invisible" so that facts "inconsistent with the ideological scheme either go unnoticed or get explained away" (38). By erasing differences and highlighting similarities, a sufficient sameness is established. "Identity, then, is a process not merely of discovering or acknowledging a similarity that precedes" a given moment; rather, it is a process "of inventing similarity and downplaying difference" (Bucholtz and Hall 2004: 371, cf. Bourdieu 1984).

From a geopolitical perspective, the tactic of adequation is also at play when disparate nation-states find themselves confronted by a common enemy. The situation is often conducive for the states to set aside potentially salient differences between themselves and emphasize situationally relevant threats to form an alliance, e.g. the USSR and United States during World War II. In the BWOTN, however, this process is imposed from without so that a connection between Iraq and al Qaeda is created not from the perspective of the two entities themselves but from the perspective of the Bush administration.

In the plot of the BWOTN, potentially salient differences between Iraq and al Qaeda are erased on their behalf in order to position the two as a cohesive enemy alliance against which the United States is fighting. Potentially salient differences include bin Laden's aim of replacing Hussein's secular regime with a fundamentalist theocracy. A statement made by bin Laden in a tape played on Aljazeera television on February 11, 2003 illustrates this animosity. In an English translation published by the BBC, bin Laden states his "belief in the infidelity of socialists. [...] Socialists are infidels wherever they are, whether they are in Baghdad or Aden" (bin Laden 2003). Such differences are especially interesting in light of the image of a strong alliance that emerges in the BWOTN.

An important consequence of the adequation of the two in the BWOTN is justification of a war to achieve the administration's pre-9/11 policy objective of "regime change in Iraq."[5] That is to say, rather than attempting to justify a separate, unrelated war, the BWOTN legitimizes a strike against Iraq vis-à-vis a "war on terror" already in place against al Qaeda. "Hence, externally imposed identity categories generally have at least as much to do with the observer's own identity position and power stakes as with any sort of objectively describable social reality" (Bucholtz and Hall 2004: 370). The linchpin in the rationale, of course, is the adequation of Saddam Hussein's Iraq and Osama bin Laden's al Qaeda so that a strike against one is justified by its equivalence to a strike against the other.

Of particular interest in this analysis, therefore, is the way adequation can be used from an outside position of power to impose sufficient sameness upon others in a process of *imposed* adequation, or adequation from without. This imposed adequation in the BWOTN is achieved through (1) a rhetorical coupling of past actions of "terror" carried out by Saddam Hussein with actions of "terror" conducted by al Qaeda to position the two entities in a category that is morally and politically equivalent, (2) a discursive matching of complementary roles each is capable of playing in an alliance – Iraq as a potential source of support (shelter, funding, arms, etc.) for terrorists and al Qaeda as a potential benefactor of such support, and (3) a narration that invokes a *historical-causal entailment* (Bruner 1991) between the past events of 9/11 and future possible events resulting from a supposed Iraq/al-Qaeda alliance. The next section moves into a close analysis of these aspects of the narrative.

Analysis

Positioning in a morally and politically equivalent category

An important strategy in the BWOTN is the positioning of both entities within the same conceptual category defined by the concept of terrorism, and marked by similar lexical descriptors such as "terror", "terrorism", and "terrorist." The potentially divergent motivations and goals of the secular military state of Iraq and the non-state fundamentalist religious organization of bin Laden are ignored, and both are characterized by words associated with the notion of terrorism. For example, in excerpt 1, taken from the October 2002 speech given in Cincinnati at the beginning of the lead-up to the Iraq war, the threat from Iraq is narrated as stemming from "its drive toward an arsenal of *terror*" (lines 8–9) rather than, say, a drive toward enhanced military capability to deter, defend or spread national interests as other nation-states do.

Excerpt 1[6] (Bush 2002)
    1   tonight I want to take a few minutes to discuss a grave threat to peace
    2   and America's determination to lead the world
    3   in confronting that threat
    4   the threat comes from Iraq

    5   it arises directly from the Iraqi regime's own actions
    6   its history of aggression
    7   and its drive
    8   toward an **arsenal**
    9   of **terror**

The notion of terrorism is repeatedly juxtaposed with an important rationale for waging war against Iraq: the possession – potential or real – of weapons of mass destruction (WMD). This rhetorical linking is highlighted in the continuation of excerpt 1, where we see the alternation between "weapons" and lexical descriptors related to the notion of terror at the end of the lines, such as "terrorist groups" (line 14), "terrorism" (line 20), and "terror" (line 21).

Excerpt 1, cont. (Bush 2002)

10   eleven years ago
11   as a condition for ending the Persian Gulf War
12   the Iraqi regime was required to destroy its **weapons of mass destruction**
13   to cease all development of such **weapons**
14   and to stop all support for **terrorist groups**

15   the Iraqi regime has violated
16   all of those obligations

17   it possesses and produces chemical
18   and biological **weapons**
19   it is seeking nuclear **weapons**
20   it has given shelter and support to **terrorism**
21   and practices **terror**
22   against its own people

Implied meanings are often deeply embedded in political speech. That is, as Chilton (2004) states, "if hearers do indeed make mental representations that involve such [implied] meanings, then it is on the basis of minimal cues, which, incidentally, the speaker could disavow on the grounds that 'he never *actually said* that' [explicitly]" (122). The rhetorical structure of this delivery weaves together an image of these two issues of "terrorist groups" and military "weapons of mass destruction" as inseparable. In other words, Iraq's potential for WMD and the issue of international terrorism parallel each other rhetorically to the effect that the issue of terrorism is constructed as a natural concomitant to Iraq's military capabilities (or desires). This coupling sets the foundation for an implied link with the specific terrorist organization of al Qaeda, the group most vividly associated with the notion of terrorism and 9/11. Such a link is reinforced throughout the BWOTN by reiterating the precipitating event of 9/11, which acts as a pivot around which the rest of the narrative revolves, as seen in excerpt 2 where the precipitating event is mentioned in line 4.

Excerpt 2 (Bush 2002)

1   we also must never forget
2   the most vivid events
3   of recent history

    4   on **September the 11th**
    5   2001
    6   America felt its vulnerability
    7   even to threats that gather
    8   on the other side of the earth
    9   we resolved then
    10   and we are resolved today
    11   to confront every **threat**
    12   from any source
    13   that could bring sudden **terror**
    14   and suffering
    15   to America

The sameness of the threat posed by al Qaeda (represented by the *terror* of 9/11) and the threat of Iraq (represented by *weapons* of terror) are constructed as situationally relevant in the BWOTN. That is, any potential difference is portrayed as one of *degree*, rather than of *kind*. This sameness of kind, but difference of degree is further supported in excerpt 3.

Excerpt 3 (Bush 2002)
    1   the attacks of **September the 11th**
    2   showed our country that vast oceans
    3   no longer protect us from danger
    4   before that tragic date
    5   we had only hints of **al Qaeda's plans**
    6   and **designs**
    7   today **in Iraq**
    8   we see a **threat** whose **outlines**
    9   are far more **clearly defined**
    10   and whose consequences
    11   could be far more deadly
    12   **Saddam Hussein**'s actions have put us on notice
    13   and there is no refuge
    14   from our responsibilities

In excerpt 3, "al Qaeda's plans and designs" (lines 5–6) are equated with the "outlines" of a threat that are "clearly defined" in Iraq (lines 8–9). The difference between the two is that al Qaeda's plans have already been enacted in the "attacks of September the 11th" (line 1) while the "consequences" of the Iraqi threat have yet to be experienced. An implicit comparison is effectively drawn between the two in a way that depicts a presumed threat from Iraq (of a similar kind to that enacted by al Qaeda) without stating concrete evidence to support knowledge of such a threat.

Bach (1994) classifies an utterance such as that seen in lines 10–11 ("whose consequences could be far more deadly") as an instance of *semantic underdetermination*, in that no complete proposition is conveyed; rather, line 11 requires *completion* to fulfill the proposition. "In these cases, instead of building on what the speaker had made explicit, the hearer infers a distinct proposition" (Bach 1994: 154–155). The obvious inference from the context is a comparison between future possible actions carried out by Iraq with those previously carried out by al Qaeda, as alluded to in line 1, so that the kind of acts perpetrated by al Qaeda only differ to potential ones by Iraq in degree (and location and time).

Again, note the structure in this excerpt that moves from the precipitating event of 9/11 (line 1) to future possible events, and alternates between the two actors, al Qaeda and Saddam Hussein. The syntactic parallelism that rhetorically juxtaposes the two actors reinforces the conceptual link between them. As van Dijk (1991) points out, a common function of parallelism is to emphasize "negative properties of opponents" (219). In this case, the function is to *adequate* the negative properties of one opponent with another. The effect is that the devastation of 9/11 as embodied by the perpetrators, al Qaeda, subtly blurs with the actions (and hypothetical future actions) of Saddam Hussein.

The erasure of distinctive differences between the terrorist organization and the nation-state is further illustrated in excerpt 4.

Excerpt 4 (Bush 2002)
    1   all that might be required are a small container and **one terrorist**
    2   or **Iraqi intelligence operative** to deliver it

    3   and that is the source
    4   of our urgent concern about **Saddam Hussein**'s links to international **terrorist groups**

Excerpt 4 builds on the notion of similar plans discussed in excerpt 3, and adequates "one terrorist" (line 1) with an "Iraqi intelligence operative" (a reference that immediately follows in line 2). One "or" the other is capable of carrying out the same kind of act. The *conventional implicature* (Grice 1975) generated by the disjunctive "or" places these two actors in a similar category, operating under similar motivations with similar goals. These conditions are presumably necessary if there is to be sufficient collaboration between the nation-state and terrorist groups to supply and deliver "a small container" comprised of WMD.

The surrounding context of 9/11 implies that "one terrorist" could be a member of al Qaeda, further strengthening the identity of terrorists (implicitly, al Qaeda terrorists) with the Iraqi regime. While the scenario in lines 1–2 is hypothetical, indicated by the modal "might" in line 1, it is immediately followed by an existential presupposition in line 4 that introduces the notion that *there are* links between "Saddam Hussein" and "terrorist groups." The implicit proposition contained within a presupposition pops up whether the presupposition is congruent with a listener's previous knowledge or not. Where an explicit statement may give a listener time to pause and challenge a stated fact at odds with their knowledge, the same fact embedded in a presupposition may simply be subject to what Lewis (1979) terms "accommodation"; that is, the "proposition may be added to the interpreter's memory as a 'fact' of reality" (Chilton 2004: 63). This may especially be true when a listener doubts their previous knowledge (or is given reason to doubt their knowledge) and is therefore inclined to abdicate judgment to a person in a position of power with access to classified information, such as the President. The proposition implied in this presupposition is then strengthened by providing allusions to real links between Saddam Hussein and actual terrorists – that is, terrorists in a general sense (seen in the continuation of excerpt 4 below).

Discursive matching of complementary roles

The notion of ties between Saddam Hussein and terrorist groups is further elaborated to adequate Iraq and al Qaeda through complementary roles each is capable of playing: on the one hand, Iraq as a potential *source* of support for non-state organizations (e.g. shelter, funding, arms, etc.), and on the other, al Qaeda as a possible *recipient*, or benefactor of support from state actors. The continuation of excerpt 4 plays upon this theme by mentioning Iraq's past support of (non-al Qaeda) individuals involved in acts of terror, which sets up a "track record" that can be used as a basis for inferring potential Iraqi support of al Qaeda.

Excerpt 4, cont. (Bush 2002)
    5   over the years
    6   Iraq has provided safe haven to terrorists
    7   such as **Abu Nidal**

          [8 lines left out about Abu Nidal]

   16   Iraq has also provided **safe haven to Abu Abbas**

          [3 lines left out about Abu Abbas]

   20   and we know that Iraq is continuing to **finance terror**
   21   and gives assistance to groups that use **terrorism** to undermine
   22   Middle East peace

The use of the present perfect in this excerpt, e.g. "has provided" (line 6), "has also provided" (line 16), "is continuing" (line 20), leaves the time frame unspecified and implies an ongoing action that extends beyond the precise allusions to, for example, "Abu Nidal" (line 7) and "Abu Abbas" (line 16). Moreover, the use of the present perfect in line 20, "we know that Iraq is continuing to finance terror," presupposes a past pattern of financing terror.

Ochs and Capps (2001) quote legal scholar Ronald Dworkin (1986) on the *doctrine of precedent*, "the doctrine that decisions of earlier cases sufficiently like a new case should be repeated in the new case." Ochs and Capps (2001) note that we search for "familiar characteristics and analogies with previous situations that have come into public light and often pass judgement accordingly" (209). The naming of specific individuals who have carried out past acts classified as terrorism, e.g. Abu Nidal (line 7) and Abu Abbas (line 16), and their relation to Iraq builds on precedent. The use of tense in this excerpt further strengthens the notion that these are but a few instances of an ongoing, established pattern of support for terrorism in the Middle East.

Another legal concept is that of circumstantial evidence, or facts that can be used to infer other facts without direct evidence. These past ties to different individuals responsible for acts of violence throughout the Middle East set up a pattern that may plausibly be repeated in the case of al Qaeda, but without pointing to direct evidence of a concrete relationship; nor are motivations (or lack thereof) for such a relationship addressed. Weak linkage to al Qaeda is, however, provided in excerpt 5.

Excerpt 5 (Bush 2002)
  1   we know that **Iraq** and **al Qaeda** have had high-level contacts
  2   that go back a decade
  3   some **al Qaeda** leaders who fled Afghanistan
  4   went to **Iraq**
  5   these include one very senior **al Qaeda** leader who received medical treatment
  6   in Baghdad
  7   this year
  8   and who has been associated with planning for chemical
  9   and biological attacks

Al Qaeda is mentioned three times in this excerpt. The ambiguous fact stated in lines 1–2 of "contacts that go back a decade" further builds upon the established pattern laid out earlier. The collocation "high-level contacts" is frequently used in international relations to indicate diplomatic ties between governments. The notion of "high-level contacts" between Iraq and al Qaeda implies a significant relationship. The image of this type of relationship is supported by mentioning two pieces of evidence. The first – that "some al Qaeda leaders who fled Afghanistan went to Iraq" – conceptually stitches together the war in Afghanistan with Iraq. The second piece of evidence is that one of those members of al Qaeda who fled Afghanistan was "one very senior al Qaeda leader who received medical treatment in Baghdad" (lines 5–6). While this does not completely bridge to the implied meaning of "high-level contacts" in line 1, it creates a well-built scaffold of circumstantial evidence that allows hearers to fill in their own imagined details.

The precedent of Iraq as a source for terrorists (e.g. providing safe haven, finances, medical treatment) and al Qaeda as a terrorist group (presumably looking for and benefiting from such types of support) provides for a plausible synergistic matching of interests that follows naturally from their positioning in a politically equivalent category. The fear of the supposed alliance's potential threat is spelled out in the narrative by explicitly laying out potential consequences in excerpt 6.

Excerpt 6 (Bush 2002)
    1   **Iraq could** decide on any given day
    2   to **provide** a biological or chemical **weapon** to a **terrorist group**
    3   or individual **terrorists**
    4   **alliance with terrorists could allow the Iraqi regime to attack America**
    5   without leaving
    6   any fingerprints

Signaled with the modal auxiliary "could" in lines 1 and 4, the potential consequences are nevertheless made vividly clear: an "alliance with terrorists could allow the Iraqi regime to attack America" (line 4).

Following Sacks (1992: 258), Ochs and Capps (2001) note that second stories are "linked by interaction and theme to the telling of prior stories in conversation" (209). In this excerpt, a hypothetical story (future Iraqi actions) is linked to previous experience (9/11) under the overarching theme of the "war on terror." The credibility of the hypothetical scenario spelled out in excerpt 6 flows naturally from the previous categorization of Iraq and al Qaeda as entities of a similar kind with shared objectives. Their potential to fulfill complementary roles legitimizes the scenario as at least plausible, if not credible.

Implied causal entailment

The adequation of Iraq and al Qaeda is reinforced throughout repeated tellings of the BWOTN, where a sequence of events is presented as a natural, common sense progression. Excerpts 7–9 illustrate how the wars in Afghanistan and Iraq are depicted as pieces of a whole, or fronts of a global "war on terror."

Excerpt 7 (Bush 2003b)
   1   America and a broad coalition
   2   **acted first in Afghanistan**
   3   by destroying the training camps of terror
   4   and removing the regime
   5   that harbored al Qaeda

Excerpt 8 (Bush 2003a)
   1   in the **battle of Afghanistan**
   2   we destroyed the Taliban
   3   many terrorists
   4   and the camps where they trained

Excerpt 9 (Bush 2003a)
   1   the **battle of Iraq** is *one* **victory** in a **war on terror**
   2   that began on September the 11th 2001
   3   and still goes on

The precipitating event of 9/11 leads to action in Afghanistan "where America and a broad coalition acted first," illustrated in excerpt 7 from Bush's September 2003 address to the nation. The utterance "acted first" (line 2) presupposes more actions to come and that "Afghanistan" is merely a piece of a bigger whole. In excerpt 8, taken from Bush's May 1, 2003 speech to announce the end of major combat operations in Iraq, this conceptualization is emphasized by referencing the war in Afghanistan as the "battle of Afghanistan" (line 1). In the same speech (excerpt 9), the conflict in Iraq is also described as a battle, the "battle of Iraq" (line 1), where the war in Iraq is positioned as "one victory in a war on terror that began on September the 11th, 2001 and still goes on." The language in these excerpts breaks these events into sub-events within a conceptual frame of a larger war.

Bruner (1991) cites "the imposition of bogus *historical-causal entailment*" as a strategy that guides the cobbling together of stories into larger narratives (19). "For example," notes Bruner, "the assassination of Archduke Ferdinand is seen as 'causing' the outbreak of the First World War" (19). The structure of the BWOTN sequentially positions a series of events that start with an abstract, in Labovian (1972) terms, that introduces the theme of an ongoing "war on terror" precipitated by the events of 9/11 (see again excerpt 9 for an example of this in the May 1, 2003 telling of the BWOTN). As Bruner (1991) points out, the precipitating event

breaches the normalcy, or canonicity of everyday life. This sets up the pivotal conflict around which the complicating action unfolds and the characters in the narrative (Osama bin Laden/al Qaeda and Saddam Hussein/Iraq) are identified. In
the BWOTN, the events in Afghanistan and Iraq, and other elements of the administration's foreign policy, are positioned as natural progressions that stem from
this precipitating event (rather than disparate foreign policy objectives). This general progression of events can be seen in excerpt 10.

Excerpt 10 (Bush 2003a)

   1   from **Pakistan** to the **Philippines** to the **Horn of Africa**
   2   we are **hunting down al Qaeda** killers

             [7 lines left out about successes against al Qaeda]

 10   the **liberation of Iraq**
 11   is a crucial advance
 12   in the **campaign against terror**
 13   we've removed an **ally**
 14   of **al Qaeda**
 15   and cut off a **source**
 16   of terrorist **funding**
 17   and this much is certain
 18   no **terrorist** network will gain weapons of mass destruction from the **Iraqi
       regime**
 19   because the regime is no more (applause)

Plausibility is a key element of narrative. Ochs and Capps (2001) state that, "Credibility depends in part upon the plausibility of a chain of objective events that can
be corroborated. Narrators, however, strategically couch these events within subjective events that cannot be contradicted" (284). For example, the statement that
"the liberation of Iraq is a crucial advance in the campaign against terror" (in excerpt 10, lines 10–12) is a subjective evaluation. Yet, the effect of its positioning
among the naming of a series of objective events and places set out in the plotline
lends credence to the relationship between Iraq and the string of events in the surrounding text. Fairclough (1995) also notes that where an "unsubstantiated piece
of interpretation is positioned after the carefully substantiated account…the aura
of objectivity has been established, and interpretation now perhaps stands a good
chance of passing as fact" (84).

    A historical-causal entailment is therefore subtly implied through the struc-
ture of the BWOTN, so that one might believe war against Iraq would not have
taken place absent the precipitating event of 9/11, or at the very least, the precipitating event made such actions all the more urgent and crucial given the con-

structed identity of Iraq and al Qaeda as allies. When the flow of such events and statements as those adumbrated above fits seamlessly with the whole, Bruner (1991) states that the "telling preempts momentarily the possibility of any but a single interpretation" (9).

Silverstein's (2003) examination of presidential speeches draws on Russian psychologist Lev Vygotsky's concept of "thinking-in-complexes" to offer a similar understanding (21–24). A "complex" categorizes a series of items in terms of sameness or "equivalence" so that thinking-in-complexes allows us to take a disparate pair of items and see "at least a local 'family resemblance'" in their juxtaposition, even when "the whole lot of things might still be very diverse overall" (Silverstein 2003: 21). Silverstein goes on to note that politics is all about the merging of issues; "issues must be brought together – given plot and characters, rhyme if not reason" (Silverstein 2003: 24). This weaving together of issues is evident in the BWOTN, where the post-9/11 response to al Qaeda morphs into the separate administration goal of "regime change in Iraq." There is no "Iraq War" in the BWOTN, only the "Battle of Iraq" within the "War on Terror." The "war on terror" moniker – now ubiquitous in public debate and discussion, and even used by some media when reporting on events in Iraq – provides for what Silverstein calls a "captioning label or image," which makes "the whole analogical series" take on "a definitive identity – in fact retrospectively a *necessary* identity that we now recognize as so many examples of one underlying principle, conceptually implicit, even immanent" (Silverstein 2003: 23). That underlying principle of the "war on terror" structures the perceptual experience of a nation. The BWOTN not only provides a way to conceptualize the events of 9/11 and their aftermath, but does so in a way that merges those events with ideologically inspired policy objectives.

Discussion

Any form of communication is a joint endeavor between speaker and hearer that relies on common ground to succeed (Clark 1996). In this way, even one-way political speeches can be thought of as an interactive process; and in political discourse heavily laden with implicit meaning, the background an interpreter brings to the process is certainly vital to deriving intended (or unintended) messages. The effectiveness of Bush administration rhetoric in the imposed adequation of two disparate actors in world affairs can be seen in Congressional approval for action against Iraq and the dominance of ideas from the BWOTN in political debate in the country. In addition, public opinion polls like those mentioned in the introduction also provide an interesting perspective on the uptake of ideas espoused (whether implicitly or explicitly) by the administration.

These polls shed light on public beliefs regarding the adequation of Saddam Hussein's Iraq and Osama bin Laden's al Qaeda in two ways. First, they show that a large number of Americans believe Iraq and al Qaeda were involved in a supportive political alliance prior to 9/11. Specifically, the April 2004 PIPA poll showed that 57% of Americans felt this way, including 45% who believed "evidence that Iraq was supporting al Qaeda had been found" (PIPA 2004a). Second, they show that some Americans go further to believe that Iraq aided and abetted al Qaeda in carrying out the events of 9/11. The same April 2004 PIPA poll found 20% to "believe that Iraq was directly involved in the September 11 attacks" (PIPA 2004a). The first result is in line with an easily retrievable interpretation of the BWOTN, but the second result is even more fascinating since administration rhetoric in the BWOTN and elsewhere does not go so far as to directly implicate Iraq in 9/11.[7] The message in the BWOTN paints a picture of a potential relationship, but more damning interpretations require additional interpretive work on the part of the audience.

The discursive strategies in political narratives often build an incomplete scaffold that requires the audience to rely on "bridging assumptions" – i.e. ideologies and shared background knowledge – to build relations of coherence (Fairclough 1995: 123, cf. Fairclough 1992, Brown and Yule 1983). The ideological assumptions an audience brings to the task of interpretation help shape resulting meanings. Moreover, an audience more sympathetic to a speaker is likely to view the speaker as more trustworthy and see the narrative as more credible. It is not surprising, then, to find in the same April 2004 PIPA poll that those who believed Iraq had supported al Qaeda were supporters of Bush. Another study by PIPA in October 2004, just before the November elections, provides a similar breakdown. This study found that 75% of Bush supporters versus 30% of Kerry supporters had the impression that Iraq "gave al Qaeda substantial support," while 20% of Bush supporters to 8% of Kerry supporters had the impression that Iraq was "directly involved in 9/11" (PIPA 2004b).

Hegemony and "common sense"

In addition to the role ideology plays in the interpretation of discourse, it is also appropriate to discuss ideology with regard to Gramsci's (1971) notion of hegemony. The identity of Iraq and al Qaeda constructed in the BWOTN is but one perspective on two issues in recent American history: the events of 9/11 and policy towards Iraq. An alternative formulation forwarded by Bush administration critics views the response against al Qaeda after 9/11 and the objective of "regime change in Iraq" as completely separate and unrelated. In this scenario, lack of evidence of a connection between Saddam Hussein and Osama bin Laden is highlighted and the notion of the two engaged in a political alliance comes across as a gross misconception at best, and as outright deception at worst. Insofar as "ideology involves the representation of 'the world' from the perspective of a particular interest" (Fairclough 1995: 44), these opposing narratives represent the world – and structure shared experience – from the perspective of different ideological interests. The narratives put forth by each of these perspectives are part of an ideological struggle played out in language.

Effective political speech couches partisan interests and actions inside "the claim that these actions are within the general moral order, and hence not justified only by partisan, self-serving grounds" (van Dijk 1998: 258). The BWOTN constructs an image of sociopolitical reality in one way, while the opposing narrative constructs a different image. Of course, neither is forwarded as a partisan perspective; but rather, both are presented as the "truth" or "simply as the way things are." Hegemony occurs when the representation of the world forwarded by one ideological perspective is taken for granted or becomes naturalized as a "common sense" conception of reality. "Ideological dominance and hegemony is 'perfect' when dominated groups are unable to distinguish between their own interests and attitudes and those of dominant groups" (van Dijk 1998: 102). While the BWOTN and its ideas, such as the *adequation* of Iraq and al Qaeda, receive ongoing challenges both domestically and abroad, its inertia in American politics is clearly evident. In many ways, the ideas inherent in the BWOTN form a basic understanding of 9/11 and Iraq that many Americans have accepted as "common sense." "Common sense" beliefs live long lives even in light of empirical counter-evidence or logical refutations. "Remember," writes Wittgenstein (1969) in *On Certainty*, "one is sometimes convinced of the *correctness* of a view by its *simplicity* or *symmetry*, i.e., these are what induce one to go over to this point of view. One then simply says something like: '*That's* how it must be'" (14).

Symbolic power and the legitimacy of words

The capacity of narrative to define sociopolitical reality and advance a particular perspective as "common sense" relies on the symbolic power wielded by the speaker to give the message credibility and the impetus to achieve widespread circulation in the media. According to Bourdieu (1987b), symbolic power is "*worldmaking* power" in that it can impose a "legitimate vision of the social world and of its divisions" (13).

Overlying the rhetorical strategies of the BWOTN is the *symbolic capital* possessed by the narrator based on his "accumulated prestige or honour" (Bourdieu 1991: 14). This symbolic capital consists of *social capital* in the form of acquaintances and networks that give him (as President) access to special information and classified intelligence, and *cultural capital* in the form of political credentials and his position as President of the United States. In essence, the symbolic capital[8] of the President – his place within the *field of power* as a dominant leader in world affairs – gives him "nomination power", or the power to impose a credible definition of sociopolitical identities in the world (Bourdieu 1986, 1987a). In this way, *identities-on-paper* become *identities-in-reality*, to use a variant on Bourdieu's (1985) explication of social classes (727, cf. Swartz 1997: 150). Identity, therefore, is itself an *effect* of culture and sociopolitical interaction undergirded by relations of power.

When social actors engage in identity work to achieve, for example, sufficient sameness among groups previously viewed as distinct, those identities may be taken up and given legitimacy by other social actors in a process of mutual social reinforcement. In the BWOTN, the discursive construction of an Iraq-al Qaeda alliance from without creates the conditions for that identity to potentially be taken up from within, creating an ensuing *spiral effect*. Put another way, in times of war, *the enemy of my enemy may become my friend*, so that a de facto alliance among otherwise disparate groups may, at least discursively, be given legitimacy from their perspective, as well. In the same February 2003 speech by bin Laden cited in the introduction, where bin Laden denounces Saddam Hussein as an infidel, he seemingly acquiesces to the imposed adequation forced upon al Qaeda and Iraq by Bush and states, "Under these circumstances, there will be no harm if the interests of Muslims converge with the interests of the socialists in the fight against the crusaders" (bin Laden 2003, February 12). Similarly, critics of the Bush administration – as well as a report released by the CIA's think tank, the National Intelligence Council (NIC 2005, cf. Priest 2005[9]) – have pointed to the way the US invasion of Iraq effectively created a haven for terrorists like al Qaeda where none previously existed. In this way, the link hyperbolized in the BWOTN actualizes itself in a self-fulfilling manner.

Conclusion

Identity formation is a social achievement, accomplished in large part through language. The discursive tactic of adequation works to erase differences and elevate similarities deemed to be situationally relevant. This analysis illustrates how the discursive strategies of the BWOTN lead to the adequation of Iraq and al Qaeda. As shown, adequation is a tactic not only used by a group to identify itself, but used from an outside position of power to impose sufficient sameness on others for political purposes. In this case, the *imposed adequation* in the BWOTN helps legitimize and forward a rationale for the US invasion of Iraq. Moreover, the resulting vision of the world and concomitant actions has spiraled into real effects for all parties involved. As Nelson (2003) writes, "Human conflict begins and ends via talk and text" (449). The power of political narrative to structure experience and define sociopolitical reality plays an important role in defining the identities that shape actions and interaction on a global scale.

Notes

1.   I owe special thanks to Kira Hall, Paul Chilton, and Chad Nilep for providing invaluable comments on earlier formulations of this paper.

2.   The 9/11 Commission's final report, released on July 22, 2004, states, "But to date we have seen no evidence that these or the earlier contacts ever developed into a collaborative operational relationship. Nor have we seen evidence indicating that Iraq cooperated with al Qaeda in the developing or carrying out any attacks against the United States" (NC 2004: 83). In addition, a Senate Intelligence Committee (2006) report, released in September 2006, further details lack of a connection.

3.   The specific functions of opinion polls in democratic societies or an analysis of their methodologies and reliability is beyond the scope of this paper. These studies, conducted by reputable research centers in the US, are simply used here to frame the key issue at stake: the capacity of political discourse to impact social understandings.

4.   The study of persuasion has been treated extensively within the domain of rhetoric, including work on Argumentation Theory (e.g. Kienpointner 1991, van Eemeren and Grootendorst 2004).

5.   It is no secret that "regime change in Iraq" was part of Bush administration foreign policy prior to taking office, well before the events of 9/11. For discussions of this policy, see Cirincione (2003), as well as Jhally and Earp (2004).

6.   The line breaks in the excerpts represent rhetorical pauses in the speech, following work by James Paul Gee (1986) in the "Units in the Production of Narrative Discourse," and help to highlight syntactic parallelism. Full transcripts and video recordings of these speeches can be found online at www.whitehouse.gov.

7.   At least explicitly, this is the case; even though implicit hints are present that may lead to such an interpretation. Moreover, when pressed, administration officials have been forced to expressly deny any Iraqi collaboration in 9/11 (even while maintaining the idea of a significant connection), e.g. Vice-President Dick Cheney's June 17, 2004 appearance on CNBC after the 9/11 Commission released Staff Statement No. 15, a twelve page preliminary report that concluded no "collaborative relationship" existed between Iraq and al Qaeda. See Hodges (2007) for further analysis of these issues and this particular interview. More recently, President George W. Bush found himself in this position when asked by a reporter at a White House Press conference what Iraq had to do with September 11. "Nothing," Bush immediately replied, "except for it's part of—" and Bush went on to reiterate elements of the BWOTN (Bush 2006).

8.   One might also talk of *political capital*—as Bush himself did at a November 4, 2004 press conference after victory in the US presidential election—as the symbolic power needed to effectively assert legitimacy. Bush: "Let me put it to you this way: I earned capital in the campaign, political capital, and now I intend to spend it" (2004).

9.   Priest's (2005) coverage of the National Intelligence Council's report notes, "President Bush has frequently described the Iraq war as an integral part of U.S. efforts to combat terrorism. But the council's report suggests the conflict has also helped terrorists by creating a haven for them in the chaos of war."

References

Bach, K. 1994. "Conversational impliciture." *Mind and Language* 9(2):124–162.

Bin Laden, O. 2003, February 12. Text of Osama bin Laden tape played on Aljazeera television (translated into English by the BBC). Available: http://news.bbc.co.uk/1/hi/world/middle_east/2751019.stm.

Bourdieu, P. 1984. *Distinction: A Social Critique of the Judgment of Taste.* Cambridge, MA: Harvard University Press.

Bourdieu, P. 1985. "Social space and the genesis of groups." *Theory and Society* 14(6):723–744.

Bourdieu, P. 1986. "The forms of capital." In *Handbook of Theory and Research for the Sociology of Education*, J.G. Richarson (ed.), 241–258. Westport, CT: Greenwood Press.

Bourdieu, P. 1987a. *Choses Dites.* Paris: Editions de Minuit.

Bourdieu, P. 1987b. "What makes a social class? On the theoretical and practical existence of groups." *Berkeley Journal of Sociology* 32:1–18.

Bourdieu, P. 1991. *Language and Symbolic Power*, G. Raymond and M. Adamson (trans.). Cambridge, MA: Harvard University Press.

Brown, G. and Yule, G. 1983. *Discourse Analysis.* Cambridge: Cambridge University Press.

Bruner, J. 19991. "The Narrative Construction of Reality." *Critical Inquiry* 18: 1–24.

Bucholtz, M. and Hall, K. 2004. "Language and identity." In *A Companion to Linguistic Anthropology*, A. Duranti (ed.). Malden, MA: Blackwell.

Bush, G.W. 2002, October 7. Speech in Cincinnati, Ohio. Available: http://www.whitehouse.gov/news/releases/2002/10/20021007-8.html.

Bush, G.W. 2003a, May 1. Speech aboard the USS Abraham Lincoln off the coast of San Diego. Available: http://www.whitehouse.gov/news/releases/2003/05/20030501-15.html.

Bush, G.W. 2003b, September 7. Address to the nation from the White House. Available: http://www.whitehouse.gov/news/releases/2003/09/20030907-1.html.

Bush, G.W. 2004, November 4. Presidential Press Conference at the White House. Available: http://www.whitehouse.gov/news/releases/2004/11/20041104-5.html.

Bush, G.W. 2006, August 21. Presidential Press Conference at the White House. Available: http://www.whitehouse.gov/news/releases/2006/08/20060821.html.

Chilton, P. 2004. *Analysing Political Discourse.* London: Routledge.

Clark, H. 1996. ""Communities, commonalities, and communication." In *Rethinking Linguistic Relativity*, J.L. Gumperz and S.C. Levinson (eds.), 324–358. Cambridge: Cambridge University Press.

Cirincione, J. 2003, March 19. "Origins of regime change in Iraq." *Carnegie Endowment for International Peace Proliferation Brief* (6)5. Available: http://www.ceip.org/files/nonprolif/templates/Publications.asp?p=8&PublicationID=1214.

Fairclough, N. 1992. *Discourse and Social Change.* Cambridge, MA: Polity Press.

Fairclough, N. 1995. *Media Discourse.* London: Arnold.

Foucault, M. 1980. *Power/Knowledge: Selected Interviews and Other Writings*. New York: Pantheon Books.

Gee, J.P. 1986. "Units in the Production of Narrative Discourse." *Discourse Processes* 9: 391–422.

Gramsci, A. 1971. *Prison Notebooks*. New York: International Publishers.

Grice, H.P. 1975. "Logic and conversation." In *Syntax and Semantics*, P. Cole and J.L. Morgan (eds.), Volume 3. New York: Academic Press.

Hodges, A. 2007. "The political economy of truth in the 'war on terror' discourse: Competing visions of an Iraq/al Qaeda connection." *Social Semiotics* 17(1): 5–20.

Irvine, J.T. and Gal, S. 2000. "Language ideology and linguistic differentiation." In *Regimes of Language: Ideologies, Polities, and Identities*, P. Kroskrity (ed.), 35–83.

Jhally, S. and Earp, J. 2004. *Hijacking Catastrophe: 9/11, Fear and the Selling of American Empire*. Northampton, MA: Interlink Publishing.

Kienpointner, M. 1991. "Rhetoric and argumentation." *Philosophy and Rhetoric* 24(1): 43–53.

Labov, W. 1972. "The transformation of experience in narrative syntax." *In Language in the Inner City: Studies in the Black English Vernacular*, W. Labov (ed.), 354–396. Philadelphia: University of Pennsylvania Press.

Labov, W. and Waletsky, J. 1967. "Narrative analysis: Oral versions of personal experience." In *Essays on the Verbal and Visual Arts,* J. Helm (ed), 12–44. Seattle: University of Washington Press.

Lewis, D. 1979. "Scorekeeping in a language game." In *Semantics from Different Points of View*, R. Bauerle, U. Egli and A. von Stechow (eds.). Berlin: Springer-Verlag.

Marquis, C. 2004, January 9. "Powell admits no hard proof in linking Iraq to al Qaeda." *New York Times*. Available: http://www.nytimes.com/2004/01/09/politics/09POWE.html?ex=108286 5600&en=7a8bc8cab6337ff4&ei=5070.

National Intelligence Council. 2005. *Mapping the Global Future*. Report of the National Intelligence Council's 2020 Project. Available: http://www.dni.gov/nic/NIC_globaltrend2020.html.

NC. 2004. *The 9/11 Commission Report: Final Report of the National Commission on Terrorist Attacks upon the United States*. New York: W.W. Norton.

NC – see National Commission on Terrorist Attacks upon the United States.

Nelson, D.N. 2003. "Conclusion: Word peace." In *At War With Words*, Dedaić, M.N. and Nelson, D.N. (eds.), 449–468. New York: Mouton de Gruyter.

NIC – see National Intelligence Council.

Ochs, E. and Capps, L. 2001. *Living Narrative: Creating Lives in Everyday Storytelling*. Cambridge, MA: Harvard University Press.

Pew – see Pew Research Center for the People and the Press.

Pew Research Center for the People and the Press. 2002, October 10. "Americans Thinking About Iraq, But Focused on the Economy: Midterm Election Preview." Available: http://people-press.org/reports/display.php3?ReportID=162.

PIPA – see Program for International Policy Attitudes.

Priest, Dana. 2005, January 14. "Iraq new terror breeding ground: War created haven, CIA advisers report." *Washington Post*, A01.

Program for International Policy Attitudes. 2004a, April 22. "US Public Beliefs on Iraq and the Presidential Election." University of Maryland. Available: http://www.pipa.org/OnlineReports/Iraq/IraqReport4_22_04.pdf.

Program for International Policy Attitudes. 2004b, October 21. "The Separate Realities of Bush and Kerry Supporters." University of Maryland. Available: http://www.pipa.org/OnlineReports/Pres_Election_04/Report10_21_04.pdf.

Riessman, C.K. 1993. *Narrative Analysis*. London: Sage Publications.

Sacks, H. 1992. *Lectures on Conversation*. Cambridge: Blackwell.

Senate Intelligence Committee. 2006, September 8. Report of the Select Committe on Intelligence on Postwar Findings about Iraq's WMD Programs and Links to Terrorism and How They Compare with Prewar Assessments together with Additional Views. Available: http://intelligence.senate.gov/phaseiiaccuracy.pdf.

Silverstein, M. 2003. *Talking Politics: The Substance of Style from Abe to 'W'*. Chicago: Prickly Paradigm Press.

Swartz, D. 1997. *Culture and Power: The Sociology of Pierre Bourdieu*. Chicago: University of Chicago Press.

Van Dijk, T. 1991. *Racism and the Press*. London: Routledge.

Van Dijk, T. 1998. *Ideology*. London: Sage Publications.

Van Eemeren, F.H. and Grootendorst, R. 2004. *A Systematic Theory of Argumentation: The Pragma-dialectical Approach*. Cambridge: Cambridge University Press.

Wittgenstein, L. 1969. *On Certainty*. New York: Harper and Row.

CHAPTER 5

Discourses of freedom

Gender and religion in US media coverage of the war on Iraq

Katherine Lemons

Introduction

"Emboldened by the fall of Saddam Hussein, Iraqi women are pushing for political freedoms many of them have never enjoyed. But as they do, a rising tide of religious zeal threatens even the small victories they have won" (Banerjee 2004). So runs the first paragraph of Neela Banerjee's February 26, 2004 article as it appeared in the *New York Times*'s temporary section, "The Struggle for Iraq: Equal Rights." The rhythm of the paragraph draws the reader into a drama between freedom and unfreedom, between liberation and oppression and between the rational and the irrational. Saddam Hussein, the oppressive dictator, falls, but as women try to push into the space he has left open, winning several unnamed "small victories," the rise of another irrational force, a "tide of religious zeal," threatens to overwhelm them, thwarting their efforts. While "political freedom" finds itself in the company of previously withheld enjoyment for which women "push," religion becomes a metaphorical tide. A "rising tide," although sometimes calculable, and possibly anticipated, is nonetheless unstoppable, irrational, and ruthless, indiscriminately sweeping up anything and anyone in its path. A tide is propelled by the inertia of its own internal movement, taking into account few external factors. Religion here metaphorically *becomes* this rising tide. The momentum of the tide is the zeal of the religious, and its movement and volume "threatens" the rational battles from which Iraqi women have emerged victorious. Women and rationality will both, it appears, be victims of this tidal wave of irrational religious zeal.

Banerjee's article pointedly participates in a discursive economy pervasive in US media treatment of the country's war on Iraq.[1] The discourse of which her article is a part relies upon two notable tropes: the comportment of the female body as a mark of relative progress, and Islam as a force of repression. In this essay, I will closely read several *New York Times* articles, tracing these tropes as indicative of assumptions about gender in Islam and about the proper role of religion in a liberated society. Among the effects of this discourse and the normative assumptions that underlie it, I will argue, is a refusal to recognize and to engage critically with different conceptions of liberation and of religion. This is in part because the discursive economy in which these articles participate is governed by Lockean liberal conceptions of freedom as negative liberty and of religion as a set of practices and beliefs indifferent to the state (Locke 1980, 1990).[2] Negative liberty entails the right to pursue one's ends only to the extent that the pursuit of these ends does not interfere with anyone else's freedom. For Locke, people are by nature free to enjoy "all the rights and privileges of the law of nature" and thereby have the power "to preserve his property, that is, his life, liberty and estate, against the injuries and attempts of other men [sic]" (Locke 1980: 46). This is most commonly glossed as a freedom *from* interference, and it assumes as its subject an autonomous individual whose highest ends are achieved through the uninterrupted pursuit of property and other goods.[3] This conception of liberty extends to a freedom of religion as a practice indifferent to and therefore both protected from and unable to interfere with the State. Religion, for Locke, must be tolerated by the State because religion itself ought not to concern external right or law, but only its own private practice and the salvation of those who participate in it (Locke 1990: 20). The religious tide with which Banerjee's article begins appears to be antithetical to the Lockean notion of religion as it threatens precisely to interfere with everything that stands before it, *especially* the political standing of women. Both religion and the standing of these women are the focal points of the article.

The gendered body

Banerjee's article presents the reader with five different women pursuing their rights. Fatennal Ramahi, the final woman introduced, is emblematic, as "the new possibilities and dangers [for women in Iraq] collide" in her life. The article's description of Ramahi begins awkwardly, with a combined reference to her work history and her social standing as a multi-lingual Iraqi woman.

"Fluent in English and German, Ms. Ramahi stopped working for the last 13 years because she was unwilling to inform on foreign employers," we read. Her fluency in English and German serve as the prelude to her introduction into the article. English and German ally Ramahi with a foreign, non-Arabic speaking world. Her refusal to work is presented as a response to a presumed demand in Iraq that she participate with her boss in what we imagine to be a project of betrayal in a xenophobic, closed world. We are given no sense of why our protagonist was asked to inform on her foreign colleagues, and only know that doing so was a condition of keeping her job. The paragraph continues: "Depressed about staying at home, Ms. Ramahi, a 45-year-old mother of four, began wearing the hijab a few years ago. When she began work, she took off the scarf." The structure of this sentence mirrors perfectly that of the first sentence in the paragraph, where the subordinate clause "fluent in English and German" prepared us for Ramahi's entrance. However, the adjectival clause that introduces Ramahi here links her not to the foreign, outside, enlightened world represented by English and German, but to the home and a depression intimately bound to it. In her depression and in the midst of the moral house-arrest that has brought it on, Ramahi has become a "45-year-old mother of four." The sentence cascades to its finish: the hijab. Depressed, homebound, and a mother, work and fluency in other languages forgotten, Ramahi covers herself. The hijab is not only the culmination and emblem of a depression and subordination, although it is these; it is also a retreat from view of the woman who first appeared to us a sentence ago.

This veil and the entanglement of its history with the history of European colonialism gives the particular diagnosis of veil-induced depression by the *New York Times* a disconcerting force that we can only articulate through a brief return to the history of colonial discourses on the veil.[4] In Frantz Fanon's writings on the Algerian Revolution, the veil figures as a source and site of argument between the Algerians and the French (Fanon 1965). The veil marks for the French a source of moral legitimacy for colonial activity. Fanon argues that once the French have established the veil as their point of intervention, it becomes for the Algerians the space of resistance through such movements as the "cult of the veil," in which wearing the veil is valorized as a sign of defiance against the French. Thus, for both the French colonizers and for the Algerians they colonize, the female body and its comportment become sites of a debate over progress and the question of legitimate occupation. Fanon writes that using the "discoveries" of sociologists and ethnologists who described Algerian society as matrilineal, colonial administrators developed their policy: "If we want to destroy the structure of Algerian society, its capacity for resistance, we must first of all conquer the women; we must go and find them behind the veil where they hide themselves and in the houses where the men keep them out of sight" (Fanon 1965: 37–38).[5] In order to control Algerian society, the French must control its women. Such control requires an unveiling, and thereby a revealing of the Algerian woman, an act which is defended as a moral obligation by the French and which at the same time serves as a symbolic challenge to the authority of Algerian men. The female body has become the externalization and the physical site of a contest between French and Algerian. Although women actively participate in the politics of resistance enacted through the veil, this is a battle between two power structures, the French and the Algerian, and there is little indication that the women upon whose bodies it is symbolically played out are themselves at issue. The veil as the centerpiece of a dispute about power thus rests upon and reiterates certain assumptions about the value of women as tokens of possession and control.

Leila Ahmed's account of the history of discourses on the veil in colonial Egypt looks at the instrumentalization of the veil as a symbol of oppression made possible in part through the manipulation of the language and impulses of feminism (Ahmed 1992: 151). Ahmed argues that in colonial Egypt, the veil became a prominent symbol of the oppression of Egyptian women for the British colonizers and was subsequently picked up as the locus of argument about the relative barbarism of Islam. A discourse of relative civilizational development in turn legitimated, through the use of European feminist language, ongoing British intervention in Egyptian affairs. Ahmed notes the irony of this situation when she writes:

> Even as the Victorian male establishment devised theories to contest the claims of feminism, and derided and rejected the ideas of feminism and the notion of men's oppressing women with respect to itself, it captured the language of feminism and redirected it, in the service of colonialism, toward Other men and the cultures of Other men (Ahmed 1992: 151).

Ahmed goes on to note that this feminist language deployed in the service of colonialism worked differently and through different idioms in different contexts, but always rested upon the same assumption that a determination of cultural superiority confers legitimacy on impositions upon the culturally inferior. Ahmed presents us with a situation in which a progressive position in one domain threatens the existing power structures while in another it is useful to those who wish, by undermining other structures of power and legitimacy, to secure their own dominance. A language of feminism employed in Britain threatens the dominance of the British patriarchy, while in Egypt it undermines the Egyptian patriarchy and favors the British patriarchy as salvific. Feminist language and, as in Fanon, discussion of the veil, have become tools for domination as well as sites of contestation.

When we read the *New York Times* article through this history of thought, its assumptions about the veil and about the relationship between removing the veil and liberation – evident in the facile links between the home, depression and the hijab – emerge clearly. Wearing the hijab marks a subservience to one regime of authority associated with oppression, invisibility and backwardness and removing the hijab marks liberation. This liberation, though, can be seen as subordination to another regime of authority, one in which visibility, transparency and, as we will see, a certain relationship to the world as a productive worker, is assumed.[6]

Ramahi's return to work coincides with such a discursive shift. In this short sentence, "When she returned to work, she took off the scarf," work is the impetus and precondition for the removal of the scarf, and the removal of the scarf as an inversion of all that wearing it entailed, marks a re-emergence or a liberation. The scarf here is "the scarf," preceded by a definite article rather than a possessive pronoun: this is not *her* scarf, but stands metonymically for the scarf in general. The two interconnected actions: entry into the capitalist work-force and removal of the veil, inaugurate the present in which we find Ramahi. She is now available for a different kind of evaluation and valuation than she was as the depressed, veiled mother of four. Now her work can be recognized, for it has value as part of the capitalist economy as it has emerged from the non-valued realm of reproductive labor. Her liberation from the veil also makes possible a different kind of evaluation, as she now participates differently in an economy of visibility.

The article continues: "'I feel back to my own self,' she said in her office, her lush auburn hair brushing the neck of her black sweater. Pointing at her smiling face, she said, 'This is the real me.'" The transformation is now complete in the rediscovery of a true self. This self is available to be discovered only when the veil is removed and work outside the home is recommenced. The "own self" claims interiority as a possession, something alienable from the person and, therefore, recuperable by it. Yet this self can be regained only when Ramahi is unveiled. Authenticity of self and visibility to others are in Ramahi necessarily coincident. She speaks these words as the removal of her veil reveals and sexualizes her. The image of Ramahi's hair is sensual, conflating her renewed self with her sexuality such that the expression of sexuality accompanies the discovery of the true self. Demonstrable sexuality as a sign of liberation often accompanies discourses on the veil and on unveiling. The removal of the veil marks a liberation from physical constraint, while simultaneously rendering the female body visible and thereby sexualized.

The sexualization of the female body as a mark of liberation that we notice here also emerges in other articles. An article about teenage girls in occupied Iraq is permeated by images of frustrated girls whose concerned parents prohibit them from wearing fashionable, tight Western clothing (Sengupta 2004). In the article, Yosor Ali al-Qatan "stares longingly at a hip-hugging pair of pink pinstriped pants," Mariam Saeed complains about the constraints on her mobility as she sits, for the first time all year, beside the pool at a private club, and Sali Ismail gazes at the television on which "women in skin-tight clothes and frosty lipstick pranced around improbably to Egyptian love songs." In contrast, one mother appears "cloaked in a mountain of black nylon" and another tries to convince her daughter to dress more conservatively and to cover her head. Although the article is purportedly about violence and the constraints it places on the lives of teenage girls, its gaze frequently and surreptitiously strays to the deprivation concomitant with a new danger associated with wearing tight clothing. The article forges a link between the

constraints on clothing choices for the women of Baghdad and the violence of occupied Iraq through religion. Sengupta writes:

> The perils and pressures bearing on the lives of teenage girls here offer a snapshot of
> the changes bedeviling Iraq. In the past several months, the new access to satellite
> dishes, Internet cafes and cellphones has given these young women a new window
> on the outside world. But creeping religious conservatism, lawlessness and econom-
> ic uncertainty have also been conspiring against them in peculiar ways.

The paragraph's central narrative is that the progress the American invasion
brought to Iraq has been consistently and strangely undermined by the joint forces of religious conservatism, lawlessness and economic uncertainty. The first
change that "bedeviled Iraq" was the change that opened the world for Iraqi wom-
en. The implication that satellite dishes, Internet cafes and cell phones are new
implies that the world prior to the American invasion was one in which all contact
with the "outside world" was impossible. As soon, it seems, as these technological
conduits of progress were introduced, and with them the possibility of liberation
through expanded horizons, they began to be undermined by stealthy forces
creeping in and conspiring against them. Sengupta strings the three culprits together in one sentence, implying that religious conservatism, lawlessness and economic uncertainty have acted in tandem to undermine the possibility of progress,
especially the progress of women. Indeed, as the article unfolds, it appears that it is
religious conservatism that reinforces lawlessness, particularly in the form of ab-
ducting young uncovered girls, and that economic uncertainty serves to enhance
and encourage the ill-effects of the other factors.

Later, Sengupta writes:

> Even though the last years of Saddam Hussein's rule had brought new restrictions
> on women's freedoms, the simultaneous collapse of the police state that had kept
> public order and the new leeway for religious clerics to demand stricter compli-
> ance with Islamic law have increasingly narrowed girls' lives.

Once again, the collapse of the police state and the emergence of religion occur
together in the article. Although there is no explicit argument here about a causal
relation between the two, it appears that both have, without exception, a narrow-
ing influence on the lives of young women. Apparently, stricter compliance to Islamic law necessarily means increasing restriction on the lives of girls. This assumption refuses the possibility that Islamic law, like any other, rests not merely on
compliance but also on interpretation.[7] The assumption that this law can be followed without mediation and that following Islamic law necessarily implies unjust
restrictions on the lives of girls does two additional things: it first implies that all
Islamic law is repressive and secondly implies that the Islamic law is only followed

by women under coercive conditions. The police state, which loses its coercive status as it comes to represent *good* coercion, has been overtaken by the *bad* coercion of the religious cleric. The simplistic argument offered here denies that the police state could be anything but better than rule by clerics. However, assessments of gender parity based on clothing constraints indicate that now, the true enemy of freedom has emerged. Scattered throughout the discussion are the discarded tight, pink clothing that the teenagers are no longer allowed to wear and the head scarves that have become increasingly common replacements for them. The message is clear and it rests on the presupposition that the revelation of the sexualized female body is an act of liberation.

Fanon's *A Dying Colonialism* is again relevant here, as he discusses the complexity of the act of unveiling for the female subject who unveils as part of a strategic politics of resistance and for the European male who watches her. For the European man, the unveiled Algerian woman becomes available by revealing her as one reveals a secret, while veiling does the opposite: it hides the woman and marks an infuriating limit to visibility and therefore to reciprocity of vision and of the "sexual encounter" of the gaze (Fanon 1965: 44). The European wants to see, and the desire to see is part of the desire to possess the colonized through the possession of colonized women. The limitation imposed on sight by the veil exacerbates a frustration and aggression toward the colonized. However, when Algerian women unveil, their physical appearance, no longer so marked, resembles that of the European, thus calling into question the difference between French and Algerians. At this moment, then, the European who once desired the removal of the veil, along with those Algerians who contested its disappearance, demand that the woman return to what he formerly referred to as the cloister of her veil. We see something of this dynamic in Banerjee's and Sengupta's articles, for when we ask *how* the Iraqi woman appears here, we must answer that she appears unveiled, she appears therefore available to the gaze of the reader's imagination. She appears sexualized, in some way graspable, possessible. With this unveiling, she becomes available to the sexual economy of vision and visibility as she is reified as a sexual object. This sexualization emphasizes the gendered nature of this self even as it becomes available in other ways as a good liberal subject.

The final paragraphs of Banerjee's article make explicit another way in which this liberal subject emerges. She appears, we will see, in a particular relationship to religion, one demanded by a secular liberal regime.

> Though she is a religious Muslim who prays and fasts, her decision to take off her scarf amounts to a grave transgression in the eyes of some, and they let her know it.
> 'The other day, I was crossing the street when a boy who was the same age as my son began shouting at me, very, very bad words,' Ms. Ramahi said, her smile vanishing as she looked down at her desk, unwilling to repeat those words. 'I hear

those words in my head still. I keep asking myself, "Why didn't you talk to him?" Then I thought, "I don't dare."

This is where the article ends, with the specter of violence emanating from the unrepeatable words of a Muslim male child. The child, with whom Ramahi should have a mother-child relationship, is instead the menacing future: he is already a violent, intolerant threat as a child and he is therefore the harbinger of a violent and unenlightened future in which Other men continue to threaten Other women.

The argument this article puts forward about the proper place of religion is intimately bound to its unwillingness to concede a space for Islam that is not more violent toward women than secular governance. The final move Banerjee makes returns us to that other, related discussion about the role of religion. The contrast Banerjee makes as she describes the affront caused by this devout Muslim's removal of her scarf is a classic comparison of religiosity as an apparent, literally *worn* display, something unavoidable and public, to religiosity enacted in the private practices of prayer and fasting. The comparison clearly favors the latter form of religiosity. While religion is acceptable, it is so only if its presence and performance are circumscribed within the private realm. The veil is simultaneously a visible demonstration of a religiosity that refuses to limit itself to the private sphere and the mark of a specific religion, Islam, about which assumptions open up an undefended link between religiosity *of this kind and through this act* and the oppression of women.

Ahmed articulates this dynamic in her discussion of Egypt, where she examines political uses of the idea that Islam oppressed women by patriarchal colonialists whose claims were based in scant and inaccurate knowledge of Islam and Muslim societies (Ahmed 1992). The veil is only an issue if it appears within a context that assumes a specific relationship between gender and religion in Islam. That assumption, as present now as in colonial Egypt, hampers attempts to rethink the double deployment of religion and gender to the political end of constructing an enemy to be fought and a victim who needs to be saved. Also entailed in the language here is the assumption that the religiosity demonstrated through the private practices of fasting and prayer is an equivalent religiosity to that of which wearing the veil may be a part. The removal of the veil, for the writer, is therefore not an actual shift or substantive change vis-à-vis religion, but is instead "a grave transgression *in the eyes of some*." The removal of the veil matters politically rather than religiously. This may indeed be the case, especially in Iraq, which has for years been a secular country; however, the unquestioned assumption that every religiosity can and ought to be rendered invisible to the public sphere if modernity is to be achieved remains problematic.

Islam and the liberal state

The re-emergence of Islam in Iraq haunts these articles as it challenges the assumption that religion *ought* to remain private, or even that it is desirable to all people that it only have a place in a person's private life. Sabrina Tavernise's article, "Aftereffects: Rights and Tolerance; Iraqi Women Wary of New Upheavals," reproduces this classical liberal discomfort with the participation of religion in political discussion. Tavernise's article takes place in a Baghdad beauty parlor where, on a Friday afternoon, women talk politics (Tavernise 2003). She writes: "While thousands of people fled to mosques for prayer services, the women here debated the difficulties of democracy while getting cuts and colors." A tide of humanity moving toward the mosque sets the scene. The verb "fled" implies a need to escape and imposes an urgency on the mosque-bound stream. The people flee *en masse*, Banerjee's "rising tide of religious zeal" incarnated in a moving crowd. Against this tide of people Tavernise introduces a small group of women going about the task of beautification. Not only are these women separate from the crowd and from the religious craze it represents, they are firmly gendered, spending their time on beauty, working to express themselves as sexualized beings. We see here the antithesis between individuation through beautification and absorption into the religious horde presented through the distinction of several nameable, modern women in the beauty parlor, and an unnamable mass of non-gendered people moving in a frenzy toward the mosque. Situated within a domain marked by the absence of men and of religion, the women discuss politics.

Tavernise offers a glimpse into the substance of the conversation: "What... if the people elect a religious leader? Would the Americans allow that to happen even if the Iraqis wanted it? And where would that leave Iraqi women?" The three questions enact a tension between the concern that the American occupiers will ignore Iraqi opinion, signaling a failure of democratic self-determination, and an implied fear that Iraqi opinion would, if granted such self-determination, subject Iraqi women to the rule of a religious leader. The article develops the second possibility:

> As enormous change sweeps Iraq, some women are viewing newfound religious freedoms nervously. Iraq does not have a history of religious fundamentalism. Its women enjoyed near parity with men for several decades through the 1970's. But the current situation is something new. Exhausted Iraqis are looking for answers in the chaos and power vacuum that has ensued since the war ended.

Religious freedom appears to be a threat exclusively to women, for it is women, not men, who worry about "religious freedoms." The article juxtaposes the women's nervousness about "religious freedom" with a history free of fundamentalism, which implies that freedom of religion in Iraq means the introduction of fundamentalism. The final sentence argues that the absence of fundamentalism has historically meant parity for women, indicating through the juxtaposition of parity and fundamentalism, which has been metonymically connected to religion, that religious freedom in Iraq is the condition for the oppression of women. The newness of this situation, then, is that Iraqis in the midst of a chaotic and violent situation are looking for consolation toward the mosque from which, we are told through a series of metonymically-related terms, emanate fundamentalism and a concomitant oppression of women.

The meaning of the "religion" to which Iraqis flee becomes increasingly clear as the article continues. The owner of the beauty salon declares: "I want to live a joyful life out in the open," followed by: "I don't want a government of religion... Religion is a private thing." Nimo Din'Kha Skander, the salon's owner, speaks the position of a secular liberal subject. Her desire for a joyful and open life as she understands it is antithetical to a religious government because a religious government thwarts the relegation of religion to the private sphere thereby contaminating the openness of the public sphere. When she says that religion "is" a private thing, Din'Kha Skander argues that this is the position religion ought to hold. The ideal of openness and joy that Din'Kha Skander attributes to the secular shift of religion to the private sphere carries with it the claim that public religion implies closure and misery, antitheses of freedom. Once again, the operative concept of freedom resembles the freedom of Lockean liberalism, for the freedom Din'Kha Skander hopes to enjoy is a freedom to pursue her interests and ends unconstrained by others. Religion figures here as the threat to that unencumbered pursuit of freedom, as it refuses to heed the Lockean demand that it remain indifferent to the public sphere (Locke 1990: 42). Indeed, for Locke, "true and saving religion consists in the inward persuasion of the mind" (Locke 1990: 20), or in Din'Kha Skander's terminology, "religion is a private thing." For Locke, this means explicitly that the State does not have a right to interfere with religion and implicitly that religion that does not comply with this inwardness does not qualify as true and therefore tolerable religion. Din'Kha Skander's particular notion of freedom and of the conditions for joy coincide with this Lockean liberal position.

However, not all Iraqi women share Din'Kha Skander's dedication to the liberal privatization of religiosity. "During the past decade, younger women have grown more literal with their Islam," the article continues. Tavernise's example is the increasing number of girls who wear head scarves in public, and her source is a United Nations official who attributes the appearance of the scarf to "constraints and privations" in the lives of young girls, among them limitations on travel that hampered the possibility of exposure to "Western values." Isolation in Iraq seems to have resulted in religious revival, and religious revival increased conservatism, marked in this article by an increase in religious practice. However, the unnamed composite subject "younger women" that enacts the renewed conservatism only appears in the article as a citation in the stories of the named, secular, educated women featured in the article. The voices and opinions of religious women and of women wearing the veil are given no space. The article continues:

> At the same time, women's rights were being curtailed by Mr. Hussein's edicts. For instance, women younger than 45 have not been allowed to travel alone, but have had to be accompanied by brothers, fathers or sons. The restrictions as well as the recent social conservatism have come as a blow to older, educated women, who fought against head scarves, arranged marriages and other constraints.

Older, educated women oppose head scarves and arranged marriages. The opposition to these two practices represents opposition to the kind of enclosed and therefore backward existence offered to women of the younger generation. Although the older women, who had the chance to travel and were thereby exposed to "Western values," cringe at the resurgence of practices of veiling and arranged marriage, deprived of rights and progressive social surroundings, younger women join the stream of people fleeing toward the mosque for solace in a time of chaos and disorder. The women are presented as doubly-duped: at once by Hussein's legislated limitations and by social conservatism. The presupposition is that veiling and arranged marriage are not possible "free choices" in the same way that unveiling and choosing not to marry might be, which means that the appearance of the veil can only mean constraint, never liberation. The article follows this logic as it quotes older women reminiscing about the pride with which they took off the hijab and refers to one woman who studied in Beirut and "...was so focused on her career as a diplomat that she never married." *This* is liberation, runs the subtext of the article. This decision to refuse the confines of marriage and a life in the home makes this woman's life history the history of the only true liberation and the only real progress.[8]

 The possibility that the article cannot entertain is that the emergence of Islam as a force in the lives of Iraqis, both men and women, may not be the result of coercion and may not represent regression. The discomfort that we sense in the article is a discomfort with certain performances of religiosity. That these performances (the donning of the veil the persistent and problematically paradigmatic example) appear in relation exclusively to women is incidental to the source of the discomfort, which is the publicness of religiosity. That it is the educated, older women featured in the narrative of the article who dispute the making-public of religion is a comment on this constellation of assumptions: education is a sign of membership in modernity, and public religion, being antithetical to modernity, cannot possibly be supported by such educated women. The entry of religion into the public sphere threatens modernity identified as possible only within a secular context. The threat is both to the supremacy of the religion-free state in political affairs and to the self-defined "Western world" that identifies with such secularism. Both the metaphor of the "rising tide" of Islam and the expression of worry on the part of the secular, liberal subjects of the article express a notion that religion in the public sphere constitutes a failure of modernization. The woman's body, although immaterial to the discomfort expressed in the articles I am reading, nonetheless serves as its locus, both because of the assumptions about the role of gender in Islam and because it is on the bodies of women that the public display of religion can be most easily noted. It is thus to the treatment of women's bodies as signs that I will now turn.

The discomfort with public and political religion that we see in this article emerges from an implied threat of intolerance that makes educated women, who in the terms of the article are "Westernized," nervous. In an article about the United States's 2002 war on Afghanistan, the pretext of which was partially justified as an act of liberation of Afghan women to the texture and type of freedom supposedly harbored by women in the West, Lila Abu-Lughod argues that the pressing question raised by the war, especially for feminists outside of Afghanistan, is how to think about difference. She asks: "Can we only free Afghan women to be like us or might we have to recognize that even after 'liberation' from the Taliban, they might want different things than we would want for them? What do we do about that?" (Abu-Lughod 2002: 787). She goes on to note that the challenge to progressives is to engage in

> ...the hard work involved in recognizing and respecting differences – precisely as products of different histories, as expressions of different circumstances, and as manifestations of differently structured desires. We may want justice for women, but can we accept that there might be different ideas about justice and that different women might want, or choose, different futures from what we envision as best? (Abu-Lughod 2002: 787–788)

Abu-Lughod presents an appeal to carefully and critically examine normative assumptions about liberation. Imagining liberation, for Abu-Lughod, must entail imagining liberation as a concept whose form alters within different contexts. Liberation, then, comes to mean the possibility for defining, within and not outside of the constraints imposed upon a person by her history, the substantive meaning of "liberation." To instead demand as this and other articles do, that liberation can be substantively assessed using one pre-established set of indicators, is to assume that the concept of "liberation" is itself not situated but universal. It is also to suggest a neutrality that, as Abu-Lughod notes, can only be given in bad faith where the terms of evaluation are themselves strongly normative. Within the normative constraints imposed by the liberalism of the *New York Times*, religion appears in opposition to rights, and Islam in particular is represented as antithetical to the freedom that rights purportedly secure. Thus, the representational scheme within which these articles make sense is such that the articles fail both to engage critically with discourses on the veil and to recognize that there are differences also among those who engage in the practice of veiling. Abu-Lughod points to the manner in which the normative liberal notion of liberation positions religiosity and the female Muslim body that cannot, as markedly Muslim, be liberated. The female body as the second and more explicit trope of the discourse on the war in Iraq demands serious analysis.

Conclusion

In this essay, I have looked at representations of Iraqi women in the *New York Times* since the official beginning of the war on Iraq by reading several articles that participate in a discourse and regime of representation with which readers of these media sources are familiar. I have argued that what we see in these representations are the normative assumptions entailed in current discussions of liberation, assumptions that have robust but reprehensible histories. The discourse of which these articles are a part is one whose strongest and most unexamined normative assumptions lie in its use of the female body and Islam both as sites of discussion and as measures of progress. The specific normativity of these articles resembles a strong Lockean liberalism, which appeals to notions of negative liberty and of secularism incompatible with the conception of Islam presented in and produced by this discourse. The imposition of certain normative assumptions about liberation and feminism elides difference and the possibility of recognizing the legitimacy of different forms of liberty. Because the female body and Islam are governed by such strong normative assumptions in the US media, the media fail to provide discursive space wherein the simplicity of the arguments represented might be fruitfully contested and the complexity and nuance of different positions might emerge. For this reason, the task of reading becomes ever more important. Although such a reading practice does not provide a new and "better" normative frame, it does help in the expository work required for the process of becoming aware of the discursive power in which these articles participate.

Notes

1. The one claim that supersedes those made by other journalists is the implicit assumption that under the rule of Hussein women's status was, in the liberal terms of evaluation available on

the pages of the *New York Times,* superior to its current condition. In this, other articles are in accordance with Banerjee's assumption that the presence of certain sorts of religiosity necessarily means a diminished status for women. See, for example, Kristof (2003), Sandler (2003), and Sengupta (2004).

2.   Although I will focus on Locke's articulations of the concepts of freedom and of the appropriate place of religion in relation to politics, both are concerns that appear throughout the classical liberal cannon. John Stuart Mill, for example, argues that the three central elements of human liberty are: first, the liberty of thought, feeling, opinion and conviction and their expression; second, the liberty of "doing as we like, subject to such consequences as may follow;" and third, of combining together with other individuals who espouse the same principles of liberty. All three components of liberty require that such freedoms are pursued only if they do not negatively affect the ability of other members of society to freely pursue their liberties (Mill 1993: 16–17). Mill goes on in the same passage to claim that no society is free that does not respect these particular liberties (17). For a succinct discussion of the concept of freedom in the liberal tradition, see Gray (1995). On liberalism and secularism, see Kant (1998) and Locke (1990).

3.   This position is presented in opposition to positive freedom, or the freedom *to* act. The relationship between the two freedoms is complex and they often inform and provide the conditions for one another, as is the case explicitly in Kant's work (for a thorough discussion of freedom in Kant, see Allison (1990)). However, for the purposes of the present argument, I will limit myself to a brief discussion of negative liberty.

4.   There are a number of important texts that carefully and critically engage the question of female subjectivity within such regimes of representation looking at different practices which I will not be able to engage here. Among these are Lata Mani's (1998) *Contentious Traditions* that engages the practice of *sati,* or widow-burning in India as a site of struggle between colonial forces and elite Indian men and Gayatri Spivak's (1988) essay "Can the Subaltern Speak?"

5.   The original French reads: "Si nous voulons frapper la société algérienne dans sa contexture, dans ses facultés de résistance, il nous faut d'abord conquérir les femmes; il faut que nous allions les chercher derrière le voile où elle se dissimulent et dans les maisons où l'homme se cache" (Fanon 2001: 19).

6.   It is helpful here to think of Gayatri Chakravorty Spivak's (1988) argument in "Can the Subaltern speak," in which she discusses the impossibility of speech in relation to female participants in *sati,* or widow-burning, as a "violent shuttling" between available discourses.

7.   As Roxanne Euben (1999) notes in her book *The Enemy in the Mirror,* one attribute of fundamentalism is that it *claims* to be simple adherence to law when it is in fact one of many interpretations thereof. The elision of interpretation in Sengupta's account reveals the writer's assumption that Islam is, in this sense, always and everywhere "fundamentalist": it implies that the laws of Islam are clear and direct, available for application without the need for mediation.

8.   Saba Mahmood gives an important analysis of the located nature of desire and particularly of the desire for specific types of freedom in her work on the women's piety movement in Egypt. She looks at the virtues and the roles cultivated by the women involved in this movement and argues that it is crucial to progressive scholarship to be able to engage the actions and desires of these women not as instances of false consciousness, but as desires produced within different fields of subjectivation to those of Western feminists. She writes, "...if we accept the notion that all forms of desire are discursively organized (as much of recent feminist scholarship has argued), then it is important to interrogate the practical and conceptual conditions under which

different forms of desire emerge, including desire for submission to recognized authority. We cannot treat as natural and imitable only those desires that ensure the emergence of feminist politics" (Mahmood 2005: 15).

References

Abu-Lughod, L. 2002. "Do Muslim Women Really Need Saving? Anthropological Reflections on Cultural Relativism and Its Others." *American Anthropologist* 104 (3): 783–790.

Ahmed, L. 1992. *Women and Gender in Islam*. New Haven: Yale University Press.

Allison, H.E. 1990. *Kant's Theory of Freedom*. Cambridge: Cambridge University Press.

Banerjee, N. 2004, February 26. "Iraqi Women's Window of Opportunity for Political Gains is Closing." *New York Times*, section A.

Euben, R.L. 1999. *Enemy in the Mirror*. Princeton: Princeton University Press.

Fanon, F. 1965. *A Dying Colonialism*. Haaken Chevalier (trans). New York: Grove Press, Inc.

Fanon, F. 2001. *L'An V de la révolution algérienne*. Paris: La Découverte.

Gray, J. 1995. *Liberalism*. Minneapolis: University of Minnesota Press.

Kant, I. 1998. *Religion within the Boundaries of Mere Reason*. Allen Wood (trans). Cambridge: Cambridge University Press.

Kristof, N. 2003, June 24. "Cover Your Hair." *New York Times*, section A.

Locke, J. 1980. *Second Treatise of Government*. Indianapolis: Hackett.

Locke, J. 1990. *A Letter Concerning Toleration*. Amherst, New York: Prometheus Books.

Mahmood, S. 2005. *The Politics of Piety*. Princeton: Princeton University Press.

Mani, L. 1998. *Contentious Traditions*. Berkeley: University of California Press.

Mill, J.S. 1993. *On Liberty and Utilitarianism*. New York: Bantham Books.

Sandler, L. 2003, September 16. "Veiled and Worried in Iraq." *New York Times*, section A.

Sengupta, S. 2004, June 24. "For Iraqi Girls, Changing Land Narrows Lives." *New York Times*, section 1.

Spivak, G. 1988. "Can the Subaltern Speak?" In *Marxism and the Interpretation of Culture*, C. Nelson and L. Grossberg (eds), 271–313. Urbana: University of Illinois Press.

Tavernise, S. 2003, May 5. "Aftereffects: Rights and Tolerance; Iraqi Women Wary of New Upheavals." *New York Times*, section A.

CHAPTER 6

Arabs in the morning paper

A case of shifting identity

Gregory Ian Stoltz

Introduction

In the wake of September 11, 2001, Arabs have come under increased scrutiny. Media representations and public discourse proclaim that Arabs are "public enemy #1 – brutal, heartless, uncivilized religious fanatics and moneymad cultural 'others' bent on terrorizing civilized Westerners, especially Christians and Jews" (Shaheen 2001: 2). The "war on terror" has incited both fear of Arabs as "others" and fear of overreaction to those fears, such as internment. This network of concerns exists in both the popular press and in academic circles, where Japanese internment is still a painfully real memory. Violence against Arabs has increased tremendously in America. It is precisely at times like this that it becomes imperative to investigate the social construction of ethnic identities.

Purpose of study

While researching the Palestinian-Israeli conflict as reported in the *New York Times* I noticed a slippage in the use of the term "Arab." Different aspects of identity were indexed with the same term. Sometimes the term referred to an ethnicity, sometimes a religion, sometimes something else entirely. This conceptual vagueness suggests that the writers and editors of the *New York Times* do not take adequate care in choosing nomenclature, perhaps as a result of a lack of understanding or a lack of appropriate research and review. This vagueness reaches millions of readers a day in a country now at odds with several nations in the Arab Middle East. This investigation seeks to uncover the range and distribution of interpretations or "senses" of the word Arab that are used in print news discourse. Merging quantitative methods and Critical Discourse Analysis (CDA), I draw conclusions about the causes and effects of this vagueness phenomenon.

Theoretical framework

Foremost among the issues that come to light in this investigation is the power of the media vis-à-vis the power of words. With the advent of CDA (cf. Fairclough 1989) and the recent budding interest in language and war, the power of words has come to the forefront of linguistic anthropological attention (Dedaić and Nelson 2003). Words in the media represent more than simply referential meaning, for "political power cannot be divorced from the power of words" (Dedaić 2003: 1). CDA concerns itself with how one group controls or influences another through the form and content of talk and text. This control is often exerted below the level of conscious awareness. This is precisely the phenomenon at work when receivers of news perceive the media as an unbiased window on the world. "Anything that is said or written about the world is articulated from a position; language is not a clear window, but a refracting, structuring medium" (Fowler 1991: 11). Osam (2003) explains that discursive power is usually expressed in control over discourse topics, types, and styles, along with sheer access to specific discourses (151). These are the most common sites of research for CDA.

Economic and political constraints on corporate media, along with the realities of the editorial process and media monitoring, require an amazing subtlety of methods. The media, news in particular, is so subtle and communicates with such authority that the public often doesn't realize the extent to which it has been influenced. The repetition of messages and message structures has a habituating effect, causing ideas to become normalized. This repetition, coupled with the subtle ways in which news discourse encodes ethnic information, causes discriminatory attitudes to appear normal. After conducting almost 200 interviews, van Dijk reports that "people often refer to the media when expressing or defending ethnic opinions" (van Dijk 1988b: 151). He insists that the subtlety of news discourse is vital to its success. Put another way, "if discrimination were always exerted openly, where it is prone to challenge and criticism by other social actors, its effects possibly would be more limited" (Gotsbachner 2001: 750). The effect on public opinion is real whether or not people are aware of the influence of media.

The analysis that follows mobilizes theoretical points from Critical Discourse Analysis, anthropological theory, and the field of language ideology. In addition to the basic research agenda of CDA, I use Huckin's (2002) notion of *dispersed intentionality*, locating intentionality in institutions as well as individuals. From sociology I borrow the idea of *racial projects*, endeavors on the part of individuals or institutions to define individuals racially (Omi and Winant 1994). Out of the work on linguistic ideology I focus on *erasure* (Gal and Irvine 1995). One of three semiotic processes proposed by Gal and Irvine, erasure is the process by which ideology "renders some persons or activities or sociolinguistic phenomena invisible"

(974). These theoretical points are brought to bear in explaining trends in the usage of the term "Arab" in American print journalism, exemplified by the *New York Times* and the *Christian Science Monitor*.

Historical background of discrimination against arabs

The treatment of Arabs in the West and by the US media is a function of cultural history. Khleif (1990) places the origins of anti-Arab sentiment in Europe in the 11th Century. He looks to the Crusades, in which White Europeans sought to rid their holy land of the quintessential Other: dark-skinned Muslim invaders of their sacred land. This ideology came slowly west as "the legacy of the Crusades and an expansionist, mercantilist Europe… seeped into pre-1776 America and later on, with the technology and advanced industrialism of the 20th century in the US, added to the 'heathen' and 'enemy' stereotype" (27). Some place the origin of anti-Arab sentiment even earlier, before the advent of Islam (Suleiman 1988). The Byzantines viewed Arabs in their empire as primitive, morally suspect nomads. These ideas spread as the Islamic empire grew and spread across the globe. American colonists compared themselves to the Hebrews and hostile Native Americans to Arabs (Suleiman 1988). This metaphor persists in American cinema even today (Shaheen 2001). As Arabs began to move west, and even more so when Middle-East politics began to erupt anew, the status of Arabs in popular perception declined (Mousa 2000).

Jumping forward to the wake of the September 11th tragedy, Arabs in the United States and beyond are still viewed with hostility. The perpetrators of the attacks on the World Trade Center were Arabs, as were the conspirators who made their actions possible. This, along with the subsequent "War on Terror" and the war in Iraq, has caused increased suspicion, scrutiny, and violence against Arabs domestically. This violence depends on a "fungibility of 'Middle Eastern-looking' or 'Muslim-looking' people with the individuals who committed the September 11 attacks and leaves Arabs, Muslims, and South Asians enormously vulnerable" (Ahmad 2002: 103–104). In the days immediately following September 11th, at least five people were killed around the United States as a result of their apparent ethnic identity. The true nature of the victim's ethnicities was not important because each victim was equally guilty of being un-White, un-Occidental.

Methods

Data collection

In order to investigate the range of usages and lack of specificity I collected 1,000 tokens of the word "Arab" from the *New York Times*. These tokens came from electronic versions of the newspaper between August 2, 2002 and December 17, 2002. The search was carried out using Lexis-Nexis Academic Universe. Specifically, the program was instructed to search for all instances of "Arab" and "Arabs" in the *New York Times*. Tokens were eliminated if they came from editorials, news summaries, or were part of proper names, such as the "Arab League" or "United Arab Emirates." Editorial tokens were eliminated because editorials are by nature polemical and intended to present particular opinions. They make no claim to objectivity and are subject to different editing requirements. News summaries were excluded because they contain identical phrases restated from articles in the body of the paper. Proper names are not relevant to this analysis because they are frozen expressions that refer to particular entities.

The newspapers

The *New York Times* was a prime candidate for this type of analysis for several reasons. The simplest is the sheer size of its readership. According to the New York Times Company website, paid readership varied between 1.1 million weekday readers and 1.6 million Sunday readers as of September 29, 2002 (New York Times 2004a). The company itself, the *New York Times* Company, whose revenues for the year 2002 exceeded $3 billion (New York Times 2004b), owns an additional eighteen newspapers, eight television stations, forty websites, and two radio stations (New York Times 2004c). This tremendous corporate presence allows the *New York Times* an almost unlimited amount of resources for gathering and reporting the news. Perhaps this is part of the reason the *New York Times* has attained the cultural status it has in the United States, that of the newspaper of record. The nature of the *New York Times* as a huge business enterprise was also an important factor in selecting it because it allows us to investigate the potential effect of corporate ownership on particular content and presentation.

For the purpose of comparison I also collected 1,000 tokens from the *Christian Science Monitor*. I analyzed issues of the *Monitor* from February 8th, 2002 to December 16th, 2002 in order to obtain the tokens. The *Monitor* had fewer instances of "Arab" per week because the paper contains fewer articles and has no Sunday edition. The *Monitor* is a very different sort of paper than the *New York Times*. It is privately owned by the First Church of Christ, Scientist. Founded in

1908 by Mary Baker Eddy, the founder of The First Church of Christ, Scientist, the paper hails itself as a "uniquely independent voice in journalism" (Christian Science Monitor 2004). No precise circulation data are available for the *Christian Science Monitor,* but its circulation is certainly less than that of the *New York Times.* It is this focus, along with financial independence, that makes the *Monitor* different than the *Times.*

The tokens

Most of the tokens came from breaking news articles chronicling conflict in the Middle East. Many of the articles containing "Arab" come from a series in the *New York Times* called "Threats and Responses." This in itself is telling with regards to the orientation of the *New York Times* towards Arabs and the Arab world. A very small minority of the tokens concerned Arab-Americans or Arab culture. A representative sample token follows:

> The administration appears to have pulled back from pressing the road map, out of sensitivity to Mr. Sharon's objections – but not to have abandoned it entirely, out of sensitivity to the Europeans and Arabs. [Weisman 2000]

Each token includes the entire paragraph containing the word "Arab." This is important in order to divine the particular interpretation of the usage. Were the tokens considered at the level of the article as a whole rather than the paragraph level, the interpretation would surely have been different and probably more complete. However, in order to facilitate the timely analysis of 2,000 tokens, it was necessary to arbitrarily impose the paragraph-level limit.

After a preliminary inspection of the tokens, several patterns appeared. "Arab" appeared repeatedly in particular phrases and contexts. The most common of these were "Arab world" and "Arab country/countries." Even in instances when the phrase was novel, there were a limited number of meanings indexed by "Arab." These were ethnicity, region, nationality, religion, and language. Many tokens involved more than one of these interpretations. It is the number and distribution of these that comprises the quantitative portion of this research. Consider the following token, in its paragraph:

> This is a war not between Israelis and Palestinians, they say, but between Jews and Arabs. It began long before Jews took the West Bank, they say, and it would continue if they gave it up, until they surrendered Haifa as well and left the region. [Bennet 2002]

In this token, a direct contrast is drawn between Jews and Arabs by way of their proximity in the sentence. In truth, Jews and Arabs do not define a binary set (cf.

Udovich and Valensi 1984; Shohat 2003). There exists to this day a significant population of Arab Jews. Currently, over 1 million Arab Jews live in Israel (Shohat 2003: 54). The *New York Times* itself published an editorial by Herbert Hadad about his identity as a Jewish Arab (Hadad 2001).

This issue hinges upon our definition of "Arab." Although it is beyond the scope of this investigation to suggest a precise definition of Arab identity, some standard in terminology is in order. "It is not surprising that the concept of identity defies precise description… A degree of conceptual vagueness is therefore inevitable, but not so cripplingly as to deny us the possibility of an informed treatment of identity-related subjects" (Suleiman 2003: 5). Following Suleiman, I consider an Arab to be someone for whom Arabic is an associated language. An associated language

> may comprise a set of shared lexical items, involve the use or knowledge of just the name of the language which a group's ancestors may have spoken, or it may actually be a particular language used by all members of the group in all situations [Eastman and Reese 1981: 113–114].

This idea was also shared by the pan-Arabists, who sought to define Arabism on linguistic grounds in order to avoid excluding Christian and Jewish Arabs (Chalala 1987). Nevertheless, tokens in which Arabs are contrasted with Jews suggest that Arab is a religion, and one that is fundamentally incompatible with Judaism. This, of course, assumes that one takes Judaism at face value as a religion.

Tokens not placed in overt contrasts still presented definable interpretations. The procedure for such identification is more subjective than the search for overt contrasts. However, as will be discussed below, inter-rater reliability was high enough to suggest that the methodology was sound. Consider the following token:

> Creating an Arab majority on the great Mesopotamian plain north of Baghdad is not a new policy for Iraq. Nor is it an innovation by Mr. Hussein, who, like all Iraqi leaders since the state's founding in 1921 is an Arab, from the Sunni sect of Islam, to which most Kurds belong. But Mr. Hussein, especially since his 1991 Gulf War defeat and the creation of the Kurdish enclave, has accelerated efforts to drive minorities out, and bring Arabs in, to the region that sits atop some of the world's greatest oil reserves. [Burns 2002a]

In this token, Saddam Hussein is already described as a Sunni Muslim from Iraq. This identifies his religion, denomination, and nationality or civic membership. Qualifying these layers of identity by adding the Arab label is an ascription of ethnic identity. Time and time again the *New York Times* concerns itself with exactly these aspects of identity. Each term – Sunni, Muslim, Iraqi, Arab – all build on each other to create a sort of "identity profile" the paper uses in order to define actors as unique intersections of demographic dimensions. After reading enough articles containing

enough tokens of Arab, one comes to expect each layer of identity. While not all layers are always present, they appear in an implicational hierarchy. Many times, as in
the case of the previous token, the surrounding context provides confirmation of a
particular sense. In the preceding token, the ethnic sense is confirmed through an
opposition created semantically between Arabs and Kurds.

Consider also the following token:

> Russian commanders say rebels killed in last week's battle in Ingushetia included
> a Turk, a Georgian and two Arabs of undisclosed nationality (Myers 2002).

This token uses proximity to equate Arabness to the state of being Turkish or
Georgian and then specifically excludes nationality as a possible sense. The two
Arabs killed in Ingushetia were Arabs because that is their ethnicity, not because
they were citizens of an Arab state or "the Arab world." Nevertheless, several tokens were completely ambiguous based on context. As a group, the coders decided
to eliminate these tokens from the corpus. This brought the number of tokens
from the *New York Times* from 1,000 to 943 and the *Christian Science Monitor*
from 1,000 to 959.

The most prevalent sense suggested for Arab was not religious or ethnic, but a
regional one. These tokens use phrases like "the Arab world" or "Arab countries"
to suggest the idea of an Arab part of the world. This Arab region is contrasted
with America, Europe, or "the West." Consider the following:

> Egypt's president… said in Cairo that if you strike at the Iraqi people because of one
> or two individuals and leave the Palestinian issue unresolved, not a single ruler in
> the Arab world will be able to curb the popular sentiments (Sanger 2002).

This is a characteristic example of the regional sense. The phrase "Arab world" itself constituted just above 10% of all the instances of Arab for both newspapers.

Less common, but still prevalent was the invocation of a national identity.
These tokens suggest the existence of an Arab nation that transcends the boundaries of individual states. It is precisely this idea that has been at the heart of several
major waves of Arab nationalism, of which pan-Arabism is one. Hourani (1991)
cites Michel Aflaq, one of the founding theorists of the Ba'ath Party, as an important modern proponent of this idea. This rhetoric has pervaded the worldview of
the authors of the *New York Times*. They overtly contrast Arabs to Frenchmen
(Aenille 2002) and to Americans (Sachs 2002).

The linguistic sense of "Arab" was found least often. In this case "Arab" was
used as synonymous with Arabic. This was used in phrases such as "in a cursive
Arab script traced in gold" (Burns 2002b) and "four Arab language cable television
stations" (Rohter 2002). This did not occur with nearly the frequency of the other
senses, but it was still common enough to be noted and coded.

Coding procedure

The procedure for coding the tokens started with a detailed reading of the paragraph. Several subsequent readings were often necessary in order to apprehend the interpretation at work. Each token was coded for the meaning it presented, including the possibility that a token could have more than one interpretation. Each token was also coded for whether or not it was involved in a contrast. I was aided in the coding by three undergraduate laboratory interns. The interns and I all rated the same set of 50 tokens and reviewed our ratings. We discussed discrepancies and each rated a new set of 50 tokens. We repeated this process until we reached 87% inter-rater reliability. Given the subjective nature of the coding judgments, we considered 87% an acceptable level of agreement. Based on this high level of agreement, I am confident in the soundness of the coding methodology.

Frequency counts were obtained for each sense and each combination of senses using the SPSS statistical package. The goal of the statistical analysis was to see the range of ways in which "Arab" is used. A quantitative approach was germane to this goal because it shows the prevalence of each sense versus the other senses, as well as the most common combination of meanings. Assuming the methodology is sound, numerical data show the pervasiveness of the misidentification phenomenon in a way qualitative Critical Discourse Analysis could not.

In addition to the larger project of counting individual senses and co-occurrences of senses, I also investigated several smaller phenomena. I focused particularly on phrases such as "Arab and Muslim world(s)" and "Arab nation." For example, consider this token from the *Christian Science Monitor*:

> Those include continued progress in the war on terrorism – including problems of Iraq and the US image in the Arab and Muslim worlds – and to secure global energy supplies (LaFranchi 2002).

This passage uses the phrase "Arab and Muslim worlds." The following day the Monitor published a story including the following paragraph:

> That mixed message is evident in the sudden Chinese courting of the Arab and Muslim world, just as sensitivities there are heightened by a perceived lack of US involvement in the Israel-Palestine standoff. President Jiang has recently been in Iran and Libya; Premier Zhu Rongji was in Egypt. The Lebanese president is in Beijing this week. [Marquand 2002]

This token uses the phrase "Arab and Muslim world." I also selected one reporter from the *New York Times*, James Bennet, and counted the number of times he drew comparisons involving Arabs, Jews, and/or Muslims. I chose Bennet because he wrote a significant number of articles on the Middle East during the research period, 59 to be exact. These analytic points were small in scope compared to the major quantitative project, but they provide interesting data that support the same research objective.

Collapsing data

Owing to the fact that more than one sense can be invoked for each token, a large number of sense permutations are possible. Some of these were marginal while others composed a significant portion of the total. Because some tokens are ambiguous, I combined the categories that only involve one sense with their contrastive counterparts and labeled these "unambiguous" tokens. These are the tokens whose senses are most obvious to the researcher and also to the casual reader. These senses are obvious because the context points only to one sense, with no distracters. The single tokens and their contrastive versions can be grouped together because they still only involve one sense. The contrast refers to a fact of the context, altering not the nature of the sense, but the prominence. Contrastive tokens present even clearer, more obvious senses to the reader and the analyst. In these contrasts, the context clues are overt and in close proximity to "Arab" in the sentence. The contrastive tokens caused far fewer disagreements among the four data coders.

Results

Frequency counts obtained from SPSS yielded a large amount of data. Thirty four sense permutations occurred. Some, like "ethic regional religious" had only one occurrence. Others, like "regional" with 296 tokens, were much more common. The data in the large, combined corpus were spread considerably but unevenly between the five senses. The entire corpus, with both papers combined, is represented in Figure 1.

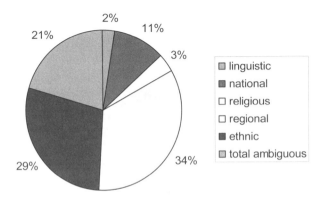

Figure 1. Sense distribution across total corpus

As we can see from the graph, the majority of unambiguous tokens fall into the regional and ethnic categories. These represent 63% of all tokens. Ambiguous tokens, those that invoke more than one sense (and as many as four), represent 21% of all the tokens in the total corpus. The remainder are split between national, religious, and linguistic tokens; these constitute 16.9%, or 321 tokens.

The next set of results presents the comparison between the two papers. For most senses, the papers shared similar results. For instance, in both, the largest category is regional. These results are illustrated in Table 1.

Table 1. Unambiguous Tokens

	New York Times		Christian Science Monitor		Totals	
Sense	Total	Percentage	Total	Percentage	Total	Percentage
linguistic	34	3.6%	11	1.1%	45	2.4%
national	124	13.1%	86	9.0%	210	11.0%
religious	47	5.0%	19	2.0%	66	3.5%
regional	315	33.4%	330	34.4%	645	33.9%
ethnic	227	24.1%	316	33.0%	543	28.5%
ambiguous	196	20.8%	197	20.5%	393	20.7%
total tokens	943	100.0%	959	100.0%	1902	100.0%

In both papers the unambiguous regional tokens, that is the regional tokens plus the contrastive regional tokens, compose around 34% of all tokens.

While the unambiguous regional tokens were comparable across the two papers, there was a discrepancy in the ethnic tokens. The unambiguous regional and ethnic tokens are represented in Figure 2.

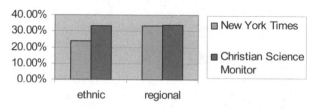

Figure 2. Unambiguous ethnic and regional tokens

Of the Monitor's unambiguous tokens, 33.0% use the ethnic sense, compared to 24.1% in the New York Times.

The two papers differ also in the way they use contrastive tokens. It is difficult to assess the true significance of these figures because the totals are small, but the differences are striking nonetheless. The contrastive tokens are represented in Figure 3.

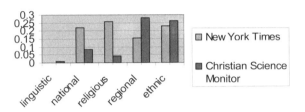

Figure 3. Unambiguous contrastive tokens

From this graph we can see that in the *New York Times,* 22% of all contrasts are national and 26% are religious, compared to the *Monitor's* 8.3% and 4.1%, respectively. The *Monitor's* contrasts are 28.1% regional and 26.4% ethnic, compared to the *Times'* 15.4% and 22.8%. Again, it is difficult to assess the statistical significance of the difference because the quantities are small. There are only 123 contrastive tokens in the *New York Times* and 121 in the *Christian Science Monitor.* This means that a difference of 27 contrastive religious tokens accounts for a difference of 22%. Although these quantities are small they are not unimportant. They illustrate the way in which consumers of different media are exposed to different messages. The *New York Times* perpetuates the idea that Arabs and Jews compose a binary set, while the *Christian Science Monitor* does not. It focuses more heavily on the idea of Arabs as an ethnic group.

The minor research points mentioned earlier also yielded interesting results. The *New York Times* has one instance of the phrase "Arab and Muslim world" and two instances of the phrase "Arab and Muslim worlds." The *Christian Science Monitor* has three instances of "Arab and Muslim world" and two instances of "Arab and Muslim worlds." James Bennet, the prolific *New York Times* reporter, used the phrase "Jews and Arabs" 16 times, the phrase "Muslims and Jews" four times, and the phrase "Muslims and Arabs" only once.

Discussion

The first striking feature about the quantitative results is the tremendous similarity between the two papers. Both papers make heaviest use of the ethnic and regional meanings. Both papers use approximately 21% ambiguous and 13% contrastive tokens. Both papers used the national sense about 25% of the time. Critically, both papers used the linguistic sense less than 5% of the time. This is remarkable because although it is a prominent definition of Arabness for scholars and political advocates, it is the least common sense in the corpus.

That the two papers, which I have argued are very different in purpose and form, show such similar sense distributions cannot be purely coincidental. Since media producers are exposed to media images expressing the cultural myths and narratives of the West just as the consumers are, both tend to share the same ethnic and racial ideas. Journalists are "routinely subject to intense ideological pressure, and it would seem likely that such ideology becomes internalized to the point where it is unconscious, as part of what Bourdieu would call the writer's habitus" (Huckin 2002: 367). Media scholars have argued since the 1920's that the messages we receive via our media become internalized. Critical Discourse Analysis argues that as a result these messages are reified and reproduced. This is not to argue that there is a conscious effort by writers and editors to mislead and malign; on the contrary, "one can believe that news is a practice without believing that news is a conspiracy" (Fowler 1991: 2). Fowler argues that the ideology is already present in the language and that writers and editors, who have little control over this ideology, simply reproduce it through their prose.

This brings us to Huckin's (2002) useful notion of *dispersed intentionality*. He argues, basing his claim on the philosophy of Wittgenstein, that intentionality can reside in institutions as well as individuals. What follows from this is that

> the intentionality that goes into decision-making at the semantic level (i.e. *the selection of words and phrases*, the crafting of sentences and the construction of overall coherence) may be blind to a secondary level of ideological leanings governed by powerful organizational interests (Huckin 2002: 367, emphasis added).

These organizational interests include the basic commercial imperative that news organizations need to attract and retain paying readers and advertisers; and also, according to Herman and Chomsky's (1988) model, a need to appease governmental sources of information. The *New York Times* and *Christian Science Monitor* both exhibit the dispersed intention to present a confusing, totalizing picture of Arab identity. I do not claim that individual editors and authors, like James Bennet, *consciously* choose to misrepresent, but no matter where the intentions reside, the picture of Arabs that results is a confusing one.

Even if a particular occurrence of "Arab" has a clear meaning, the general meaning of the term "Arab" is still uncertain. An instance of a word refers to all previous instances of that word, creating a dialogue between utterances (Bakhtin 1984). In the dialogue in the current data set each mention of "Arab" evokes all previous mentions, piling uncertainty atop uncertainty. In one paragraph an Arab is someone who is Muslim. In the next he or she is someone who is the opposite of an American. In a third, Arab connotes the language adorning the walls of the mosque. The reader is left with a sense of a monolithic Arab identity. This is precisely the reason so many scholars find that Americans do not differentiate Arabs from Muslims (for example, Naber 2000; Shaheen 2001; Suleiman 1988).

When we consider the results from the count of "Arab and Muslim world" and "Arab and Muslim worlds" we begin to see how this happens. The invocation of the Arab and Muslim world, which occurred once in the *New York Times* and three times in the *Christian Science Monitor,* suggests that the Arab world and the Muslim world are one and the same. This oversimplification ignores the fact that "the majority of Muslims are neither Arab nor Middle Eastern, but Indonesian, Malaysian, Filippino, Indian, and Chinese" (Naber 2000: 43). The phrase "Arab and Muslim worlds" more accurately characterizes the overlap between Arabs and Muslims for what it is, partial and incomplete, although this is perhaps just this author's reading. This phrase occurs twice in each paper. By including both characterizations of Arabs, the papers confuse readers about the actual demographics of Arabs and Muslims.

This confusion is an example of what Gal and Irvine (1995) describe as the semiotic process of *erasure*. Erasure is the process by which

> [f]acts that are inconsistent with the ideological scheme may go unnoticed or get explained away. So for example, a social group or a language variety may be imagined as homogeneous, its internal variation disregarded (974).

In the case of Arabs, the complex and multi-layered nature of Arab identity is erased when the label is used inconsistently. Readers cannot form a definite, unified conceptual scheme for who Arabs are. Instead they become a nebulous mass consisting of Arab Muslims and any other dark-skinned residents of the Middle East who are not obviously Jewish. Suleiman (1988) concluded after studying ethnic opinions among teachers of social science in Kansas that educated Americans did not know Turks and Persians from Arabs, or Shiites from Sunnis. As soon as it seems that a clear picture of Arabs is emerging in the newspaper text, the context changes and Arabs become somebody else.

It may be hard for Americans to define what exactly makes someone an Arab, but it is clearly not hard to present oppositions between Arabs and non-Arabs, as the contrastive tokens teach one to do. From reading the *New York Times*, a reader learns that Arabs are not Jews. Of the *Times'* 123 contrastive tokens, a plurality contrasts Arabs with others on the basis of religion. This occurs almost exclusively in the phrase "Arabs and Jews." Consider also the text of James Bennet's 59 articles. They include 16 instances of the phrase "Jews and Arabs", four of "Muslims and Jews", and one "Muslims and Arabs." "Muslims and Jews," which comprises a binary along one axis, is only one fourth as frequent as "Jews and Arabs," which does not. Contrastive tokens, which represent 12.8% of the entire corpus, bear a large functional load because they create binary oppositions that become natural with repetition. After exposure to countless repetitions of the phrase "Arabs and Jews," the American media consumer becomes habituated to the set and internalizes its logic. The notion that one cannot be Arab and Jewish becomes self-evident and taken for granted.

The large amount of regional tokens in both papers serves the goal that Edward Said (1978) labeled in *Orientalism*, namely, they create an opposition between the West, which is assumed to be democratic and free, and the East, which is assumed to be backwards, misogynistic, and totalitarian. The discursive construction of Arabness as a nebulous, unpredictable concept, which is undoubtedly an example of Orientalism, is a *racial project* of the highest order. Racial projects are discursive efforts at constituting a group as a race, which is, according to Omi and Winant (1994), "a concept which signifies and symbolizes social conflicts and interests by referring to different types of human bodies" (55). For surely, even though the North American juridical system has difficulty deciding whether Arabs are white (consider the "racial prerequisite" cases cited in Haney-Lopez 1996), the average American (like those polled by Suleiman) has no doubt that they are "dark-skinned" and different. What is most important to realize about racial projects is that they "connect what race means in a particular discursive practice and the ways in which both social structures and everyday experiences are racially organized, based on those meanings" (Omi and Winant 1994: 56). The discursive construction of Arabs as a group that is different from "Us" and incompatible with who we are has ramifications in the social status of Arabs in America and in their everyday lives. This plays out particularly in the post September 11th era, with racial profiling and violence against alleged Middle Easterners on the increase.

At the beginning of this project I decided to include the *Christian Science Monitor* as a form of "experimental control," by which the *New York Times* could be judged. The results of that comparison have been surprising. The remarkable similarity between the usages in each paper was not expected. Neither was the fact that the *Christian Science Monitor* had more regional tokens. Being the supposed "objective voice" did not stop the *Monitor* from making heavy use of the notion of the "Arab world," one of the most powerful of Orientalist phrases in the corpus. The repeated mention of the "Arab world" racializes Arabs by setting their very existence apart from the West. Note that the set of Arab countries are not referred to as "the Arab nation," as the pan-Arabists of yesteryear would have hoped. Instead, the Arab countries are discursively constituted as an entirely different world.

The *New York Times'* reputation for being particularly biased against Islam, as Said (1981) argues so convincingly, made its greater use of the religious sense of the word Arab unsurprising. The *Times* made religious contrasts six times as often as the *Monitor*. This comparison is particularly odious because it contributes to the oversimplified notion that the conflicts in Israel and Iraq are simply religious wars. This focus on religious differences masks the vital issue of nationalist struggle in both conflicts. It is as pernicious as it is common to frame the conflict in religious terms. Focusing on differences only deepens the cognitive divide in the conflict; whereas Aharoni (2003) argues that emphasizing commonalities is an important step in Israeli-Palestinian reconciliation.

Conclusion

Language has political power that belies its referential use. The power of language comes from its ability to both create and reinforce concepts. The *New York Times* and *Christian Science Monitor* are able to simultaneously reiterate the notion that Arabs can be defined vaguely – through shifting references and by contrast to all that is Western and free – and strengthen this notion through repetition and novel examples. It is vitally important to examine the ideas we have about ethnic groups and attempt to divine the sources of these ideas. In the process we learn as much about the subtle ways in which ideology is encoded as we do about the complicated nature of identity, ethnic or otherwise.

References

Aenille, C. 2002, September 22. "For lovers of risk, there's Iraqi government debt." *New York Times*, 3–8.

Aharoni, A. 2003. "The forced migration of Jews from Arab countries." *Peace Review* 15(1): 53–61.

Ahmad, M. 2002. "Homeland insecurities: Racial violence the day after September 11." *Social Text* 72(3): 101–115.

Bakhtin, M. 1984. *Problems of Dostoevsky's Poetics*. Minneapolis: University of Minnesota Press.

Bennet, J. 2002, April 28. "Mideast turmoil: The settlements; despite violence settlers survive and spread." *New York Times*,1:1.

Burns, J.F. 2002a, August 11. "Kurds must endure Iraq's 'nationality correction.'" *New York Times*, 1:4.

Burns, J.F. 2002b, December 4. "Threats and responses: UN team; test of power: Inspectors tour an Iraqi palace." *New York Times*, A1.

Chalala, E. 1987. "Arab Nationalism: A bibliographic essay." In *Pan-Arabism and Arab Nationalism*, T. Farah (ed.), 18–56. Boulder: Praeger Publishing.

Christian Science Monitor. 2004. "About the Monitor." Available: http://www.csmonitor.com/aboutus/about_the_monitor.html.

Dedaić, M. 2003. "Introduction: A peace of word." In *At War with Words*, M. Dedaić and D. Nelson (eds.), 1–23. New York: Mouton de Gruyter.

Dedaić, M. and Nelson, D. 2003. *At War with Words*. New York: Mouton de Gruyter.

Eastman, C. and Reese, T. 1981. "Associated language: How language and ethnicity are related." *General Linguistics* 21(2): 109–116.

Fairclough, N. 1989. *Language and Power*. London: Longman.

Fowler, R. 1991. *Language in the News*. New York: Routledge.

Gal, S. and Irvine, J. 1995. "The boundaries of languages and disciplines: How ideologies construct difference." *Social Research* 62(4): 976–1001.

Gotsbachner, E. 2001. "Xenophobic normality: The discriminatory impact of habitualized discourse dynamics." *Discourse and Society* 12(6): 729–759.

Hadad, H. 2001, September 30. "Soapbox: For a Jewish Arab, feelings of shame." *New York Times*,14WC:7.

Haney-Lopez, I. 1996. *White by Law*. New York: New York University Press.

Herman, E. and Chomsky, N. 1988. *Manufacturing Consent: The Political Economy of the Mass Media*. New York: Pantheon.

Hourani, A. 1991. *A History of the Arab Peoples*. New York: MJF Books.

Huckin, T. 2002. "Textual silence and the discourse of homelessness." *Discourse and Society* 13(3): 347–372.

Khleif, B.B. 1990. "Ethnicity as a social movement: The case of Arab Americans." In *Sociologus* 40(1): 19–37.

LaFranchi, H. 2002, April 30. "For Bush, a bigger personal role in Mideast." *Christian Science Monitor*, 2.

Marquand, R. 2002, May 1. "US meets China's heir apparent: Who's Hu?" *Christian Science Monitor*, 7.

Mousa, I.S. 2000. "Arab/Islam phobia: The making of the media in the West." In *Civic Discourse and Digital Age Communication in the Middle East*, L. Gher and H. Amin (eds.), 71–82. Stamford: Ablex Publishing.

Myers, S.L. 2002, October 5. "Russian recasts bog in Caucasus as war on terror." *New York Times*, A1.

Naber, N. 2000. "Ambiguous insiders: An investigation of Arab American invisibility." *Ethnic and Racial Studies* 23(1): 37–61.

New York Times. 2004a. "The New York Times." Available: http://www.nytco.com/company-properties-times.html.

New York Times. 2004b. "Excerpt of company finance report." Available: http://www.nytco.com/pdf-reports/2002_10-K_Selected_Financial_Data.pdf.

New York Times. 2004c. "Business units." Available: http://www.nytco.com/company-proper-ties.html.

Omi, M. and Winant, H. 1994. *Racial Formation in the United States*. New York: Routledge Publishing.

Osam, K. 2003. "The politics of discontent: A discourse analysis of texts of the reform movement in Ghana." In *At War with Words*, M. Dedaić and D. Nelson (eds.), 149–177. New York: Mouton de Gruyter.

Rohter, L. 2002, December 15. "South America region under watch for signs of terrorism." *New York Times*, 1:32.

Sachs, S. 2002, September 9. "Threats and responses; Government ready to fingerprint and track some foreign visitors." *New York Times*, A16.

Said, E. 1978. *Orientalism*. New York: Vintage Books.

Said, E. 1981. *Covering Islam*. New York: Vintage Books.

Sanger, D. 2002, August 28. "In talks with envoy, Bush assails Hussein, but Saudis are firm in opposing war." *New York Times*, A8.

Shaheen, J. 2001. *Reel Bad Arabs.* New York: Olive Branch Press.

Shohat, E. 2003. "Zionist discourse and the study of Arab Jews." *Social Text* 21(2): 49–73.

Suleiman, M. 1988. *Arabs in the Mind of America.* Brattleboro, VT: Amana Books.

Suleiman, Y. 2003. *The Arabic Language and National Identity.* Washington, DC: Georgetown University Press.

Udovich, A.L., and Valensi, L. 1984. *The Last Arab Jews: The Communities of Jerba, Tunisia.* New York: Harwood Academic.

Van Dijk, T.A. 1988. *News Analysis.* Hilsdale: Laurence Erlbaum Publishing

Weisman, S.R. 2000, December 12. "Abrams back in capital fray at center of Mideast battle." *New York Times*, A1.

CHAPTER 7

Visual discourses of war

Multimodal analysis of photographs of the Iraq occupation

David Machin

Photographs from different wars over the past 150 years reveal that war has changed. But additionally, the ways that these photographs represent war – what they include and exclude, the kinds of settings and action they show, the kinds of social actors that are depicted – reveal that the discourses about war that were dominant in each society at each time, have also changed. These discourses reveal how the powerful try to shape the way that populations might come to think about the nature and meaning of war.

One hundred and fifty years ago photographs from the Crimean war showed British officers in ceremonial uniforms posing proudly in settings that could have been just about anywhere. There were no images of corpses, enemies or devastated civilians. Regular lower class soldiers and enemy Russian soldiers were not depicted. The discourses revealed in these photographs represent war as a natural colonial activity and the upper-class soldier as noble, dignified and proud.

In the 1970s, photographs from Vietnam show napalmed villagers and US soldiers looking lost and terrified. This was the only war where people in the West saw some of the actual *ongoing* effects of bullets and explosives on bodies and society. Often such photographs are only seen and considered long afterwards, such as in the case of WWI, the 'war crimes' photographs of the German Wehrmacht, and images of the Allied bombing of Dresden during WWII. The photographs from Vietnam reveal discourses that were critical of the meaning of the war as it was happening.

During the first Gulf war, photographs found in the press in the US and Europe were mainly of military technology or anonymous photographs of troops in training taken prior to the war. These images reflected discourses about the importance of the superiority and precision of American technology (Griffin 2004) and hid the true role of aerial bombardment of troops and civilians in the conflict.

In these three cases the photographs reveal something of the changes in the nature of warfare and also something of the dominant discourses that represented war. Studies of the linguistic representation of war over the past hundred years, in the form of the war rhetoric of politicians, have shown that the dominant discourses of the meaning of war and the nature of enemies have remained pretty much the same (Lasswell 1927, Orwell 1946, Chilton 1985, Lazar and Lazar 2004, Graham et al 2004). But an analysis of war photography reveals that the visual rhetoric has changed. Perhaps images index more accurately how discourses of war have changed.

Photographs of the war in Iraq

In this chapter I use multimodal discourse analysis and social actor analysis to look at photographs of the Iraq conflict that appeared in the European and American press in 2005–2006. I will say more about these approaches in the relevant sections. The specific images that I analyze, including images of soldiers, civilians, and Iraqi prisoners abused at Abu Ghraib, are taken from the Getty and Corbis image banks. The image banks have been the source of the majority of the photographs of Iraq that I have collected from British and European newspapers. These stock images have been a dominant source of war images now for over a decade (Griffin 2004).

This reliance on commercial image banks, which hold millions of syndicated photographs, is part of a broader change in the use and nature of the photograph. Image banks offer images that are technically of high quality, cheap, easily searchable and accessible. Above all, the images that are kept in these databases have high *meaning potential*. This means that the images can be used not to show specific instances, to document particular moments in time and place, but to symbolize the generic. This increased use of image bank photographs to represent war is part of a broader change in the use of photography in the mass media. Rather than documenting, the photograph is increasingly central as part of layout and used symbolically (Machin 2004).

These photographs can be used to represent instances of 'suffering', 'combat', 'enemies' and 'civilians' in general. Therefore any editor wanting to have an image on a front page of a newspaper or magazine to accompany a text, say about an attack on a village, can choose from many hundreds that show soldiers, civilians or enemies. A good multi-purpose image can earn about £100,000 a year as it is licensed out around the planet (Machin 2004).

The analysis in this chapter is of 20 images each of allied soldiers, Iraqi militia, and civilians. Additionally I looked at 15 images of prisoner abuse. These reflected the images that were seen daily in the press in Europe and the US at the time. Of course it was possible to find some more challenging images, for example in the weekend magazine supplements of left-of-centre newspapers. But it is reasonable to think about the images I have chosen as reflecting the mainstream and everyday representation of the conflict in Iraq. The aim is to reveal what kinds of participants are depicted as being involved in the conflict. In what kinds of settings are they shown and what are they shown doing? As we shall see, all of these are quite different to what we saw in Vietnam, Crimea and the first Gulf war. Very different discourses of war are being realized.

Representing the participants

I begin by looking at how the participants in the conflict are represented – the US and allied soldiers, the enemy and the civilians. I use an approach from social semiotics called 'social actor analysis.' Drawing on linguistics, this allows us to think about the way that classification is realized both linguistically (c.f. Van Leeuwen 1996) and visually (c.f. Van Leeuwen 2000, Machin and Van Leeuwen 2005). This allows us to systematically examine how soldiers, enemies and civilians are positioned for the viewer in the photographs.

Individuals and groups

Participants can be referred to as individuals or *en groupe*. This can make a massive difference to the way that events are represented. Linguistically, 'collectivization' is realized by plurality or by means of mass nouns or nouns denoting a group of people (e.g. *clan, militia, terrorists*). Visually this is realized by shots which show groups or crowd shots. The members of the groups or crowds can be 'homogenized' to different degrees. They can all be shown wearing the same clothes, performing the same actions or striking the same poses. 'Individualization' is realized linguistically by singularity (e.g. a woman), and visually by shots that show only one person. Visual individualization is a matter of degree. It can be reduced by increasing distance, making individual traits less easy to observe. Collectivization can also be achieved by focus on the generic features of a group of people so that they are turned into types. For example, a news photograph of Muslim people in London might foreground those individuals wearing traditional clothing.

In the images I selected, the US and British soldiers are shown both as individuals, as in image 1, and as part of small teams, as seen in image 2. They are shown in close-up so that they can be seen as individuals and so that we can identify with them, and they are shown in groups to emphasize that they are soldiers. Unlike photographs of previous wars we rarely see them in extremely large groups as was the case in images from WWII. In that war it would have been more important to show sheer size of force, an image linked to nationalism and the strength and invincibility of the nation. In the case of Iraq we can be told linguistically how many allied troops are in Iraq, but we are not shown this visually.

Image 1

Image 2

Image 3

Image 4

Image 5

Image 6

Image 7

Image 8

This shows that the US soldiers are individuals, who we can identify with, and therefore are expected to act more decently and humanely, although they are always also collectivized in small groups or teams. This is important in the context of humanitarian / peacekeeping discourse. Images showing massive military forces, bases, convoys or huge numbers of soldiers would be too powerful. This would look more like an invasion and less like something done with care and thought. Smaller numbers showing teams emphasizes closer coordination rather than massive force.

The enemies are always collectivized, as in image 3. If they are shown alone and in close-up then they are made generic through appearance – they all wear the same clothes or carry guns in an unruly manner. Therefore they are shown to not be regular army, but a collection of motley individuals. The trend is that those individuals that most represent the generic will be the subject of the photograph or will be brought to the fore.

Civilians are mainly collectivized, as in image 4. They are normally shown *en masse*. They are shown praying, as in image 5, carrying a coffin or shroud in the street, or simply standing around watching the allied soldiers. Typically the only civilians shown in close-up are children or women as in image 6. In these cases some kind of difference will be indexed: the child could be holding an automatic weapon, the woman could be wearing clothing that signifies an ethnic type. Both of these emphasize difference and particular kinds of effects of the conflict. For decades National Geographic magazine has sent these kinds of images of women and children around the planet. The message is that in different parts of the world, that which is most cherished to us, and that which is most innocent, is corrupted (Lutz and Collins 1993). These women and children are not presented as enemies themselves but as part of the corruption of normality caused by the enemy, which can be restored by the humanitarian acts of the Western forces. Here lingers the idea that war is between equal forces comprised of men. In fact, in such as war of occupation it will be less easy to tell enemies from 'innocent victims.'

Categorization

The linguistic and visual representation of participants can also *categorize* them, regardless of whether they are also 'individuated' or 'collectivized.' Visual categorization is either 'cultural' or 'biological' or a combination of the two. Cultural categorization is realized through standard attributes of dress, hairstyle, body adornment, etc. Biological categorization is achieved through stereotyped physical characteristics. Such categorization may be used to invoke both positive and negative connotations as in the case of racist stereotypes, but it may also be meant to invoke positive connotations, as in 'Action Man' type stereotypes of masculinity or 'Barbie' type stereotypes of female attractiveness.

In the photographs, as is shown in images 1 and 2, the American and allied soldiers are categorized culturally through the clean military uniform of the modern soldier and the technology that they wear on their helmets in the form of night vision and intercom radios, and carry in the form of their high-tech weapons. This emphasizes the sophistication and authority of these soldiers. There is also some 'biological' categorization. Soldiers shown on patrol have 'Action Man' style square jaws and muscular build. Soldiers shown writing home in the classic war photograph style, on the other hand, may be more youthful and slimmer built.

In contrast, the enemy is culturally categorized through wearing clothing that western viewers have come to associate with al Qaeda or other generic Islamic fundamentalists. These are often shown as tatty and weathered. Other militias are shown as wearing largely civilian clothing, as is seen in image 3. These are not official army and are never shown in ways that individualize them. It is also usual, as is seen in image 3 to depict militia from a very low camera angle, as is the convention for depicting power or threat.

So enemies differ from US soldiers by being badly dressed, badly armed, without order and discipline, and a motley collection of individuals. The enemy also generally holds weapons that are now iconic of non-official forces – the AK-47 and the Rocket Propelled Grenade. They hold these pointing upwards in undisciplined fashion, again iconic of resistance movements throughout the 20th century. This is not how US soldiers are represented. They hold guns in ways that emphasize readiness or 'at ease.' The way the militia members hold their guns is more like the way cowboys were depicted holding their guns in Westerns, signifying a less regimented and individualistic pose.

Weapons are also included in situations that are out of place for a Western viewer, for example at prayer, as seen in image 5. This means that these participants are shown as being in disorder – the correct boundaries are not being maintained. All of this chaos contrasts with the measure, order and legitimacy of the US soldiers. The anthropologist Mary Douglas (1966) pioneered thinking about the importance of culturally constructed boundaries for locating the meaning of phenomenon that are seen to contaminate or be inappropriate. Drawing on her analysis we can see that from a Western perspective automatic weapons should not be found in the hands of children or during religious events. Where they do appear, they are not to be explained or understood but are seen as alien, as 'dirt.' This means that a western viewer will not consider that perhaps if you are a 10 year old, and your parents have been killed, and your house has been bulldozed by an occupying force, then you may wish to defend yourself, and may wish to take your gun to your prayer meeting. In the Western model, the guns are contaminating and should be removed to restore order.

The non-official, bandit-like enemies, armed to the teeth, which we find in the photographs of Iraq, are easily understood in the context of the dominant discourses of the *enemies of freedom,* which refers to global terrorist networks. At the time any enemy of the US or West could be categorized in this way. Their political motives need not then be considered. This discourse had been gathering force from the 1960s when American people were familiar with the idea of their society being under threat from evildoers around the world. Kennedy spoke of Free World security "being slowly nibbled away at the periphery" by world terrorists and subversion (Barber and Neale Ronning 1963: 31). In the 1980s Ronald Reagan signed the National Security Decision Directive 138 approving pre-emptive attacks on terrorists (McClintock 2002). The Bush administration's post Sept 11th document, the National Strategy for Combating Terrorism (White House 2001), lays out a vision for a new world order based on the need to keep an eye on the 'enemies of freedom.' "The world must respond and fight this evil that is intent on threatening and destroying our basic freedoms and our way of life" (1). What this means is that these undisciplined militia can, with little effort, be seen, not as civilians who wish the US and British to leave their country, who may be concerned by the economic situation being imposed by the governments of these countries, but as generic *enemies of freedom.*

Maintaining the differences between civilians and enemies is an important element of the contemporary legitimation of war. As Colin Powell said in 2003 regarding the Iraq war, "We have not been attacked by an army, but by rebel groups that do not represent the people of Iraq." The civilians, therefore, *do* 'represent the people' on whose behalf the war is fought. The Western media generally deny legitimacy to any kind of groups that are not official to a particular nation state, even if that nation state was created, as in the case of Iraq, by the arbitrary map drawing of the European colonial powers (Lewis 1999, Halliday 2003).

The civilians are categorized culturally through clothing and postures that indicate lower socio-economic groups, as in image 4. No middle-class civilians are represented. We might argue that since the US and allies have decided not to allow the Iraqis to run their own country that it is important that we do not see images of the kind of sophisticated, educated class of Iraqis that could easily manage their own affairs.

Agency and action

Here I look at agency in the images (who does what) and action (what gets done). This is an approach that draws on the functional semiotic theory of Halliday (1985). He was interested in the ways that action and transaction were linguistically communicated. Through his analysis, texts could be analyzed to show how people were represented as behaving, i.e. who was shown as being active and who as passive. Such representations are deeply ideological. For example:

(1)   A thousand Palestinians had been killed.

In this sentence there is no actor even though we are offered facts and a description of a situation. In this way the agents, or those who carried out the killing, remain anonymous.

In order to be specific about analyzing this process of agency and action, Halliday used the terms 'actor', 'goal', 'process' and 'circumstance'. For example, in a news item we might find the following sentence:

(2) *The allies protected civilians in Baghdad.*

The actors in this case are the allies who carry out the process of protecting. The goal is the civilians, who are to be protected, and the circumstance is Baghdad. In this sentence it is the allies who have the agency, or power. The Iraqis are the goal and have no agency. As we will see, we can also use these concepts to think about the *visual* representation of actors and what they are shown doing.

Halliday also distinguished different kinds of processes. Just because someone is depicted as being an actor involved in processes, it does not follow that they are active agents, even when they are not the goal. This is important as processes can give the impression of agency where there is none. So we must ask what kind of process it is and what kind of role the participants must play in that process.

- *Material* – doing something in the world; e.g. "The soldier killed the terrorist."
- *Behavioral* – acting without outcome; e.g. "The soldier whistled."
- *Mental* – thinking evaluating, sensing; e.g. "The soldier was worried."
- *Verbal* – saying; e.g. "The soldier talked about democracy."
- *Relational* – being like, or different to something else; e.g. "The militia had crude weapons (in contrast to the US soldiers)."
- *Existential* – existing, appearing; e.g. "He was in Baghdad."

So an actor can be represented as being very active or busy, but in fact achieving very little. For example, a heroine in a romantic novel might be engaged in a lot of action, but this may involve a lot of *existential* processes, such as being in different places, about *mental* processes, such as wishing, missing, hoping, and *behavioral* processes such as watching and listening. All this produces no outcome on the world. She is not an active agent and is not depicted as having power over the world.

In the analysis below I look at the actors in the Iraq conflict and what they do and achieve *visually*. I ask what kinds of goals and what kinds of processes characterize the participants.

By comparison, in photographs from the war in Vietnam, US soldiers were seen engaged in material processes as actors firing guns, dropping napalm on villages. They were also shown as 'goals', as the recipients of processes having been themselves shot. They were also shown carrying out behavioral processes, as simply suffering, running through woodlands, or in existential processes lying in fields. Many photographs show mental states emphasizing the chaos and lack of purpose to the war, as soldiers were shown as confused, afraid, bewildered. Also in photographs from this war, civilians are shown as goals, having been burned, thrown out of their villages and suffering and dying. These representations of actors and action reflect dominant discourses at the time which were highly critical of the war.

The photographs from Iraq show the US and allied soldiers mainly as engaged in behavioral processes of observing and searching, as in images 1 and 2. Poses also suggest mental processes of calmness and consideration. Classic is image 1 where the soldier keeps guard, vigilant but peaceful and disciplined. This indicates the order that the US and allied forces bring, giving a sense of peacekeeping. They are not shown acting aggressively in any kind of process. Occasionally they are shown in shooting poses, but not actually firing. Material processes find them hunting for militia, but mainly they seem to wait and watch. These are the civilized actions of the peacekeeper rather than acts of destruction.

The soldiers are also shown in behavioral processes reading letters from home. In other material processes they pick up young children on homecomings. This is a humanizing action. Close-up shots of soldiers' faces show mental processes of thoughtfulness and tenderness.

The goals of the soldiers are never clear. While we find the occasional photograph of militia, there is no clear enemy. In fact, of course the enemy and civilians may be the same. This is one reason there are few representations of goals and of the enemy. Circumstance is also generally vague. Soldiers are often shown in quite anonymous streets or open spaces. There is little sense of a living, sophisticated city when we have been told the photograph shows Baghdad, for example. I will return to the decontextualized nature of the settings in the next section.

The enemy in Iraq is shown as engaged in behavioral processes, standing or sitting, holding their weapons pointing in the air, as in image 3. They are not shown carrying out any material processes such as attacking. Poses indicate mental processes of aggression, although there are few close ups. Primarily in this case the enemy is shown in terms of relational processes. This means that they are shown behaving in a way that emphasizes their difference. In this case, according to Kress and Van Leeuwen (1996) we can think of the enemy as being carriers of meaning rather than as actors. So they carry meaning through their postures and dress, in contrast to the US soldiers.

Earlier photographs of civilians from the conflict showed them engaged in material processes of looting, although there was much debate as to how much this had been staged (Talbot 2003). Here the civilians are agents in what for the allies can be described as a process of civil disorder, again requiring the presence of peacekeeping forces. But soon photographs showed civilians existentially as just being in the photograph, perhaps waiting, as in image 4, watching the soldiers as they patrol or guard. In these photographs there is little clear sense of the mental processes of the civilians. These people are shown without agency.

In the case of civilians, mental processes are represented in the cases of close-ups of children or women, who look questioningly out of the frame (image 6). These are the same children who are shown carrying automatic weapons. Such images show the child's need to be protected, for his society to be put back in order, to return to normality through the calmness of the US or allies.

The only time that the civilians are shown as being active are in photographs of street demonstrations where they wave images of a leader, or where they carry a shrouded body through the streets as mourners. But these are behavioral processes that do not bring about change. Or faces show helplessness, therefore revealing that the civilians are the 'goal', victims of suffering created by the enemy, rather than themselves being actors. The peacekeepers are therefore required.

Finally, the US soldiers were shown in the material process of abusing prisoners (image 7). There was outrage that a number of Iraqi prisoners were naked and humiliated, seemingly, it was claimed by the military, for the fun of a small number of out-of-control rogue US soldiers. We are now familiar with the idea that we will read criticisms of the armies that are claimed to represent us. But the outrage expressed about these images is one indication that we do not have the resources to talk about this new kind of war, one not between the more or less equal forces of two nation states fought on a battle field, but one of counterinsurgency and guerrilla attacks on superior forces.

The tactics of the US for dealing with insurgency since the end of WWII have been to use small groups of elite soldiers to train local forces to destabilize governments. After WWII with the birth of the UN it was no longer possible for countries to simply go to war with another to take territory, resources or political advantage. At the heart of this approach was brutality aimed at psychological and physical terror. Discourses of old war emphasize gentlemanly conduct in war, at least for the 'good' side, even though during WWII espionage and terror were key tactics for all participants. It seems that we are not equipped with the discourses to see this kind of abuse as a regular part of warfare, although on one level we are not surprised when it happens.

We also need to put this abuse into context and see it as a symptom of something bigger. The conflict in Iraq is just one small part of a long history of activity by the

Western powers in the region, map making and appropriating resources. Iraq itself was created by the British in the 1920s by throwing together three geographically and ethnically diverse Ottoman provinces, and in the process breaking part of one of the provinces off to create Kuwait. Even when Iraq gained independence, Britain remained in charge of the military, creating much resentment. This was followed by the alliance politics of the US in order to compete with the Soviet Union and to maintain control over access to oil. The region was described by Washington as one of "the greatest material prizes in world history" (US Government 1945). US oil companies had already undertaken extensive exploration of the region in the 1930s. This has continued to be the reason for US concerns of 'stability' in the region and is one of its reasons for its support of Israel (Green 1984) and also of 'moderate' pro-Western regimes. Billions of dollars in military aid have been and still are ploughed into the region to secure governments friendly to the US (Stoff 1980). These policies, taking effect in a region already under strain from the earlier colonial meddling, have caused chaos. The case of a number of prisoners being abused is only one small aspect of this whole situation. Indeed to target only the abuse is to target only one *symptom* of the causes of the situation.

Could the response to the photographs be about the horror becoming visible? At the time of writing, fox hunting, the pursuit and killing of a fox by a pack of trained dogs, had just been banned in the UK. Yet each year billions of animals suffered horrifically, kept in battery farms and fed on a cocktail of drugs and anti-biotics. What might be at issue here is the public nature of the abuse. In the Crimean war, death and combat were not seen in photographs, but could be represented in oil paintings where brave soldiers fought and died in poetic poses. In different eras it is clear that there are appropriate domains for different kinds of representations. Of course later these can then be revisited and used for evidence, even where they might later be proven otherwise, of war atrocities, as in the case of the discredited photographic exhibition of the war crimes of the German Werhmacht that toured Germany and Austria in the 1990s.

The disgust shown at the photographs of prisoner abuse is also an indication of the way that the news media bring our attention to single mediagenic events rather than processes. Susan Sontag (2004) pointed to this when discussing the way that people respond to brutality in photographs. She raises the point that people generally associate true horror and brutality with memorable photographs, rather than with longer-term suffering. She suggests that this is something to do with the way that key photographs can be possessed. We can have concrete stances towards them. Also, key photographs must in their moment be remarkable. They cannot show the gradual, the casual. This is true of the news media as a whole. The gradual is not photogenic or telegenic. Could we say that we have been trained, or encouraged, by the mass media to respond in this way to isolated instances?

The soldiers carrying out the abuse were described in the media as being rogue. But this conceals two things. First, war brutalizes its participants. Read any war novel written by former front-line soldiers such as *The Naked and the Dead*, *Cross of Iron* or *A Rumor of War* for more insight into this. This is something that is not discussed. Second, professional soldiers have always been from the lower socio- economic classes, people who have few other options in life. In his semi-autobiographical novel about the Gulf War, *Jarhead*, James Swafford does not paint a sophisticated, educated view of the marines. Yet, discourses from WWII remain about 'our boys', about honorable, brave soldiers, acting in the name of their people.

Finally, one big criticism made of the images of the abuse of prisoners was that it showed 'our boys' who should behave better. But these soldiers are not 'our boys' in the sense that they were in WWII. These are professional soldiers. Further, in modern peacekeeping warfare, increasing numbers of personnel work for private military organizations. Dynacorp and Global Risk now provide large parts of the forces present in most conflicts. This number has soared since the US Defense Department spent $300 billion on private forces between 1994 and 2002 (Singer 2004).

Modality

Modality refers to the way that we communicate how true or how real a representation should be taken. This is a way of analyzing images that has been inspired by linguistic analysis, allowing us to reveal what is offered to us as certain and what is concealed. We can think therefore of modality as levels of reality or certainty. In linguistics, Halliday (1985) told us that language provides us with resources to express kinds and levels of truth. Consider the two following statements.

(3) *It is possible he is in Iraq.*

(4) *It is certain he is in Iraq.*

The first of these statements (3) has lower modality than the second (4). There is less certainty. Therefore a representation that expresses high modality claims to represent closely what we would expect to find in the real world. One use of this observation is that it allows us to look at what aspects of a written or spoken representation are offered to us as certain and what are distanced from the real world, avoided or edited out. Looking at what is reduced in modality, taken out, left in, or emphasized, therefore, allows us to reveal something about the ideology of that representation.

The same can be said for photographs or any visual representation (Kress and Hodge 1979, Kress and Van Leeuwen 1996). But in place of words such as 'possible' or 'might', there are other techniques whereby modality can be reduced and reality be avoided or changed. In the case of photographs we can look at the detail of the subjects of the image and of the details of the setting. Has this been reduced, or sharpened? Is it different than would be seen if we were there? If it is reduced then we can ask why. This reduction in attention to detail works in the same way as words such as 'possible' and 'might.' We can also examine arrangement of the elements in the image. Do they resemble the way that elements would normally be seen in the world? Do the colors in the images appear as they would if we were there?

Settings

In images from the US occupation of Vietnam, we see lots of detailed settings: burning villages, bloody injured soldiers, shot-up jungle, squalid encampments, and the inside of helicopters during combat. These are recorded in high modality. Light, shadow and color, where the images are in color, are as we might expect in the real world.

The images from Iraq are very different. Settings are often decontextualized as in images 1 and 2. Backgrounds are often out of focus so that details aren't clear, or are generic so that they could be just about anywhere, any building or any desert. From the flow of images that appeared in the US and European press it was impossible to get a sense of what Baghdad or other cities looked like. So we have a low modality representation of settings in Iraq. This is war that is not very realistic in terms of setting. A blurred decontextualized image is like a sentence that says 'this *might be* Iraq' rather than 'this *is* Iraq.'

It has been argued that in the West we are now familiar with decontextualized images of trouble spots around the world. Commentators on US movies about conflict in the Middle East have said that terrain is often ignored or shown as generic (Blunt 1994). These are not specific places inhabited by people with real lives. They are just faraway places where there are bad people – *enemies of freedom* as George W. Bush might call them.

The result of there being no background or clearly discernable setting has an effect of drawing emphasis to the participants. Photographs which show individuals or groups against a fuzzy background focus attention on the foreground of the image. Clearly we are to think about the participants rather than the place itself. Just as we do not see middle class Iraqis, we do not really see Iraq.

Color

Colors in photographs from Iraq are pleasing to the eye, given added saturation and reduced modulation to create flatter colors, as in cartoons. In image 8 the colors were all saturated to emphasize the sensory nature of contact between parent and child. Color therefore is often low modality and is not as we would expect to see it were we present. This use of flattened colors, meaning that you do not see variations in levels of the color as you would when you look at, say, a colored object in the real world, often goes along with higher light tones to maintain optimism. This is to be expected in media where images have become an important part of layout (Machin 2004). Advertising and promotional photographs often look over-exposed to reduce shadows and give a sense of well-being. These images are intended to look good on the page, and are now a common feature of news media.

Arrangement of elements

We are also able to ask whether the arrangement of the elements in images resembles the way that they would normally be arranged in the real world. In photographs of Iraq this is often not the case. Images of soldiers and tanks try to give balance or interest to the image. Likewise, enemies are often shown standing in visually interesting configurations, although civilians are not. This gives a sense of stylization to the images, again reflecting their importance for layout and page design.

Such images would have looked bizarre in the context of Vietnam. But in Iraq they go unnoticed. One reason for this is that we are now familiar with the use of the image for symbolic, rather than recording, purposes. Machin (2004) showed the way that images are increasingly used to express concepts and emotions, rather than to inform and record, as they were in Vietnam. We find this in the Iraq images. We see people in prayer with automatic weapons laid out in front of them. We see soldiers guarding, quietly watchful. These images aim to symbolize peace-keeping rather than show us what is actually going on in the war.

Modality in Abu Ghraib images

In contrast, the images of the torture of the Iraqi prisoners show high naturalistic modality as seen in image 7. These images stand out greatly from the others. Lighting is poor. Focus is not used to draw out any one element. The layout of the elements in the photographs is messy, as in the real world. All of the other photographs we have analyzed so far are posed, stylized and decontextualized.

But these photographs may be the only real imagery that we get to see from the conflict. As I have already discussed, this fact is unfortunate as they encourage us to focus on a single moment in what is a century of actions which should bring shame.

One compelling aspect of these images is the way that they do index the real so powerfully. Roland Barthes (1977) has spoken of the way that such representations can index realism and truth even if they are in fact staged, through being grainier and having poor lighting. The pioneering filmmaker Frederick Wiseman used the same principles to index realism in film-making – for example, the use of harsh lighting and deliberately awkward camera movement. This does not mean, he commented, that it is a lie, but that it gives the impression of being real, that everything is shown as it is. The high modality of the abuse images, while it may represent real events, is in itself a signifier of informing, though much about the events that comprise the kind of conflict that is Iraq and the reality of war, go un-represented.

Conclusion

While the war rhetoric of politicians during the occupation of Iraq may have been very similar to other wars, photographs reveal that dominant discourses of war have changed. Ongoing war is now defined visually as peacekeeping done by small teams of professionalized, technologized soldiers, who act with restraint and care to protect weak civilians. Enemy casualties, which in previous wars have been cel-ebrated, are excluded.

These photographs are testimony to the West's denial of history and of its own responsibility for the instability in the Middle East. The wealth of the West has been built on the exploitation of the world with exactly the kind of disregard that we now find in Iraq. Yet the way we are offered access to Iraq through the news media is, as with all international events, without social and historical context. The trend towards the symbolic photograph is a further step in that direction. The re-duction in newsroom budgets means that there are less and less resources for on-going investigation and corroboration.

Of course there are increasing discourses in the West that are critical of wars as they take place, but the predominance in the mainstream media of photographs such as those analyzed here help to make the discourses of humanitarian peace-keeping the dominant definition of our time and allow us to conceal the reality of war. Are we being controlled or have we become too squeamish, preferring to keep our gore and bloodshed in the realm of movies and computer video games? The realism of photojournalism during American occupation of Vietnam was certain-ly just a blip in the history of war photography.

References

Barber, W. and Neale Ronning, C. 1963. *International Security and Military Power: Counterin-surgency and Civic Action in Latin America*. Columbus: Ohio State University Press.

Barthes, R. 1977. *Image-Music-Text*. London: Fontana.

Bill, J. 1988. *The Eagle and the Lion: The Tragedy of American-Iranian Relations*. New Haven: Yale University Press.

Blunt, A. and Gillian, R. 1994. *Writing Women and Space: Colonial and Postcolonial Geographies*. London: The Guildford Press.

Carruthers, S. 2000. *The Media at War*. London: Palgrave Macmillan.

Chilton, P. 1985. *Language and the Nuclear Arms Debate: Nukespeak Today*. London: Frances Pinter.

Dao, J. 2004, April 3. "For God, country and wallet: America's privatized armies are here to stay." *New York Times*.

Douglas, M. 1966. *Purity and Danger: An Analysis of Concepts of Pollution and Taboo*. London: Routledge.

Graham, P., Keenan, T., and Dowd, A. 2004. "A call to arms at the end of history: A discourse–historical analysis of George W. Bush's declaration of war on terror." *Discourse and Society* 15 (2–3): 199–221.

Green, S. 1984. *Taking Sides: America's Secret Relations with a Militant Israel*. New York: William Morrow.

Griffin, M. 2004. "Picturing America's 'war on terrorism' in Afghanistan and Iraq: Photographic motifs as news frames." *Journalism* 5(4): 381–402.

Halliday, F. 2003. *Islam and the Myth of Confrontation*. London: I.B. Tauris.

Halliday, M.A.K. 1985. *An Introduction to Functional Grammar*. London: Edward Arnold.

Kress, G. and Hodge, R. 1979. *Language as Ideology*. London: Routledge.

Kress, G. and Van Leeuwen, T. 1996. *Reading Images: The Grammar of Visual Design*. London: Routledge.

Lasswell, H. 1927. *Propaganda Technique in WWI*. Cambridge and London: M.I.T. Press.

Lazar, A. and Lazar, M. 2004. "The discourse of the New World Order: 'Out-casting' the double face of threat." *Discourse and Society* 15: 223–242.

Lewis, B. 1999. *The Multiple Identities of the Middle East*. London: Phoenix.

Lutz, C. and Collins, J. 1993. *Reading National Geographic*. Chicago: University of Chicago Press.

Machin, D. 2004. "Building the world's visual language: The increasing global importance of image banks in corporate media." *Visual Communication* 3(3): 316–336.

Machin, D. and Van Leeuwen, T. 2005. "Computer games as political discourse: The case of Black Hawk Down." *Journal of Language and Politics* 4(1): 119–141.

McClintock, M. 2002. *Instruments of Statecraft: US Guerrilla Warfare, Counterinsurgency and Counterterrorism 1940–1990*. New York: Pantheon.

McConnell, J. 2001, October/November. "The counterterrorists at the Fletcher School: The Reagan administration's new terrorism policy." *Boston Review*. Available: bostonreview.net/BR11.4/mcconnell.html.

Orwell, G. 1946, April. "Politics and the English language." *Horizon*.

Short, J. 1991. *Imagined Country: Environment, Culture and Society*. London: Routledge.

Singer, P. 2004. "Should humanitarians use private military services?" *Humanitarian Affairs Review*. Available: www.humanitarian-review.org/upload/pdf/SingerEnglishFinal.pdf.

Slim, H. 1995. "Military humanitarianism and the new peacekeeping: An agenda for peace." *The Journal of Humanitarian Assistance*. Available: www.jha.ac/articles/a003.htm.

Sontag, S. 2004. *Regarding the Pain of Others*. New York: Farrar, Straus and Giroux.

Stoff, M. 1980. *Oil War and American Security: The Search for a National Policy on Foreign Oil, 1941–1947*. New Haven: Yale University Press.

Talbot, A. 2003, April 19. "The looting of Baghdad's museum and library: US government impli-
   cated in planned theft of Iraqi artistic treasures." *World Socialist Web Site*. Available: wsws.
   org/articles/2003/apr2003/loot-a19.shtml.
United States Government. 1945. Foreign Relations of the United States, volume 8. Washington:
   Government Printing Office.
Van Leeuwen, T. 1996. "The representation of social actors." In *Texts and Practices – Readings in
   Critical Discourse Analysis*, C. Caldas-Coulthard and M. Coulthard (eds.), 32–71. London:
   Routledge.
Van Leeuwen, T. 2000. "Visual racism." In *The Semiotics of Racism – Approaches in Critical Dis-
   course Analysis*, M. Reisigl and R. Wodak (eds.), 333–350. Vienna: Passagen Verlag.
White House. 2003. National Strategy for Combating Terrorism. Available: whitehouse.gov/
   news/releases/2003/02/counter_terrorism/counter_terrorism_strategy.pdf.

CHAPTER 8

"Martyrs and terrorists, resistance and insurgency"

Contextualizing the exchange of terrorism discourses on Al-Jazeera

Becky Schulthies and Aomar Boum

In the aftermath of 9/11, Al-Jazeera, the Qatar-based Arabic channel emerged as a leading news source on the world media stage, challenging major Western news outlets with its controversial coverage of the United States' 'war on terror' (El-Nawawy and Iskandar 2002). Although Al-Jazeera drew a lot of criticism about its airing of bin Laden video tapes, live reporting in Kabul during the 2001 U.S. led invasion, and the footage of captured/slain American soliders in Iraq in 2003, the Arab network refuses to accept the Western portrayal of its coverage as propaganda. It continues to assert its claim to objective journalism within an Arab-Islamic view, as embodied in its motto: *al-ra'i wa ra'i al-akhar* (opinion and its counterpoint).[1]

Al-Jazeera's weekly programs provide revealing sites for "obscuring, hedging, confusing, exploring, or questioning what went on, that is, for keeping the coherence or comprehensibility of narrated events open to question" (Bauman 1986 :5). Building on the Bakhtinian notion of heteroglossia and the dialogic construction of meaning (Bakhtin 1981), we explore the processes by which Western discourses on terrorism terminology are entextualized by program moderators and guests in two Al-Jazeera talk shows, *min washington* (From Washington) and *al-sharīa wa al-hayāt* (Islamic Law and Life).[2] This paper will analyze the following questions: How do the program moderators frame Western discourses on terrorism? What linguistic, political, or social factors influence the constellation of participants called upon to analyze terrorism discourses and terms? Can the struggle over appropriate forms of discourse be seen in these programs? Is there a dialogic layering of meaning, a negotiation of terms that transform the larger dialogue on terrorism? We define Western discourses on terrorism as the body of talk by American and European political leaders and mainstream media personnel about Arab and

Islamic concepts related to terrorism, as well as their evaluations of the means by which these ideas are circulated. There are multiple conversations surrounding terrorism terminology, but most often these discourses are debated in immediate response to speeches and stances taken by American and European political leaders and reflect an on-going contest for "Arab hearts and minds" (Fine 2003).

Background: British connections and Qatari support

Qatar, a former British colony and member of the Gulf Cooperation Council, is a monarchy whose economy relies on oil revenues and industry, like many of its Gulf neighbors. In June 1995, Sheik Hamad bin Khalifa Al Thani peacefully deposed his father who was in Geneva. Hamad, a British-trained emir and a graduate of the Royal Military Academy in Sandhurst, was bent on introducing a liberal political system, adopting democratic institutions and emphasizing women's freedom and rights to education. In 1996 he annouced the abolition of the Ministry of Information, the end to media censorship, and the establishment of the General Association for Qatari Radio and Television. This led to the establishment of Al-Jazeera, one of the most popular and controversial satelite TV stations in the Arab World (Parker 1999; Maharaj 2001). Qatar's emir promised to subisdize the channel till 2001, at which point it would need to rely on advertising revenues. However, the advertising revenues have not materialized, despite the fact that Al-Jazeera has one of the largest Arab audience shares[3] (Schleifer 2003). Al-Jazeera has turned to alternative funding options, primarily the sale of exclusive footage and images to global/Western media outlets, and claims that it is breaking even while expanding its channels and programming (Schleifer 2003).

Many of the station personnel came from the BBC Television Arabic Satellite Channel, a joint Saudi-British venture that failed after the Kingdom and BBC disagreed upon editorial principles. That core group, which consisted of journalists drawn from all over the Arab world, has expanded as Al-Jazeera opened a series of training workshops for broadcast journalism in Qatar. Al-Jazeera's journalistic format combines voices and opinions of Israeli and Arab opposition leaders which had not been heard in Arab media previously (El-Nawawy and Iskandar 2002). By re-routing the flow of information away from censored and foreign produced media, Al-Jazeera forced the Arab and Western state and privately owned information structures to respond, thereby transforming the mechanisms for control of the public stage (Eickelman and Anderson 1999: 5).

Much has been written and said about Al-Jazeera's objectivity or lack thereof (Seib 2005, Hudson 2005, El-Nawawy and Iskandar 2002). Regional and international politicians and analysts comment on and seek to engage Al-Jazeera directly (by appearing in interviews on their programs) or indirectly (via other talk shows or written and spoken commentaries) on a regular basis. Some, like independent Palestinian journalist Ramzi Baroud, see Al-Jazeera as a champion of free speech leading to democracy in the Middle East.

> And because Aljazeera displayed a shockingly balanced narration of the news and provided an equal platform to all, it was hated and loved; it was an Islamist, a socialist, a radical, a conservative, a reactionary, a progressive, a demagogue, a liberal, democratic, pro-Saddam, pro-Shiite, pro Kurds, anti Israel, infiltrated by the Israeli Mossad, by the CIA, by Osama bin Laden, by everyone, by no one, all at once. In short, it was even-handed (Baroud 2002).

Abdallah Schleifer, director of the Adham Center for Television Journalism at the American University of Cairo, views Al-Jazeera as a work in progess, attempting to train its personnel in suitable reporting styles, means, and methods as it comes of age in a global media stage outside of previous parochial markets (Schleifer 2003). Others find Al-Jazeera's methods extreme, that they incite rather than inform, that they are disloyal to Arab unity and break the long-honored tacit regional agreement not to use state media to rat on one's neighbors (Ajami 2001; Waxman 2001). This has prompted diplomatic scandals and international pressure on Al-Jazeera and Qatar from countries such as Jordan, Kuwait, Iraq, and Saudi Arabia. After Al-Jazeera aired the bin Laden tapes in October 2001, U.S. Secretary of State Colin Powell protested to the Emir of Qatar (Fine 2003). Hafez Al-Mirazi, *min washington* moderator, in an interview with Secretary Powell, asked him about U.S. government policy toward "independent media in the Arab world," citing Al-Jazeera specifically:

> Powell: We believe in free and open and independent media. We believe that in order for a free, open and independent media to do its job – and its job is to serve its viewers, serve its listeners, serve its readers – then that presentation ought to be balanced and it ought to reflect all views. And it should not just be slanted to one particular point of view or the focus strictly on polemical actions, polemical activities. And so, free, open, independent, yes, but with those values comes the value of balance and perspective. And as your role of the free and independent media is to educate people, help them understand issues of the day. That's all we ask of them (DOS transcript 2004).

As he moves from abstract descriptions of independent media ("its job is to serve its viewers") to direct exhortations ("your role") and back again to a nebulous free media ("that's all we ask of them"), Powell's words reveal a complex number of voices and positions in the dialogue surrounding Al-Jazeera's broadcasting motives.

The dialogic exchange is also evidenced in the creation of rival stations, such as Al-Arabiyya and Al-Hura; the change in format, programming and presentation styles on state-owned television stations; and the unequaled media commentaries and debates surrounding Al-Jazeera in Arab, European, and American media. A case in point: during the 2004 Democratic National Convention, Hafez Al-Mirazi, Al-Jazeera's Washington Bureau chief, was interviewed by American and European journalists more often than he appeared on Al- Jazeera due to the Convention's decision to take down the Al-Jazeera logo from the media center. Al-Mirazi commented on this media navel-gazing at the Convention: "It's good that we are here. It makes it clear to people that we're covering a legitimate story, if there is such a thing as legitimate and illegitimate stories. But it is a bit self-referential. The media covering the media covering the media" (Dante 2004).

This preoccupation with Al-Jazeera's visibility and viability in the public sphere is part of the dialogue taking place on multiple planes and with multiple actors. In these exchanges it is clear that "appropriate forms of discourse" (Crapanzano 1990: 279) are being challenged – whether independent media means allowing a multiplicity of voices to appear (al-ra'i wa ra'i al-akhar), as Al-Jazeera does, or providing balanced information in media's role as educator, as Secretary Powell argues. More is going on than just a disagreement over media conventions of discussion and presentation, but also the meanings being generated by both sides, and the Arab media's influence and creation of an audience.

Heteroglossia and dialogic emergence of meaning

Bakhtin's dialogic emergence of meaning offers a useful concept from which to explore how meaning is taken outside of the individual and emerges in social interaction. In this view, dialogue is the way in which groups continuously produce, reproduce and revise culture and meaning (Crapanzano 1990). Tedlock and Mannheim identify a type of dialogue that is more than the formal exchange of ideas. They see dialogue as a functional social field where multiple voices and cultural logics contend with each other and challenge the authority of the narrator (Tedlock and Mannheim 1995: 5). Maranhão further emphasizes the collective construction of meaning:

> The speaker is successively enfeebled, first, by his lack of autonomy in the face of his addressees, who also participate in the production of meaning; second, by the dilution of his identity behind the characters, who start speaking for him and soon speak as independent voices; third, by the characters themselves having their roles attenuated by the polyphony...that is typical of ordinary life (Maranhão 1990:4).

In this heteroglossic approach, words and ideas emerge in a particular social and historical context where participants appropriate, challenge, and negotiate their meaning (Bakhtin 1981: 428).

Al-Jazeera programs are social spaces in which multiple audiences appropriate and negotiate the meaning of events. There the authority of speakers is consistently challenged and transformed, as reporters, program moderators, and broadcasters frame successive discussions as responses to previous critiques and guests, and interlocutors re-contextualize utterances made at different times and in different places by individuals not present at the time of dialogue (Bakhtin 1984). For example, much of what Al-Jazeera programs report, debate, and respond to are the comments of President Bush, who has yet to appear on any program. His words are appropriated and then debated by third party representatives or critics. *Min washington* (From Washington) is a weekly Al-Jazeera talk show hosted by Hafez Al-Mirazi in Arabic and aired predominantly from Washington D.C. Guests are usually Arabic speakers, though translation is provided for non-Arabic speakers. The program focuses on U.S. foreign policy and events that impact the Arab and Islamic World. In an episode devoted to Bush's views on the spread of democracy in the Arab world, Al-Mirazi's introduction of the guests and topics begins and ends with video clips of Bush's speeches (*min washington* episode aired May 2, 2004). Al-Mirazi sets the tone for Bush's statements on U.S. policy toward "what is known as the struggle against terrorism"[4] and thereby engages the debate on his own terms, choosing which of Bush's words to use and challenging the authority of the speaker by the lack of response inherent in the use of a video clip.

Al-Jazeera is striving to prove its adherence to Western media standards of objectivity while also catering to the ideals of the Arab-Islamic world. In an interview with *Middle East Insight* in March 2002, Hafez Al-Mirazi notes that the network covers "the news from an Arab perspective, the same way that CNN covers the news from an American perspective." This complexity of the target audience is compounded by the diversity of the production staff, which is composed of multiple nationalities, voices, interests and agendas. Yosri Fouda, Al-Jazeera London Bureau Chief, in talking about the atmosphere in the network, remarked: "it is a mixture of the tribal and the urban, the Eastern and the Western, the leftist and the rightist, and the religious and the secular" (El-Nawawy and Iskandar 2002 :28).

The events of 9/11 and the emerging American ideology toward terrorism altered the orientations of the station's audience and Western attitudes toward Al-Jazeera's representations. Previously, Western media had encouraged the controversies stirred by Al-Jazeera's reporting on regional Arab issues and applauded its methods as key to introducing democratization and freedom of speech. CBS's *60 Minutes*, the *New York Times*, *Washington Post*, and *LA Times* each ran positive features on Al-Jazeera's efforts (Mahjoub 2001).

Al-Jazeera, however, foregrounded its engagement with the international audience post-9/11 by increasing the number of programs airing from outside the Middle East, boosting the number of correspondents in non-Arab countries, marketing their exclusive images to Western news outlets, and even providing an English language version of their website. It sees itself as competing with international media giants, such as CNN and BBC for audience and influence, in addition to local Arab news channels. In June 2004, Al-Jazeera issued a code of professional conduct, which stimulated a *min washington* program surrounding issues of journalistic integrity in international media. The program moderator, Al-Mirazi began the July 15, 2004 program by reading the newly introduced Al-Jazeera professional charter, then moving on to an extensive summary of historical changes to American media code of ethics, and an explicit comparison between CNN's professional standards and those of Al-Jazeera. The guests on the program were the Al-Jazeera General Manager, CNN Executive Director of News, the American Association of News Producers President, and the president of a media watchdog association. But the program did not just respond to international discourses on transparency in Al-Jazeera's reporting policies. Al-Jazeera's General Manager stressed the importance of this code for educating and creating an informed audience – recognition that Al-Jazeera is at the intersection of engaging global and local dialogues and audiences.

Jihad (Holy War) and/or terrorism:
Islamic contextual reference and dialogic process

Dialogue and its processes are central to Bakhtin's heteroglossia. The constant dialogic interaction(s) of meanings condition each other; the process of redefining is endless unless a powerful participant is involved, in which case meaning becomes authoritative and absolute. Holquist explains how "a word, discourse, language or culture undergoes 'dialogization' when it becomes relativized, de-privileged, aware of competing definitions for the same things" (Holquist 1981: 427). The dialogical production of the religious term *al-jihad* (jihad) takes place between different individuals (ordinary citizens and religious scholars), sectors of the Islamic and Arab societies (government and masses), Western nation states and other participants who are affected in one way or another by '*al-jihad*' and/or '*al-irhab*' (terrorism).[5] Dialogue concerning the concept of jihad is not only internal to Islamic societies but has also become part and parcel of the daily conversations of Western societies. Arab-Islamic and Western educational and political institutions as well as media corporations have become central dialogical actors in the process of 'relativizing' or 'de-privileging' the concept of *al-jihad*.

These interpretations and redefinitions of jihad, terrorism and violence have dialogically influenced Muslims' modern conceptualizations of jihad. Classical jurists defined jihad as:

> An effort directed against any object of disapprobation by the use of the heart, the tongue, the hands, and the sword. The jihad of the heart was directed against the flesh, called by the Sufis the 'carnal soul'. It was to be accomplished by fighting temptation through purification of the soul. The jihad of the tongue and hands was undertaken in fulfillment of the Quranic injunction to command the good and forbid the bad. And the jihad of the sword was concerned exclusively with combating unbelievers and enemies of the faith by open warfare. (Willis 1967 :398–99)

The above-mentioned forms of jihad are discussed in several Quranic verses and *hadith* (sayings of the Prophet Muhammad). For instance, according to a *hadith* narrated by Abu Hurayrah (one of the trusted companions of the prophet) and transmitted by al-Tirmidhi and Ibn Majah, "if anyone meets Allah with no mark of jihad, he will meet Allah with a flaw in him." Quranic verse 61:10–11 reads "O you who believe! Shall I guide you to a commerce that will save you from a painful torment? That you believe in Allah and His Messenger Muhammad, and that you strive hard and fight in the cause of Allah with your wealth and your lives, that will be better for you, if you but know."

In light of these statements, many Muslims have interpreted and legitimized 'suicide attacks' and/or 'martyrdom operations' towards Israel and citizens of some Western and Muslim nations. After the outbreak of the Aqsa Intifada in 2000, some Palestinians resorted to suicide bombing as a legal warfare strategy against Israel. This strategy was legitimated not only by the general public, but also by state and individual Islamic muftis and scholars. A number of *fatawa* (religious scholarly judgments or rulings on a certain issue) have been issued by Muslim clerics in favor of suicide bombings. Al-Jazeera live programs have presented many episodes after 9/11 on the relationship between Islam, violence and martyrdom.[6] The Egyptian-born Sheikh Yusuf al-Qaradawi, Sunni Studies department head at Qatar University, is one of the most prominent proponents of suicide bombers as a strategic weapon of resistance. In one of the episodes of *al-sharīa wa al-hayāt* (Islamic Law and Life)[7], he discussed these 'martyr operations' / 'suicide bombings' as part of the general *jihad fi sabil allah* (jihad on behalf of Allah).

While condemning 9/11 as terrorism, al-Qaradawi, and other scholars gave legitimacy to 'martyrdom operations' against Israel. In the wake of 9/11, there has been tremendous pressure on Arab governments to condemn 'suicide bombings.' Sheikh Muhammad Said al-Tantawi, head of Egypt al-Azhar mosque and university, declared that *sharia* does not accept killing innocent people. The imam regretted many attempts by Muslim scholars linking jihad with terrorism. This same position was upheld by Sheikh Muhammad bin Abdellah al-Sabil, member of the Saudi council of senior *'ulama* (clerics) and the Imam of the Grand Mosque in Mecca. The Saudi cleric called for all Muslims to protect the lives and property of the people of the book as prescribed in the *sharia*.

In response to these state-promoted *fatawa*, al-Qaradawi asked:

> How can the head of Al Azhar incriminate mujahedin who fight against aggressors? How can he consider these aggressors as innocent civilians...? Has fighting colonizers become a criminal and terrorist act for some sheikhs...? I am astonished that some sheikhs deliver *fatawa* that betray the mujahideen, instead of supporting them and urging them to sacrifice and martyrdom (al-Qaradawi 2001).

The wide public support for the 'suicide operations' pressured al-Tantawi to change his *fatwa* and explained that his first ruling on suicide bombing was misinterpreted. He states that:

> A man who blows himself up in the middle of enemy militants is a martyr, repeat, a martyr. What we do not condone is for someone to blow himself up in the middle of children and women. If he blows himself up in the middle of Israeli women enlisted in the army, then he is a martyr, since the women are fighters (quoted in Malka 2003: 26).

For al-Qaradawi, "Israeli society was completely military in its make-up and did not include any civilians. Men and women are soldiers. They are all occupying soldiers" (al-Qaradawi 2001). In an *al- sharï'a wa al-hayat* episode entitled *al-irhab wa al-'unf* (Terrorism and Violence, aired October 27, 2002), al-Qaradawi distinguished between 'terrorism' and 'martyrdom.' He proclaimed,

> The Palestinian who blows himself up is a person who is defending his homeland. When he attacks an occupying enemy, he is attacking a legitimate target. This is different from someone who leaves his country and goes to strike a target with which he has no dispute (al-Qaradawi 2002).

In his dialogical interpretation of the word 'suicide bombing,' al-Qaradawi rejects comparing 'suicide' to 'martyrdom.' It is distinct from 'terrorism' because it is an act of self defense and thus a legitimate form of resistance (Malka 2003 :22). While suicide is prohibited in Islam, martyrdom is one of the highest forms of religiosity. "Suicide bombings is an unjust and misleading name because these are heroic commando and martyrdom attacks and should not be called suicide operations or be attributed to suicide under any circumstances"(*sharï'a wa al-hayat* episode aired December 9, 2001). Al-Qaradawi makes a historical link between 'suicide bombing' as a modern act and jihad. He maintains:

> The martyr operation is the greatest of all sorts of jihad in the cause of Allah. A martyr operation is carried out by a person who sacrifices himself, deeming his

life of less value, striving in the cause of Allah, in the cause of restoring land and preserving dignity. To such a valorous attitude applies the following Quranic verse: "And of mankind is he who would sell himself, seeking the pleasure of Allah; and Allah hath compassion on His bondmen" (Quran 2:207). But a clear distinction has to be made here between martyrdom and suicide. Suicide is an act or instance of killing oneself intentionally out of despair, and of finding no outlet except putting an end to one's life. On the other hand, martyrdom is a heroic act of choosing to suffer death in the cause of Allah, and that's why it is considered by most Muslim scholars as one of the greatest forms of jihad (al-Qaradawi 2004).

By defining the concept of 'suicide bombings' on the basis of traditional deontological ethics, al-Qaradawi is looking backward, as a modern revivalist scholar[8], to justify "killing oneself," which Islam and many other religions prohibit because it debases human life. His attitude towards the problems of fighting Israeli soldiers draws from a fundamentalist Islamic reference to jihad, but is also modernist because it uses Hegelian or even utilitarian consequentialist ethics, which maintain that the end justifies the means. 'Suicide bombing' as a form of jihad is essentially an instrument of revival, employed for the purpose of extending the frontiers of Islam and leading the faithful back to their roots.

January 11–16, 2004, The Islamic Fiqh Council issued another legal ruling regarding Palestinian 'suicide bombing.' While reaffirming the sanctity of human life, they stressed that:

> Martyr operations are a form of jihad, and carrying out those operations is a legitimate right that has nothing to do with terrorism or suicide. Those operations become obligatory when they become the only way to stop the aggression of the enemy, defeat it, and grievously damage its power. It is not allowed to use terms such as "jihad", "terrorism", and "violence", which have become frequently used by today's mass media as scientific terms, to mean other connotations beyond their basic well known meanings. (Islamic Fiqh Council Fatwa 2004)

We can infer that these Muslim scholars' rulings on 'suicide bombing' are still part of the movement of reform and renewal within Islam. This movement is "forward-looking, implying an effort to adjust or change present customs and institutions to the demands and needs of contemporary societies" (Willis 1967:395). They are engaged in a dialogic process to define '*jihad*' and '*irhab*' that involves modern nation-states (Israel, the U.S., Egypt, Saudi Arabia, Iraq), media outlets providing a non-state forum for discussing these issues (such as Al-Jazeera), historical texts, others scholars and schools of thought, and the daily lives of individuals.

min washington (From Washington)

Al-Jazeera prides itself on being one of the only Arab satellite news networks to have such extensive international coverage, citing its 23 bureaus with seventy reporters located in the major Western capitals and Arab World.[9] The Washington Bureau consists of six reporters headed by Hafez Al-Mirazi, and during 2004 boasted two weekly programs, *From Washington* and *Race for the American Presidency*, which focused on events, characters, and discourses flowing from or forming around the United States. The format of these two programs is rather basic and the program backdrop a simple studio image whose centerpiece is the U.S. Capitol Building, rather than the bright lights of a vibrant urban center, or brilliant hues of the Doha digital studio. Unlike many of the other weekly talk shows, *min washington* does not have a regular call-in portion (although this has been included occasionally); the moderator simply frames the discussion with opening and closing statements and directs the flow through specific questions to the invited guests, even determining the turn-taking of participants. All of Al-Jazeera's program moderators have editorial independence with regard to their program content and direction – there is no oversight committee for the talk shows.[10]

As Maranhão states, "dialogue does not occur by accident but is initiated when certain elements in the historical horizon of the interpreter call his attention to particular constellations of meaning" (1990: 4–5). The choice of program topics in the last year followed the flow of current events vis-à-vis the U.S. (President Bush's State of the Union Address, release of the 9/11 Commission report, the Abu Ghraib scandal, the Democratic and Republican National Conventions), and the selection of guests was constrained by who would consent to participate, their availability in Washington or near an Al-Jazeera studio, and their ability to speak Arabic (although simultaneous translation was provided). Most often there were between three and four guests, some of whom knew Arabic and others for whom simultaneous translation was provided. During 2004 the guests were preponderantly Arab (including many Egyptians, reflecting al-Mirazi's social networks); Americans critical of U.S. government positions (including government officials and staff from previous administrations); Department of Defense or State representatives (including Secretary Colin Powell); and media personnel (newspaper and television producers and editors).

U.S. participants who wish to win the support of Arab and Muslim viewers are disadvantaged by their inability to speak Arabic. The handicap of language further complicates the intertextual polyvocalic nature of dialogue. The program moderator has the advantage of understanding both English and Arabic, following American debates surrounding events, issues, and policies, while English speaking guests have access to the dialogue via an interpreter and translations of debates.

On the one hand, translation slows the dialogic exchange, allowing interactants more time to formulate responses and standardizing turn-taking to a greater degree. On the other hand, translation is, by its nature, a process of interpretation and dialogue, further introducing possibilities for misunderstanding and misrepresentation. Unlike the United States, Israel has managed to fit into this dialogical debate. Israeli guests often speak fluent Arabic. Thus, they manage to make their point heard by relying on the same linguistic medium. Despite the difficulties inherent in simultaneous translation for a live talk program, during 2004 *min washington* hosted approximately one non-Arabic speaker per program.[11]

One of the phrases coined by Al-Jazeera in defense of its media coverage is the term "contextual objectivity." This is the idea that the "medium should reflect all sides of any story while retaining the values, beliefs, and sentiments of the target audience" (El-Nawawy and Iskandar 2002: 26). El-Nawawy and Iskandar argue that this seeming contradiction stems from the dialogic space where "Al-Jazeera determine[s] what [is] important for the public to know even as Al-Jazeera [is] itself influenced by its audience" (2002: 27). In order to win public awareness and attention, Al-Jazeera relies on and responds to local sensitivities and uses *uslub al-itara issahafiyya* [the style of emotional journalism] (2002: 57). As it presents images and information of interest to the Arab-Islamic audiences and draws on their emotions, it angles away from reporting multiple sides of a story. For example, when reporting on American operations in Afghanistan, the Palestinian-Israeli conflict, and the intermittent bombing of Iraq, images are shown of Iraqi, Palestinian or Afghani casualties rather than Israeli, American or Kuwaiti losses. This was explicitly addressed in a *min washington* program (Mohammed Alami moderated), where the invited guests included Al-Hurra (U.S. government sponsored television directed toward the Middle East) producer Mawafiq Harb as well as independent film producer Hani Salama.

> Alami: Mawafiq, if you take what Brother Hani said, that history is written by the victors, the Americans are the victors in the region, and there are some who claim the coverage of Sawa and Al-Hurra specifically – that it is media coverage for the vanquished region, coverage without any heart, that it does not feel or take the feelings of the victims into consideration.

> Harb: This is not true, with my respect to Mr. Salama. He said most of the Arabs. I think he is sitting in New York and generalizing. It is necessary that we move away from generalizations. We are not able to know the opinion of people in all matters, and we ought not generalize in this field with regard to the sympathies and feelings, and the nature of the sympathies toward the media message understood there. We understand the media message as any journalist working in any news editing room: he presents documented information. We empathize by informing in an objective and credible manner, and we distinguish between opinion

> and news. If I give you my opinion, I would say this is my opinion but news is reality and sympathies are opinions and when you want to express your feelings and emotions, there are programs, articles, many media ways and means by which you are able to express your opinions and feelings, you should not transform media associations news broadcasts into servitude to the audience (*min washington* episode airing August 20, 2004).

In this interaction, contextual objectivity and *uslub al-itara issahafiyya* are framed as the norm, rather than the exception. Al-Hurra, the U.S. backed Arab news station, is being challenged for its lack of empathy toward the feelings of the target audience. The interlocutors are both from the Arab World, have had experience in Arab and Western media bureaus, and are familiar with the context of these debates surrounding media and objectivity. This is not seen as a personal exchange, despite the use of first and second person pronouns in this face-to-face interaction. They metadiscursively challenge the official platform and objectives of the Western 'Other' via voices that index previous debates (such as Hani Salama's use of the phrase, 'history is written by the victors'), iconic terms (such as 'victims' and 'objectivity') that have been reframed and refitted for this particular dialogic moment.

Contextualizaion and the negotiation of meaning

Bakhtin emphasizes a multitude of conditions (social, historical, physiological) that affect the meaning of any word uttered at a particular time (Bakhtin 1986: 72–90; Holquist 1990: 59–66; Morson and Emerson 1990: 123–39). Participants use words that reflect the meanings of previous uses and contexts and yet each new use alters the meaning. In this sense, Bakhtin (1986) argues, "all utterances are heteroglot in that they are a function of a matrix of forces" (428).

Al-Jazeera, and specifically *min washington*, is an intersecting node of ideas, images, people, and voices that is constantly being negotiated and reshaped in the dialogic interchange between circulating cultures: Western, Arab, Islamic, American, Arab Nationalist, Secularist, Qatari, Israeli. For example, *min washington* does not use the term 'war on terror' *harb al-irhab* as utilized by American discourses, but rather *mukafaha al-irhab*, 'the terrorism battle or struggle.' Al-Jazeera uses the term martyr 'shahiid' when identifying Palestinian 'suicide bombers.' This word indexes a religious and emotional framework with which an Arab audience already identifies. On the contrary, when Al-Jazeera uses the word terrorist, it qualifies its use with the phrase '*ma yusama bil-irhab*' [the so-called terrorist]. It distances itself from the meaning this term has accrued in Western contexts by visualizing it in quotes, while at the same time indicating their epistemic stance toward the truth-value of its usage by others.

struct the dynamics of the exchange as the dialogue continues. He explains: "Power [is] a set of potentials, which, while always present, can be variably exercised, resisted, shifted around and struggled over by social agents" (Hutchby 1996: 497). This exercise of power can be seen in each *min washington* program as Al-Mirazi recontextualizes American political discourse in his introductions. He also restates and reframes guests' comments in the course of the dialogue. Both host and guests make interjections and clarifications, and speak on behalf of other individuals and institutions. In a much more heated terminology debate with an Al-Hurra producer, Mawafiq Harb, Al-Mirazi queried:

> Al-Mirazi: Is there something [wrong with] its name, Palestine? You have your reporter while closing say, "So and So from Ramallah."
>
> Harb: We will not innovate [on these] matters, rather we will rely on terms recognized previously by respected media institutions, we will call each country.
>
> Al-Mirazi (interrupting): Excuse me, [but] respected [stations] are not Arab.
>
> Harb: I did not say that. Al-Jazeera is respected and enjoys credibility.
>
> Al-Mirazi: Yes, well, Arab stations say, for example, "Palestine".… The American forces in Iraq: Another interesting topic of difference. Some question, is this station speaking about the forces with any name, is it the occupation?
>
> Harb: Its name is the coalition forces.
>
> Al-Mirazi: Fine then, if the Americans themselves were saying occupation, if the Iraqi ambassador to the U.N. was saying occupation, if the [Iraqi Ambassador] to the U.S. in Washington Ranid Rahim says occupation?
>
> Harb: There is a difference between the English and Arabic language. If we translate literally "occupation", it shows up as *ihtilal*, if we translate "resistance" into English as *muqaawama*, the word "resistance" in English does not mean the same thing emotionally as it does in Arabic.
>
> Al-Mirazi (interrupting): then resistance and occupation will not be in the political dictionary?
>
> Harb: I do not think that most of the Iraqi people today consider a bombing operation which targets Iraqi civilians is resistance. If you bring me statistics today and show me whether the Iraqi people consider what is happening today in Iraq with the killing of Iraqi civilians resistance, I say we'll call it resistance [*muqaawama*] (*min washington* episode aired January 22, 2004).

Both al-Mirazi and Harb question the efficacy of translation, and the cultural meanings accrued to particular terms. Both challenge how the other station represents the reality of Iraq and Palestine through the use of terms such as 'resistance' and 'occupation' in Arabic, whose heteroglossic nature is acknowledged by Harb. He believes that to maintain objectivity the use of such terms needs to be avoided, but in doing so he questions the long-established usage of these terms by Arab news stations such as Al-Jazeera – thus questioning the credibility and authority of Al-Jazeera. At stake is how Palestinian and Iraqi actions are interpreted by Arab audiences, which is not just an intellectual debate but a question of meaning-making.

This episode of *min washington* makes clear, as Bakhtin said, that our mouths are filled with the words of others, which implies the power of appropriation. Appropriation is a central part of Bakhtin's dialogism, in that participants must be able to "apprehend, internalize, and recreate the utterances of others" not to reshape it for "absorption and subsequent conformity to the dominant discourse of a given community," but rather to recontextualize it in advancing the discourse of the self (Bakhtin 1986: 89). While the debate is over terminology, defense of Al-Jazeera and the Arab point of view is inherent, and becomes an appropriation of an utterance to further Al-Jazeera's place and validity in the world media stage.

Conclusion

Al-Jazeera is as much in the process of creating an information audience as it is informing its audience. The Al-Jazeera enterprise is not just about responding to the Arab cultural context of oral exchange, it is about doing so within Western frames and formats and structures of information circulation. The forms and flows of these exchanges are transformed and transform as they circulate. There is constant metadiscursive negotiation of the terms employed in terrorism designations.

Whatever the political and social environment, Al-Jazeera evokes a powerful response. It has become a symbol for controversy and fulfills the Arabic proverb, *khalif tu'raf* – disagree and you will be known. Not only has the station gained visibility in the cafes, salons, and homes of the "Arab street", it has emerged in the American and Western imagination and discourses. From President Bush citing concerns of Al-Jazeera "propaganda" to President Bartlett of the television series *The West Wing* worrying about Al-Jazeera's exposure of covert US actions (October 2002 episode), Al-Jazeera's image is being appropriated on international and regional levels. Al-Jazeera has also appropriated the Arab political discourse of the surrounding nation states, apprehending and reinterpreting it. In this manner, it exposes their inconsistencies and contributes to the transnational media's influence on public debates. This form of appropriation is part of the synchronic intertextuality of Al-Jazeera in the discursive social imagination. The dialogue is occurring on both the verbal and visual planes, both with and without the consent of Al-Jazeera.

Notes

1.   Portions of this paper stem from work presented at the Middle East Studies Association Annual Meeting in 2002 and subsequently expanded at the Society for Linguistic Anthropology Conference in 2004. We owe a great debt to many scholars who have contributed to this paper and who are not cited in the bibliography, including Abdessamad Fatmi, Abdelmajid Hajji, Michael Bonine, Thomas K. Park, James Greenberg, Norma Mendoza-Denton, Ellen Basso, and Kamron Talatof.

2.   The dialogues referenced in this paper are our own translations from Arabic unless otherwise indicated.

3.   Audience statistics in the Arab World are unreliable. Al-Jazeera self-reports approximately 40 million of 300 million possible Arab viewers, including European Arabs and those in Canada and the U.S. (Rugh 2004:231).

4.   Translation of Al-Mirazi's phrase used in the episode.

5.   Bakhtin would disagree with us in terms of viewing our conversational input as an objective neutral reporting through these dialogical interactions on jihad/terrorism. Nevertheless, we decided to put these terms between quotes because we want these terms to stand as they are described by the different voices that have been reinterpreting them. Hence, words related to jihad/terror will be put between quotes. There are other names that can be defined as jihad and/or terror depending on the voice that utters them. Among these are al-'unf al-islami' (Islamic violence), al-tafjirat al-irhabiya and al-'amaliyyat al-intihariyya (suicide bombing).

6.   Among the titles of the episodes are: The United States and the Categorization of Terrorism, Terrorism and Violence, Islamic Culture and Hatred, Why Muslims are Accused with Terrorism, the Future of Independence Movements after being Accused of Terrorism, Attempts to Change Muslim Educational Curriculums, Violence between Concepts of Resistance and Terrorism, Defining Terrorism and a Terrorist and the American War in Afghanistan, Annual American Report on Types of Terrorism.

7.   One of the main live programs broadcasted by Al-Jazeera, *Sharia and Life* discusses contemporary issues from an Islamic angle, and used to be hosted by Maher Abdullah. The 78-year-old Qaradawi is a regular on the show.

8.   Personal communication with Dr. Thomas Kerlin Park and Dr. James Greenberg.

9.   Information cited by Wadih Khanifar, General Direction of Al-Jazeera in the July 15, 2004 episode of *min washingon*.

10.   Personal communication with Yosri Fouda, Al-Jazeera program host for *Top Secret*.

11.   Information gathered from the Al-Jazeera Arabic language website, which posts transcripts of programs, www.aljazeera.net.

References

Ajami, F. 2001, November 18. "What the Muslim World is Watching." *New York Times.*
Al-Qaradawi, Y. 2004, March 11. Suicide Fatwa. Available: http://www.islamonline.net/fatwa/english/fatwaDisplay.asp?hFatwaID=68511.

Al-Qaradawi, Y. 2001, December 4. Suicide Fatwa. Available: http://www.adl.org/main_Arab_ World/al_Qaradawi_report_20041110.htm?Multi_page_sections=sHeading_2.

Bakhtin, M. 1981. *The Dialogic Imagination: Four Essays*. M. Holquist (ed.), C. Emerson and M. Holquist (trans). Austin: University of Texas Press.

Bakhtin, M. 1984. *Problems of Dostoevsky's Poetics*. C. Emerson (ed. and trans.). Minneapolis: University of Minnesota Press.

Bakhtin, M. 1986. "The Problem of Speech Genres." In *Speech Genres and Other Late Essays*, C. Emerson and M. Holquist (ed.) V. McGee (trans.), 60–102. Austin: University of Texas Press.

Baroud, R. 2003. "War on Aljazeera an Assault on the Collective Arab Aspiration." Available: http://www.scoop.co.nz/mason/stories/HL0312/S00070.htm

Bauman, R. 1986. *Story, Performance and Event*. London: Cambridge University Press.

Dante, C. 2004, July 29. "A very Arab view on very American politics." *Christian Science Monitor*.

Department of State Transcript. 2004, June 16. "U.S. Secretary of State Colin Powell Interview with Hafez Al-Mirazi of Al-Jazeera Television." Available: http://www.state.gov/secretary/ rm/33631.htm

Crapanzano, V. 1990. "Dialogue." In *The Interpretation of Dialogue*, T. Maranhaõ (ed), 269–291. Chicago: University of Chicago Press.

Eickelman, D. and Anderson, J. 1999. *New Media in the Muslim World: The Emerging Public Sphere*. Bloomington: Indiana University Press.

El-Nawawy, M. and Iskander, A. 2002. *Al-Jazeera: How the Free Arab Network Scooped the World and Changed the Middle East.* Boulder: Westview Press.

Fine, J. 2003. "Al-Jazeera Winning TV Credibility War." *Transnational Broadcasting Studies Journal* 10:3 Available: http://www.tbsjournal.com/Archives/Spring03/fine.html

Holquist, M. 1990. *Dialogism: Bakhtin and his world*. London: Routledge.

Hudson, M. 2005. "Washington vs. Al-Jazeera: Competing Constructions of Middle East Realities." *Transnational Broadcast Studies* 14:1 Available: http://www.tbsjournal.com/Archives/ Spring05/Hudson.html

Hutchby, I. 1995. "Power in discourse: the case of arguments on a British talk radio show." *Discourse and Society* 7: 481–497.

Islamic Fiqh Council. 2004, January 27. Fatwa on Palestinian Suicide Operations. Available: http://www.islamonline.net/fatwa/english/FatwaDisplay.asp?hFatwaID=91481

Mahjoub, T. 2001, October 11. "Qatar's Al-Jazeera Stands Firm in its Coverage despite U.S. Displeasure." *Agence France Presse*.

Malka, H. 2003. "Must Innocents Die? The Islamic Debate over Suicide Attacks." *Middle East Quarterly* 19–28.

Maranhaõ, T. 1990. "Introduction." In *The Interpretation of Dialogue*, T. Maranhaõ (ed), 1–22. Chicago: University of Chicago Press.

Morson, G.S. and Emerson, C. 1990. *Mikhail Bakhtin: Creation of a Prosaics*. Stanford: Stanford University Press.

Norris, P., Kern, M. and Just, M. 2003. "Introduction", In *Framing Terrorism: The News Media, The Government and the Public*, P. Norris, M. Kern and M. Just (eds), 1–17. New York: Routlege.

Parker, N. 1999, August 4. "Tiny Qatar Beams Big Signal to Arab World," *The Christian Science Monitor*.

Rugh, W. 2004. *Arab Mass Media. Newspapers, Radio and Television in Arab Politics*. Westport Connecticut: Praeger.

Schleifer, S.A. 2003. "An Interview with Mohamed Jasim Al Ali, Managing Director of Al-Jazeera." *Transnational Broadcasting Studies Journal* 10:3 Available: http://www.tbsjournal.com/Archives/Spring03/jasim.html

Seib, P. 2005. "Hegemonic No More: Western Media, the Rise of Al-Jazeera, and the Influence of Diverse Voices." *International Studies Review* 7(4):60 1–615.

Tedlock, D. and Mannheim, B. 1995. *The Dialogic Emergence of Culture*. Urbana : University of Illinois Press.

Waxman, S. 2001, December 4. "Arab TV's Strong Signal: The al-Jazeera Network Offers News the Middle East Never Had Before, and Views That Are All Too Common." *Washington Post*.

Willis, J.R. 1967. "Jihad fi Sabil Allah-Doctrinal Basis in Islam and Some Aspects of Its Evolution in Nineteenth-Century West Africa." *The Journal of African History* 8(3):395–415.

CHAPTER 9

Between "us" and "them"

Two TV interviews with German chancellor Gerhard Schröder in the run-up to the Iraq war

Annette Becker

Introduction[1]

Political discourse is about taking sides. This becomes particularly apparent at times when a war, or a nation's active participation in a war, is at stake. Language plays a crucial role in the construction of ideological positions. Within political discourse, televised media interviews are a particularly dynamic genre. In this genre, political positions are publicly elicited and negotiated by two or more inter-acting participants while an overhearing mass audience is watching. Occasionally, however, despite the expectation that interviewees take sides, they strategically avoid doing so. This paper examines two German TV interviews with German Chancellor Gerhard Schröder (Social Democratic Party) in which this type of strategic blurring takes place. In both interviews, Gerhard Schröder was questioned about Germany's position on whether the United States should declare war on Iraq. Both interviews were shown in the most prominent news broadcasts of the two major German public channels and conducted by the anchors themselves. Anchor Klaus-Peter Siegloch interviewed Gerhard Schröder for the *heute journal* of the ZDF, a channel known for its predominantly Conservative orientation; and anchor Ulrich Wickert interviewed him for the *Tagesthemen* of the ARD, a channel known for being predominantly supportive of Social Democratic positions. Accordingly, in spite of their identical overall political context and topics, the two interviews showed remarkable differences regarding questioning strategies and ideological positioning. For analysis, this paper draws from critical discourse analysis, appraisal theory and pragmatics. This incorporation of various methodological perspectives is inspired by the contributions of the critical analysts in Wodak and Meyer (2001), who explicitly recommend theoretical diversity for the analysis of a particular discursive reality.

Politics, discourse and media in the run-up to the Iraq war

On January 28, 2003, George W. Bush, President of the United States, delivered his second State of the Union Address to a nationally televised joint session of the U.S. Congress. In this speech, Bush rhetorically prepared the ground for what would less than two months later become known as the Iraq War. One of his main points was that Secretary of State Colin Powell would present the United Nations Security Council (UNSC) with new proof of Iraq's possession of weapons of mass destruction on February 5. The United States would then ask the UNSC "to consider the facts of Iraq's ongoing defiance of the world" and would leave no doubt about the U.S. position: "We will consult, but let there be no misunderstanding: If Saddam Hussein does not fully disarm for the safety of our people, and for the peace of the world, we will lead a coalition to disarm him" (Bush 2003). Consequently, the crucial question everybody wanted answered by the German Chancellor was: Would Germany, one of the ten non-permanent members of the UNSC, vote for or against supporting the United States in military action against Iraq?

To advertise their respective positions, both the U.S. government and the German government made extensive use of the media, even across national borders. For instance, Colin Powell offered to be interviewed by the ZDF on January 28. The ZDF immediately rose to the rare occasion. In the ZDF's Washington studio, ZDF correspondent Eberhard Pilz gave the Secretary of State a forum for a passionate plea in favor of the U.S. position. When Pilz asked Powell how he felt about the German government's position, Powell replied, "It's a very strong difference between and among friends." On the morning of January 29, several German newspapers published an interview with Gerhard Schröder in which the German Chancellor pointed out that even if Colin Powell presented new proof for the existence of weapons of mass destruction in Iraq on February 5, the German position in favor of a peaceful implementation of UN resolution 1441 would not change. This statement was, at least partly, also designed for an international audience. On the evening of January 29, the ZDF *heute journal* (21:15–21:45) broadcast the interview between Eberhard Pilz and Colin Powell, and just a few minutes later, the interview between Klaus-Peter Siegloch and Gerhard Schröder. Within the hour, the ARD *Tagesthemen* (22:30–23:00 p.m.) showed the interview between Ulrich Wickert and Gerhard Schröder. Although both interviews had been pre-recorded earlier in the evening, they appeared, in this media context, as if they were the immediate German reaction to Colin Powell. What made the situation so difficult for both German interviewers and their prominent interviewee was that everybody, from the German public to the U.S. government, had a vested interest in the outcome. The following sections outline how such ideological positions are constructed in discourse in general and analyze the discursive resources Gerhard Schröder and his interviewers use for the construction of affiliation or disaffiliation. This is inspired mainly by the frameworks suggested by Fairclough (1995, 2003) and the frameworks for the analysis of political discourse suggested by Chilton and Schäffner (1997, 2002).

"Us" and "them" in discourse

Van Dijk (1998, 2006) defines ideologies as belief systems shared by groups, and reproduced in discourse. In ideological discourse structures, there are usually four main discursive strategies involving the distribution or withholding of positive or negative information about those who are seen as belonging to one's own group and those who are perceived as being "the others." Van Dijk subsumes these strategies under what he calls the "ideological square":

- Express / emphasize information that is positive about Us.
- Express / emphasize information that is negative about Them.
- Suppress / de-emphasize information that is positive about Them.
- Suppress / de-emphasize information that is negative about Us. (van Dijk 1998:267)

These strategies occur in political discourse where it is in the interest of the discourse participants to construct clear-cut boundaries between "Us" and "Them." This was less clearly the case in the two interviews examined in this paper. When Klaus-Peter Siegloch and Ulrich Wickert asked Chancellor Gerhard Schröder to explicitly formulate the German position, a complicated interplay of group loyalties, and social and discursive roles arose (Becker 2004, 2005a). The following sections will address three questions: Who did Schröder and his interviewers construct as "Us"? Who did they construct as "Them"? And how were these constructions negotiated? First of all, a preliminary overview of the main topics of the core sequences of interviews will be given. In the subsequent sections, the participants' use of personal pronouns, transitivity and appraisal resources as well as the role of these phenomena in the discursive construction of "Us" and "Them" will be discussed.

Main topics of the interviews

Core sequences are the central sequences of interviews, without openings, closings, pre-core sequences and pre-closing sequences (cf. Lauerbach 2004). In the core sequences of their interviews with Gerhard Schröder, both interviewers addressed the following main topics:

- The announcement of new evidence for Iraq's possession of weapons of mass destruction
- Germany's position concerning war on Iraq in the light of this new evidence
- French influence on the German position
- Differences between American and German positions

Gerhard Schröder dealt with these main topics as follows:

- New evidence for Iraq's possession of weapons of mass destruction is still unconfirmed.
- Evaluation of evidence is not up to Germany but to inspectors.
- France and Germany are close allies.
- America and Germany are also close allies.
- War should never become a normal means of politics.

As is apparent, there were similarities but also differences regarding the main topics addressed by each interviewer (IR) and interviewee (IE). In both interviews, Schröder contested the relevance of the interviewers' topics and introduced topics of his own. This is not uncommon in political interviews (Harris 1991; Galasiński 2000; Chilton 2004). Topic presentations and the ideological positioning of social actors are closely connected. Linguistic resources regularly applied for such positioning include, for instance, the use of personal pronouns (Wilson 1990; Suleiman et al 2002; Ward 2004), transitivity (Galasiński 2000; Halliday 2004), and appraisal (White 2001; Martin and White 2005).

Personal pronouns

The use of pronouns in political interaction often serves strategic purposes. For instance, as Wilson (1990) observes:

> The distribution of I/we (exclusive and inclusive) is clearly marked in political interaction, and this is perhaps not surprising. One of the major aims of a politician is to gain the people's allegiance, to have them believe that the decisions that are being made are the right ones. At the same time no one can guarantee the outcome of any political decision, and since any politician's position is dependent on the support of the people, it is also useful to have the audience believe, in some circumstances, that any actions are perhaps not only, or not fully, the responsibility of one individual. First-person pronominal forms can assist the politician in achieving these almost contradictory aims. (50)

This section examines the personal pronouns and their referents in the core sections of both interviews. The core section of each interview consists of eight question-answer exchanges. Their length is almost the same (ZDF 870 words, ARD 865 words). In the ARD interview, the interviewee is allowed slightly more discursive space (84% of the words) than in the ZDF interview (78%), shown in Figure 1.

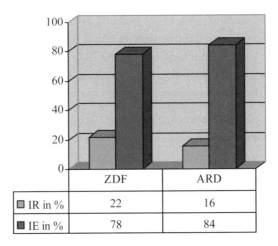

	ZDF	ARD
▣ IR in %	22	16
▣ IE in %	78	84

Figure 1. Speaking time allotted to IR and IE in both interviews

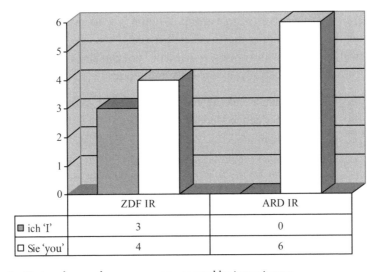

	ZDF IR	ARD IR
▣ ich 'I'	3	0
▢ Sie 'you'	4	6

Figure 2. First and second person pronouns used by interviewers

Since, obviously, there is a difference between the way interviewers and interviewees use pronouns, contributions of interviewers and interviewee will be examined separately. Of particular interest regarding pronominal perspective is the use of first and second person pronouns (Suleiman et al 2002). In their questions, the interviewers use the following first person (*ich* 'I') and second person pronouns (*Sie*, the formal and polite German pronoun for 'you', which is grammatically third person plural), including the corresponding possessive pronouns, as shown in Figure 2.

Neither interviewer uses the first person plural *wir* 'we' or the indefinite pronoun *man* 'one'. Of the two interviewers, only the ZDF interviewer, Klaus-Peter Siegloch, uses forms of the first person singular pronoun or of the corresponding possessive pronouns. These forms appear exclusively in metadiscursive utterances:

(1) KS_{ZDF-3} Aber noch einmal <u>meine</u> Frage, Herr Bundeskanzler...
     But once again my question Mr. Chancellor...

(2) KS_{ZDF-4a} Ja, Herr Bundeskanzler, aber kann <u>ich</u>'s richtig zusammenfassen...
     Yes, Mr. Chancellor, but may I sum it up correctly …

(3) KS_{ZDF-6} ... das verstehe <u>ich</u> richtig?
     … I understand that correctly?

Most pronouns used by the interviewers are address pronouns. As forms of the intimate second person singular pronoun *du* 'you' would be inappropriate in institutional contexts like a news interview, the participants use the polite address form *Sie* 'you'. Like the English *you*, the German *Sie* has ambiguous reference and can refer either to a single person or to a group. When it is used in utterances directed at a head of state, its meaning may oscillate between "you as a person," "you and your political party," "you and your government," or "you and the nation you represent." Siegloch's usage of *Sie* 'you' is mainly ambiguous:

(4) KS_{ZDF-1} Beim Thema Irak steht die Entscheidung ja nun offenbar bevor. Bleiben <u>Sie</u> dabei: Mit einem deutschen Ja im Sicherheitsrat ist nicht zu rechnen?
     Concerning Iraq, the decision seems to be imminent. Do you still insist: A German Yes in the Security Council is not to be expected?

(5) KS_{ZDF-2} Außenminister Powell hat aber nun ja auch im Gespräch mit dem ZDF noch einmal neue Beweise angekündigt für kommenden Mittwoch. Könnte das denn <u>Ihre</u> Haltung noch verändern?
     But Secretary of State Colin Powell announced in his interview with the ZDF new evidence for next Wednesday. Could this, then, change your position?

(6) KS~ZDF-6~   Aber wenn Frankreich am Ende mit "Ja" stimmt, würde das <u>Ihre</u> Position ja auch nicht verändern...
But if in the end France voted "Yes", after all, that would not change your position either...

These three usages of *you* may refer either to Schröder, or to Schröder and the German government. Only once does Siegloch appear to invite Schröder to speak on his own behalf, quoting him as follows:

(7) KS~ZDF-5~   Wird denn Deutschland auf jeden Fall genauso wie Frankreich im Sicherheitsrat abstimmen, weil <u>Sie</u> ja immer von einem Schulterschluss gesprochen haben?
Will Germany in every event vote exactly the same as France in the Security Council, as you have always spoken of solidarity with France?

In contrast, the ARD interviewer Wickert predominantly invites the German Chancellor to speak on his own behalf:

(8) UW~ARD-1~   Können <u>Sie</u> Präsident Bushs Rede zur Lage der Nation voll und ganz unterschreiben?
Can you fully and completely support President Bush's State of the Union Address?

(9) UW~ARD-2~   US-Außenminister Colin Powell will dem Sicherheitsrat nächste Woche Geheimdienstinformationen vorlegen. Sind <u>Ihnen</u> schon einmal Beweise vorgelegt worden, die den Irak belasten?
US Secretary of State Powell is preparing to present the UNSC with secret service evidence next week. Have you been shown any evidence yet which incriminates Iraq?

(10) UW~ARD-6~   Wie beurteilen <u>Sie</u> die neue US-Doktrin vom Präventivschlag?
How do you judge the new US doctrine of pre-emptive strike?

(11) UW~ARD-7~   Die U.S.A. streben eine Zustimmung der UNO für einen Angriff gegen den Irak an. Haben <u>Sie</u> mit dem französischen Präsidenten Jacques Chirac darüber gesprochen, ob er bereit sei, gegen einen Irak-Krieg sein Veto einzulegen?
The USA is striving for the consent of the UN to attack Iraq. Have you spoken to the French President, Jacques Chirac about whether he is ready to use his veto against an Iraq war?

(12) UW~ARD-8~   Wann wird, <u>Ihrer</u> Meinung nach, der Krieg beginnen?
When will, in your opinion, the war start?

Even when Wickert questions Schröder about the decisions of the German government, he addresses him personally by using "your government's decision" instead of "the German government's decision":

(13)   UW_{ARD-3} Könnten diese amerikanischen Geheimdienstinformationen die Entscheidungen Ihrer Regierung beeinflussen?
       Is there a possibility that this American secret service evidence might influence your government's decisions?

This difference in the use of pronouns results in Schröder being differently positioned in the two interviews. In the case of the ZDF interview, Schröder is addressed mainly as the representative of a social group. By contrast, in the ARD interview, he is mainly addressed as an individual.

Corresponding to this distribution of individual versus potentially collective address forms, Schröder's answers to Wickert are overwhelmingly given from an individual *I*-perspective, whereas his answers to Siegloch are chiefly from a collective *we*-perspective (Figure 3).

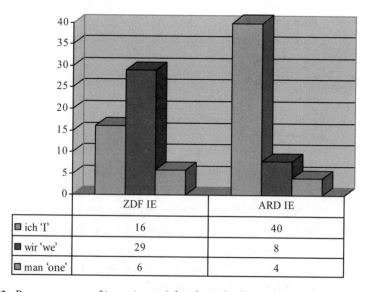

	ZDF IE	ARD IE
▣ ich 'I'	16	40
▪ wir 'we'	29	8
▣ man 'one'	6	4

Figure 3. Pronoun usage of interviewee Schröder in both interviews

Additionally, Schröder's answers to Siegloch also contain more instances of the indefinite pronoun *man* 'one.' This pronoun is often used to avoid committing oneself to either an individual or a collective perspective. Similarly, the reference of *wir* 'we' varies. In most cases, the German Chancellor uses exclusive *wir* 'we' to refer to the German government. This may switch to the inclusion of the German population in general or of the German television audience in particular, and, occasionally, to the inclusion of the interviewer:

(14) GS$_{ZDF-3}$ ...<u>wir</u> sind sehr eng mit Frankreich in dieser Frage, und das ist auch gut und richtig so, und insoweit, denke ich, sollten <u>wir alle</u> ein Interesse haben, auch in <u>unseren</u> öffentlichen Debatten nicht dazu beizutragen, dass Krieg wieder ein, na ja, fast normales Mittel der Politik wird, das darf es nicht sein, und ich denke, dass gerade <u>die Deutschen</u> wissen, warum das nicht sein darf, und äh deswegen auch verstehen, warum <u>wir</u> ganz besonders sensibel sind.

... we are very close to France in this respect and this is good and right as it is, and I think we should all be concerned not to let war again become a, let's say, every day means of making politics, even in our public debates, this is unacceptable, and I think that especially the Germans know why this can't be and therefore also understand why we are so sensitive.

Interestingly, Schröder does not say *wir Deutschen* 'we Germans' in the last line of the above example. Moreover, *die Deutschen* 'the Germans' and the sensitive persons referred to by *wir* 'we' at the end of Schröder's turn seem to belong to different groups. Schröder does not speak on behalf of the entire German population here. Instead, he constructs a contrast between *die Deutschen* 'the Germans' and *wir* 'we', meaning here: we, the German government. In the ARD, Schröder also juxtaposes himself and the German public, maintaining that he has the backing of their majority:

(15) GS$_{ARD-8}$ ...Einmal: Mich macht wirklich ernsthaft besorgt, dass <u>wir in Deutschland</u> eine Diskussion führen, als sei Krieg ein normales Mittel der Politik. <u>Ich</u> will hier sehr deutlich sagen und <u>ich</u> bin ganz froh darüber, <u>dass ich da in Übereinstimmung mit den größten Teilen der deutschen Öffentlichkeit</u> bin: Das darf es nie werden.

...First, I find it very disturbing that we in Germany are discussing war as if it were a normal means of politics. I want to be very clear about this, and I am glad that I have the backing of the major parts of the German public: this is what it must never become.

Generally, Schröder's use of the different first person pronouns corresponds closely to what Wilson (1990) has postulated concerning the differing degrees of existential involvement, or personal responsibility involved in a speaker's choice of either 'I' or the different types of 'we.' According to Wilson's scale of existential involvement, "'I' indicates a greater existential involvement" than inclusive 'we', "which in turn indicates a greater existential involvement" than exclusive 'we' (Wilson 1990:80). This is particularly striking when Schröder changes his perspective several times within a single turn where he switches between ambiguous 'we' for the public political sphere and 'I' only for metadiscursive comments on his own interview contributions:

(16)   GS$_{ZDF-8}$ Nein, wir haben deutlich gemacht äh äh, dass diese Entscheidung mit Rücksicht auf die Beratungen im Sicherheitsrat jetzt nicht an- steht, äh das ist auch eine gemeinsame Position mit europäischen Partnern, und äh unsere amerikanischen Freunde wissen, was wir zu leisten bereit sind und was nicht, und was wir zu leisten bereit sind, folgt der grundsätzlichen Position, die ich Ihnen genannt habe, das sind äh Diskussionen, die wir intern mit unseren Bündnispartnern führen, und ich sag's nochmal, an unserer Bereitschaft, Bündnis- verpflichtungen äh einzugehen und sie auch einzuhalten, ist über- haupt gar kein Zweifel erlaubt, aber es wird keine direkte oder indi- rekte Beteiligung Deutschlands an einem Krieg geben.
No, we have clearly stated er er that this decision is not at issue now, considering the discussions in the security council, this is also a posi- tion shared with European partners, and er, our American friends know what we are willing to do and what not, and what we are willing to do follows the fundamental position which I have explained to you, and these are er discussions we are conducting internally with our al- lies, and again, there is absolutely no reason to doubt our willingness to er take on and fulfill our duties as allies, but there will be no direct or indirect participation of Germany in a war.

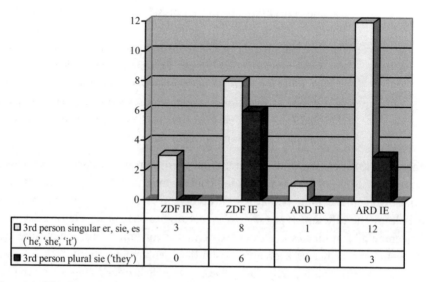

	ZDF IR	ZDF IE	ARD IR	ARD IE
☐ 3rd person singular er, sie, es ('he', 'she', 'it')	3	8	1	12
■ 3rd person plural sie ('they')	0	6	0	3

Figure 4. Third person pronoun usage by IR and IE in both interviews

In both interviews, Schröder's *wir* 'we' never includes the United States or France, nor any other nation. How, then, are the positions of nations other than Germany integrated into the discourse? Are they constructed as "Them"? Figure 4 shows the distribution of third person reference.

In the ZDF interview, the most frequent third person singular pronoun is *es* 'it' with clausal reference:

(17)   GS$_{ZDF-2}$ Zunächst einmal ist <u>es</u> so, dass äh <u>es</u> gut ist, dass...
        First of all, it is so that er it is good if ...

Other third person singular referents in the ZDF interview are abstract nouns like *unsere Position* 'our position.' Only in the ARD interview do third person singular pronouns refer to persons in the roles of acting, communicating or thinking subjects. This corresponds to the different degrees of abstraction versus personalization in the interviewers' questions, which has already been shown for the choice of address pronouns and will be taken up in the section on transitivity (Halliday 2004) below. Neither interviewer uses the third person plural pronoun *sie* 'they' at all. In the ZDF interview, Schröder's third person plural pronouns *Sie* 'they' refer three times to *die Beweise* 'proof' and besides that to *Fragen von Krieg und Frieden* 'questions of war and peace', *Bündnisverpflichtungen* 'duties as allies', and *die Inspektoren* 'the inspectors.' In the ARD interview, Schröder's *Sie* 'they' refers twice to *Einzelheiten* 'details' and once to *die Inspektoren* 'the inspectors.' Obviously, there is no clearly defined "Them" in the interviews, at least not in a strict grammatical sense. On a pragmatic level, though, there is a contrast between the German government and the German people, which Schröder indirectly constructs through his juxtaposition of *I* or *we* versus *the Germans*. The following section will discuss the linguistic representation of other nations and their representatives in the two interviews, using the concept of transitivity from Systemic Functional Linguistics (Halliday 2004).

Transitivity

The system of transitivity, as systemic functional linguists define it, "construes the world of experience into a manageable set of process types" (Halliday 2004:170). These process types may refer to the outer world, to people's inner worlds or to borderline cases. For instance, what people do in the world is labeled "material process" (e.g. *Gerhard Schröder <u>is visiting the studio</u>*), whereas what they think or feel is labeled "mental process" (e.g. *Gerhard Schröder <u>likes</u> interviews*), and their belonging to certain groups is labeled "relational process" (e.g. *Gerhard Schröder <u>is</u> German*). When the border between mental and material processes is transgressed and people do things such as laughing or crying, this is called "behavioral process."

Additionally, there are verbal and existential processes (e.g. *Gerhard Schröder <u>said</u> that there <u>was</u> a general consensus).*

As indicated above, one of the main differences between the ZDF interview and the ARD interview is the different degree of abstraction versus personalization involved – there is more abstraction in the ZDF interview and more personalization in the ARD interview. This is also mirrored in the different representations of Germany, the United States, France, Iraq, other countries, Europe, and international institutions in the two interviews. Typical of the ZDF interviewer's style is a preference for abstract nouns like *ein deutsches Ja* 'a German yes', and *die deutsche Haltung* 'the German attitude', whereas both the ARD interviewer and the interviewee prefer to use nouns with a more concrete, personal reference, as in *Ihre Regierung* 'your government' and *die Deutschen* 'the Germans.' The only person other than Schröder mentioned in the ZDF interview is Secretary of State Colin Powell. The ZDF interviewer refers to him via his title and last name, whereas Schröder uses a more familiar formulation of first and last name without title. In comparison to the ZDF interview, the ARD interview abounds in references to specific persons, both by the interviewer and by the interviewee. What is also noteworthy is the ZDF interviewer's downplaying reference to the looming war as *Thema Irak* 'the Iraq topic', where the ARD interviewer is explicit about *einen Irak-Krieg* 'an Iraq war.' Also of note is the explicit construction of the American allies as friends in both interviews. Table 1 shows how the different nations, their representatives and international institutions are introduced into the discourse. Note the greater degree of abstraction in the ZDF interview than the ARD interview.

Table 1. References used by IR and IE in both interviews

	ARD	ZDF
Germany	**Wickert (IR)** – wir in Deutschland *we in Germany* – die deutsche Öffentlichkeit *the German public* – man in Deutschland *people in Germany* – die Deutschen *the Germans*	**Siegloch (IR)** – die deutsche Position *the German position* – die Deutschen *the Germans* – Deutschland *Germany*

	ARD	ZDF

USA	**Schröder (IE)**
	– Ihre Regierung
	  your government
	– Guido Westerwelle
	– der deutsche Geheimdienst
	  the German Secret Service
		Schröder (IE)
		– ein deutsches Ja
		  a German yes
		– die deutsche Haltung
		  the German attitude
		– Deutschland
		  Germany

	Wickert (IR)
	– die amerikanische Regierung
	  the American government
	– amerikanische Sicherheitsinteressen
	  American safety interests
	– Amerika
	  America
	– die amerikanische Öffentlichkeit
	  the American public
	– die amerikanischen Freunde
	  the American friends
	– Herr Powell
	  Mr. Powell
		Siegloch (IR)
		– Colin Powell
		– man in America
		  people in America
		– unsere amerikanischen Freunde
		  our American friends

	Schröder (IE)
	– Präsident Bush
	  President Bush
	– U.S.-Außenminister Colin Powell
	  U.S. Secretary of State Colin Powell
	– amerikanische Geheimdienst-
	  informationen
	  American Secret Service information
	– die U.S.A.
	  the U.S.A.
	– U.S. Doktrin vom Präventivschlag
	  U.S. doctrine on preemptive strike
		Schröder (IE)
		– Außenminister Powell
		  Secretary of State Powell
		– die amerikanischen Verbündeten
		  the American allies

France	**Wickert (IR)**
	– Frankreich
	  France
	– der französische Präsident
	  the French president
		Siegloch (IR)
		– Frankreich
		  France

	Schröder (IE)
	– der französische Präsident Jacques
	  Chirac
	  French president Jacques Chirac
		Schröder (IE)
		– Frankreich
		  France

	ARD	ZDF

Iraq	**Wickert (IR)**
	– Irak
	  Iraq
	
	Schröder (IE)
	– Irak-Krieg
	  Iraq war
		Siegloch (IR)
		--- 	
		
		Schröder (IE)
		– Thema Irak
		  Iraq topic

Other nations	**Wickert (IR)**
	– Kosovo
	  Kosovo
	
	Schröder (IE)
	--- 	
		Siegloch (IR)
		– Afghanistan
		  Afghanistan
		
		Schröder (IE)
		– Türkei
		  Turkey

Europe	**Wickert (IR)**
	--- 	
	
	Schröder (IE)
	– Europa
	  Europe
		Siegloch (IR)
		– europäische Partner
		  European partners
		– Bündnispartner
		  allies
		
		Schröder (IE)
		--- 	

International institutions	**Wickert (IR)**
	– Sicherheitsrat der Vereinten
	  Nationen
	  United Nations Security Council
	– Inspektoren
	  inspectors
	– Herr Baradei
	  Mr. Baradei
	– Geheimdienstinformationen
	  Secret Service information
	– der Sicherheitsrat
	  Security Council
	
	Schröder (IE)
	– Sicherheitsrat
	  Security Council
	– Geheimdienstinformationen
	  Secret Service information
	– U.N.O.
	  UN
		Siegloch (IR)
		– Inspektoren
		  inspectors
		– Fachleute
		  experts
		
		Schröder (IE)
		– Sicherheitsrat
		  Security Council

As already indicated in the section on pronouns, these different degrees of abstraction versus personalization regarding the participants often correspond to particular types of processes. For instance, the ZDF interviewer uses a higher rate of existential processes, as seen in (18), whereas the ARD interviewer uses material processes more frequently, as seen in (19). Both of these examples are taken from the opening turns of the interviews.

(18) KS$_{ZDF-1}$ Beim Thema Irak steht die Entscheidung ja nun offenbar bevor. Bleiben Sie dabei: Mit einem deutschen Ja im Sicherheitsrat ist nicht zu rechnen?
Concerning Iraq, the decision seems to be imminent. Do you still insist: A German Yes in the Security Council is not to be expected?

(19) UW$_{ARD-1}$ Können <u>Sie</u> Präsident Bushs Rede zur Lage der Nation voll und ganz unterschreiben?
Can you fully and completely support President Bush's State of the Union Address?

As to Schröder's answers, the main difference in transitivity (Halliday 2004) parallels the differences in Schröder's use of pronouns. The pronoun *I* appears mainly in mental and verbal processes:

(20) GS$_{ARD-1}$ Ich finde, dass die Rede in den Punkten, die mir wichtig sind, uns weitergebracht hat...
I think that the address has brought us further on the issues which are of importance to me...

Mental processes also often have *we* as their agent, as well as material processes:

(21) GS$_{ZDF-7}$ ... dass... wir nun wahrlich keinen Grund geliefert haben, an unserem Beitrag im Kampf gegen den Terrorismus zu zweifeln...
... that...we have given no reason at all to question our part in the fight against terror ...

But whereas mental and verbal processes can also serve as hedges, material processes are frequently used to create or simulate factuality. The strongest commitment is encoded in existential processes, seen in Schröder's final turn on the topic:

(22) GS$_{ZDF-8}$ .... es wird keine direkte oder indirekte Beteiligung Deutschlands an einem Krieg geben.
... there will be no direct or indirect participation of Germany in a war.

Such monoglossic statements, as they are called within appraisal theory because they do not acknowledge the potential existence of other opinions or voices (White

2001; Martin and White 2005), are rare in these two interviews. Rather, heteroglossic engagement prevails, which, instead, does acknowledge other opinions and voices, e.g. by using hedges or similar linguistic devices. The choice of such heteroglossic options, in combination with other appraisal resources, is a very efficient tool for blurring the boundaries between "Us" and "Them" because speakers may use them to avoid commitment.

Appraisal

From the very beginning, the interviews differ in the way the appraisal systems *engagement* and *graduation* are used. The appraisal system *engagement* "includes resources that introduce additional voices into a discourse, via projection, modalization or concession; the key choice here is one voice (*monogloss*), or more than one voice (*heterogloss*)" (Martin and Rose 2003:54). For instance, *Noam Chomsky wrote another book* is a monoglossic utterance, whereas *I heard that Noam Chomsky might have written another book* is heteroglossic. Questions are generally heteroglossic. Only the "bare declarative" is defined as monoglossic (White 2001). Such unmitigated declaratives may also function as questioning turns in interviews. However, following this strict definition, there are no monoglossic questioning turns in the two interviews examined in this paper. Instead, the interviewers introduce other actual or potential voices into the discourse and invite Schröder to comment on them:

(23)   KS$_{ZDF-2}$ <u>Außenminister Powell</u> hat aber nun ja auch im Gespräch mit dem ZDF noch einmal neue Beweise angekündigt für kommenden Mittwoch. Könnte das denn Ihre Haltung noch verändern?
But in his interview with the ZDF Secretary of State Colin Powell has announced new evidence for next Wednesday. Could this, then, change your position?

(24)   UW$_{ARD-7}$ <u>Die U.S.A.</u> streben eine Zustimmung der UNO für einen Angriff gegen den Irak an. Haben Sie <u>mit dem französischen Präsidenten Jacques Chirac</u> darüber gesprochen, ob er bereit sei, gegen einen Irak-Krieg sein Veto einzulegen?
The USA is striving for the consent of the UN to attack Iraq. Have you spoken to the French President Jacques Chirac about whether he is ready to use his veto against an Iraq war?

Throughout the interview, Schröder responds to such strategies by stressing both the irrevocability of the German position and the bonds between his government and the politicians or nations mentioned by the interviewers. However, his usage of the appraisal system of engagement oscillates between monoglossic and heter-oglossic statements, both enriched with corresponding resources from the ap-praisal system of *graduation*. This system includes "[v]alues by which speakers graduate (raise or lower) the interpersonal impact, *force* or volume of their utter-ances, and by which they graduate (blur or sharpen) the *focus* of their semantic categorizations" (White 2001). This mixture between different degrees of engage-ment and graduation signals caution and confidence at the same time and is used by Schröder to navigate freely between positions. Occasionally, Schröder's use of engagement and graduation even varies in the course of a single turn:

(25) GS$_{ZDF-5}$ ... Es wird eine <u>sehr</u> enge Abstimmung mit Frankreich geben, und natürlich werden wir jeden <u>Versuch</u> unternehmen, so eng wie <u>möglich</u> zusammen zu bleiben, <u>das kann doch gar keine Frage sein</u>.
... We will co-ordinate our response with France very closely, and there can be no question about it, we will of course attempt everything possible to maintain this close relationship, this cannot be questioned at all.

This turn occurs immediately after a struggle with Siegloch over the appropriateness of the interviewer's formulations[2] of one of Schröder's previous turns. At first, Schröder signals confidence by stressing that the response with France would be coordinated 'very' closely. However, the maintenance of the relationship is subse-quently only formulated as an attempt. To counterbalance this uncertainty, Schröder then dismisses the topic altogether. When Siegloch follows this turn with a chal-lenge[3] in (26), Schröder interrupts him and rebuffs him in strong terms in (27).

(26) KS$_{ZDF-6}$ Aber wenn Frankreich am Ende mit "Ja" stimmt, würde das Ihre Po-sition ja auch nicht verändern, <u>// das verstehe ich richtig?</u>
But if in the end France voted "Yes" after all, that would not change your position either, // I understand that correctly?

(27) GS$_{ZDF-6}$ // (<u>*inaudible, spoken in overlap*</u>)/'Ich meine, wir diskutieren hier Fra-gen von Krieg und Frieden, und die diskutieren Sie in einer Weise, wenn ich Ihnen das sagen darf, entschuldigen Sie, die dieser Bedeu-tung nicht unbedingt angemessen ist.
// (<u>inaudible, spoken in overlap</u>) I mean, we are talking here about questions of war and peace, and, you are discussing them in a man-ner, if I may tell you so, excuse me, which is not quite appropriate considering their gravity.

Siegloch then challenges Schröder again, this time by constructing an explicit con-trast to the American position:

(28)   KS$_{ZDF-7}$ Das sehen vermutlich die amerikanischen Verbündeten etwas an-
ders, Herr Bundeskanzler.
The American allies would probably disagree, Mr. Chancellor.

Schröder then insists on the German position, praises Colin Powell as a person and elaborates on the understanding between America and Germany. In this turn, his engagement gradually moves from the heteroglossic to the monoglossic, supported by graduation resources. Thus, he constructs, or rather reconstructs, his confident position:

(29)   GS$_{ZDF-7}$ Ich denke, ich habe deutlich gemacht, wie die deutsche Position ist,
und ich kenne Colin Powell als einen der ernsthaftesten internation-
alen Gesprächspartner, die ich je hatte, und ich bin ziemlich sicher,
dass man in Amerika die Situation, die ich geschildert habe und die
Bedeutung, die das im Prinzipiellen für uns hat, schon verstehen
wird, zumal man dort sehr genau weiß, dass in anderen Fragen, die
äh nicht ganz äh andere Bedeutung haben, wie zum Beispiel unsere
Teilnahme an Enduring Freedom, wie unser Engagement in Afghanistan, wir nun wahrlich keinen Grund geliefert haben, am unserem
Beitrag im Kampf gegen den Terrorismus zu zweifeln oder gar in
Frage zu stellen, dass wir Verpflichtungen aus dem Bündnis heraus
nicht erfüllen. Ich glaube, da haben wir uns keine Vorwürfe zu
machen. Im Ernst macht uns auch keiner Vorwürfe.
*I think I have clearly explained what the German position is. Colin
Powell is in my opinion one of the most serious international partners
that I ever had and I am quite certain that the Americans can understand our situation as I have described it, and what this, as a matter of
principle, means to us, especially as they know very well that in other
related instances which have not entirely different gravity, take for example our part in Enduring Freedom, our participation in Afghanistan, we have given no reason to question our contribution in the fight
against terror, or even to question that we do not fulfill our duties as
allies. I think we do not have any reason to criticize ourselves. And no
one is seriously criticizing us either.*

Schröder's description of Colin Powell is full of positive *judgment*, an appraisal resource that is used to comment on moral qualities of persons (White 2001; Martin and White 2005). Nearly the same description occurs in the interview with the ARD:

(30)   GS$_{ARD-8}$ ... Äh ich denke, dass man in Deutschland besonders sensibel ist,
und das sage ich auch immer wieder den amerikanischen Freunden,
einem so int- in- äh wirklich interessanten und auch ernsthaften Ge-

sprächspartner wie Herrn Powell insbesondere: Die Deutschen haben Erfahrung mit Kriegen.

… I think that we are sensitive here in Germany, and I keep saying this to our American friends, especially to Colin Powell who I appreciate as a really interesting and serious partner: Germany has experienced war.

Interestingly, Schröder also uses a similar appraisal strategy to praise the ARD interviewer's journalistic qualities before he, nevertheless, refuses to answer the interviewer's question:

(31) GS$_{ARD-7}$ Wir stimmen uns sehr eng (.) mit Frankreich ab, aber die Gespräche, die ich mit dem französischen Präsidenten führe, in diesen Einzelheiten, ich verstehe Ihre Neugier, Herr Wickert, das ist auch gute journalistische Neugier, die werde ich Ihnen aber (.) nicht vermitteln. In jedem Falle gilt, dass wir uns sehr eng abstimmen mit Frankreich, und äh das ist die Vereinbarung, die wir getroffen haben, und die Einzelheiten dieser sehr engen Abstimmung äh, die gehören nicht in die Öffentlichkeit.

We are in close coordination with France, but my discussions with the French President, in all their detail, I can understand your curiosity Mr. Wickert, it is after all a good journalistic curiosity, but I won't be revealing these to you. In any case we will coordinate closely with France, that is our agreement, and the details of this do not belong in the public.

This time, Schröder sugars the pill of his refusal to answer by mitigating the face-threat (Brown and Levinson 1978) to Wickert by including a compliment. Why does he do so here? And why does he treat the ZDF interviewer differently? Context and topics are exactly the same in the ZDF interview. However, a brief quantitative comparison of the questioning strategies reveals that the ZDF interviewer uses more formulations and challenges than the ARD interviewer, who mainly uses topic-initiating questions. As various analyses of political interviews have shown, formulations and especially challenges are the most face-threatening strategies to a politician's public face (Bull et al. 1996) and are therefore dispreferred (Lauerbach 1999, 2001, 2003, 2004, 2006; Becker 2004, 2005a, 2005b). Therefore, it is not surprising that Schröder reacts differently to his interviewers' questions. Moreover, the difference in questioning strategies corresponds to the political orientation of the channels: The general orientation of the ZDF is more conservative than the orientation of the ARD. This is corroborated by a small but telling media reaction to the two interviews in the *Frankfurter Allgemeine Zeitung*, a major German daily newspaper known for its conservative attitude:

Es ist an der Zeit, einen Moderator zu loben, der wohl unterschätzt wird: Klaus-Peter Siegloch im "heute journal". Er tat am Dienstag[4], was in der ARD leider niemand vermochte. Er stellte dem Bundeskanzler die Gretchenfrage, die da lautet, warum die deutsche Position zum möglichen Irak-Krieg ist, wie sie ist und ob sie sich nach dem 5. Februar, wenn die Amerikaner ihre angeblichen Beweise vorgelegt haben, nicht noch ändern könne. Das wollte Gerhard Schröder nicht beantworten. Als Siegloch auf seiner Frage beharrte, musste er sich von seinem Gegenüber beleidigen lassen. Schließlich schien es, als säße da einer, der nicht mal mehr selbst an seine hohle Rhetorik glaubt. Dabei war es eine einfache, wenn auch folgenschwere Frage. (*FAZ*, 1/31/2003 :42)

It is about time to praise a presenter who seems to be underestimated: Klaus Peter Siegloch in the "heute journal". He did on Tuesday[4] what, unfortunately, no one in the ARD was capable of doing. He asked the German Chancellor the crucial question why the German position regarding the potential war on Iraq is as it is, and whether it might change after February 5, when the Americans present their alleged proof. Gerhard Schröder did not want to answer this. When Siegloch persisted asking his question, he had to face being insulted by his guest. In the end, it seemed as if there was somebody sitting there who no longer believed in his own hollow rhetoric. And it had been a simple, albeit serious question. (FAZ, 1/31/2003:42)

It seems that the FAZ writer appreciates the more antagonistic style of the ZDF interview as being more appropriate and efficient, whereas the ARD interview is disqualified as inefficient. However, an analysis of the efficiency of the different questioning strategies on the basis of the scale of evasiveness developed by Harris (1991) – who uses pragmatic criteria to formally distinguish between and empirically evaluate direct, indirect and evasive responses to questions in political interviews – shows that Schröder answers more questions, directly or indirectly, in the ARD interview than he does in the ZDF interview. This also suggests that, at least regarding these two interviews, the border between "Us" and "Them" is not constructed between Germany and any other outside nation, in spite of the different positions of Germany and the U.S., but between those supporting the Chancellor and those opposing him. Even Iraq is not constructed as "Them", and only in the ZDF interview does Schröder mention the *Kampf gegen den Terrorismus* 'fight against terrorism.' But the noun phrase "fight against terrorism" only appears within a prepositional phrase that modifies another prepositional phrase which is itself embedded in two hypotactic subclauses. Such subordinating syntactic constructions are indicative of hierarchical backgrounding (Tomlin 1985). Thus, we may assume that, at least within these two interviews, Schröder has other priorities.

Conclusion

Obviously, even in times of war, politicians orient towards complex parameters of "Us" versus "Them" relations that exist not only between nations, but also intra-nationally, between the political groups of a country and their group interests. At least this is the orientation the German Chancellor exhibits in the two interviews conducted on January 29, 2003, in the run-up to the Iraq war. In both interviews, he expresses solidarity with both the United States and France, in spite of their differing views concerning war against Iraq on the basis of the newly announced proof of weapons of mass destruction, and in spite of the fact that Germany and the United States hold different views concerning such a war, too. This has been demonstrated through the analysis of pronouns, transitivity, and appraisal and supported through a brief look at questioning strategies and foregrounding. As to nations, the construction of a clear-cut "Them" is avoided altogether. However, the Chancellor's discursive behavior conducted in channels with differing political orientations suggests subtle and not so subtle "Us" and "Them" dichotomies on an intra-national level. In both interviews, Schröder positions himself on one side of the debate over Iraq, mirroring the existing dichotomy in German politics and in the German media. Schröder's main goal, though, is the public construction of a unified "Us", with both the German government and the German nation as referents, in spite of all evidence to the contrary.

Notes

1.   My thanks go to Vanessa Tomala, Rirhandu Mageza and Nicky Prendergast for their assistance with transcripts and translations. I also wish to thank the organizers and participants of the conference *Ideologien der Lüge* at the *DFG Graduiertenkolleg Kulturen der Lüge* in Regensburg in June 2003 and the organizers and participants of the lecture series *GrenzBereiche des Lesens 2004* at the Johann Wolfgang Goethe University in Frankfurt am Main for the constructive discussions from which earlier publications focusing on other aspects of the Chancellor's interviews have benefited (Becker 2004; 2005a), as well as Adam Hodges and Chad Nilep for their helpful comments on earlier versions of this paper.

2.   Lauerbach's (2001) concept of formulations is based on Heritage and Watson (1979). Without using the term *follow-up*, Antaki (2002) analyzes how this type of interviewer turn is used in service encounters with clients with learning disabilities to repeat what he calls 'failed' questions in a personalized version that is more likely to be understood and answered.

3.   Challenges are defined as responding turns in which an interviewer questions aspects of an interviewee's response (Lauerbach 2001). Bell and van Leeuwen (1994) define challenges as confrontations with statements contradicting or weakening an IE's position: "[C]hallenges always formulate objections to the interviewee's position as stated in the interview. They always

involve a 'but' or, slightly stronger 'but surely'. They always force the interviewee in a defensive position. The interviewee is always the batsman, never the bowler" (141).

4. This is an error – both interviews were broadcast on Wednesday, January 29, 2003.

References

Antaki, C. 2002. "Personalised revision of 'failed' questions." *Discourse Studies* 4(4): 411–428.

Becker, A. 2004. "To challenge or not to challenge: Two TV interviews with German Chancellor Gerhard Schröder in the Run-up to the Iraq War." In *Ideologien zwischen Lüge und Wahrheitsanspruch*, S. Greschonig and C. Sing (eds.), 155–171. Wiesbaden: Deutscher Universitätsverlag.

Becker, A. 2005a. "'Ja, Herr Bundeskanzler, aber...': Zum Lesen von Fernsehinterviews." In *Grenzbereiche des Lesens 2004*, S. Lotz and B. Migge (eds.) Available: http://publikationen.ub. uni-frankfurt.de/volltexte/2005/884/.

Becker, A. 2005b. "Interviews in TV election night broadcasts: A framework for cross-cultural analysis." In *Dialogue Analysis IX / Selected Papers from the 9th IADA Conference, Salzburg 2003*, A. Betten and M. Dannerer (eds.), 61–71. Tübingen: Niemeyer.

Bell, P. and van Leeuwen, T. 1994. *The Media Interview: Confession, Contest, Conversation*. Kensington, NSW: University of New South Wales Press.

Brown, P.and Levinson, S. 1978. "Universals in language usage: Politeness phenomena." In *Questions and Politeness: Strategies in Social Interaction*, E. Goody (ed.), 56–311. Cambridge: CUP.

Bull, P., Elliott, J., Palmer, D. and Walker, L. 1996. "Why politicians are three-faced: The face model of political interviews." *British Journal of Social Psychology* 35: 267–284.

Bush, G.W. 2003. State of the Union Address. Available: www.washingtonpost.com/wp-srv/on-politics/transcripts/bushtext_012803.html.

Chilton, P. 2004. *Analysing Political Discourse: Theory and Practice*. London: Routledge.

Chilton, P. and Schäffner, C. 1997. "Discourse and politics." In *Discourse as Social Interaction*, T.A. van Dijk (ed.), 206–230. London: Sage.

Chilton, P. and Schäffner, C. 2002. "Introduction: Themes and principles in the analysis of political discourse." In *Politics as Text and Talk: Analytic Approaches to Political Discourse*, P. Chilton and C. Schäffner (eds.), 1–41. Amsterdam: Benjamins.

Fairclough, N. 1995. *Media Discourse*. London: Arnold.

Fairclough, N. 2003. *Analyzing Discourse: Textual Analysis for Social Research*. London: Routledge.

Galasiński, D. 2000. *The Language of Deception: A Discourse Analytical Study*. Thousand Oaks: Sage.

Halliday, M.A.K. 2004. *An Introduction to Functional Grammar (Third Edition)*. London: Arnold.

Harris, S. 1991. "Evasive action: How politicians respond to questions in political interviews." In *Broadcast Talk*, P. Scannell (ed.), 76–99. London: Sage.

Heritage, J. and Watson, D.R. 1979. "Formulations as conversational objects." In *Everyday Language: Studies in Ethnomethodology*, G. Psathas (ed.), 123–162. New York.

Lauerbach, G. 1999. "From macro to micro and back: Framing, footing, and genre in recent TV election night coverages." In *Language and Ideology: Selected Papers from the 6th Pragmatics Conference*, J. Verschueren (ed.), 317–443. Antwerp. International Pragmatics Association.

Lauerbach, G. 2001. "Implicit communication in political interviews: Negotiating the agenda." In *Negotiation and Power in Dialogic Interaction*, E. Weigand and M. Dascal (eds.), 197–214. Amsterdam: Benjamins.

Lauerbach, G. 2003. "Opting out of the media-politics contract: Discourse strategies in confrontational political interviews." In *Selected Papers from the 8th IADA Conference, Bologna 2000*, M. Bondi, (ed.). Tübingen: Narr.

Lauerbach, G. 2004. "Political interviews as hybrid genre." *Text* 24(3): 297–301.

Lauerbach, G. 2006. "Discourse representation in political interviews: the construction of identities and relations through voicing and ventriloquizing." *Journal of Pragmatics* 38(2): 196–215.

Martin, J.R. and Rose, D. 2003. *Working with Discourse: Meaning Beyond the Clause*. London: Continuum.

Martin, J.R. and White, P.R.R. 2005. The *Language of Evaluation: Appraisal in English*. London: Palgrave Macmillan.

Suleiman, C., O'Connell, D.C., and Kowal, S. 2002. "'If you, and I, if we, in that later day, lose that sacred fire …': Perspective in political interviews." *Journal of Psycholinguistic Research* 31(3): 269–287.

Tomlin, R.S. 1985. "Foreground-background information and the syntax of subordination." *Text* 5: 85–122.

Van Dijk, T.A. 1998. *Ideology: A Multidisciplinary Approach*. London: Sage.

Van Dijk, T.A. 2006. "Politics, ideology, and discourse." In *Encyclopedia of Language and Linguistics* (second edition), K. Brown (ed.), 725–740. Amsterdam: Elsevier.

Ward, M. 2004. "*We* have the power – or do we: Pronouns of power in a union context." In *Systemic Functional Linguistics and Critical Discourse Analysis*, L. Young and C. Harrison (eds.), 280–295. London: Continuum.

White, P.R.R. 2001. "Appraisal: An Overview." The *Appraisal Website*. Available: www.grammatics.com/appraisal/AppraisalGuide/Framed/Frame.htm.

Wilson, J. 1990. *Politically Speaking: The Pragmatic Analysis of Political Language*. Oxford: Blackwell.

Wodak, R. and Meyer, M. (eds). 2001. *Methods of Critical Discourse Analysis: Introducing Qualitative Methods*. London: Sage.

CHAPTER 10

Discourse of war and terrorism in Serbia

"We were fighting the terrorists already in Bosnia…"

Zala Volcic and Karmen Erjavec

> *"Hundreds of Islamic extremists who became Bosnian citizens after fighting the Serbs now present a threat to Europe and the United States… bin Laden and Muslim groups have been involved in Bosnia, Kosovo… Macedonia… throughout the 1990s… Everyone knows that Mujahidin fighters were fighting on the side of the Bosnian Muslims in Bosnia against the Serbs. Many of them still live in Bosnia today… When the Serbs went to war in Bosnia, they went to war against terrorism."*
> – A Serbian Journalist, in a personal interview, Belgrade, Serbia, 2003

Introduction

Symbolic social geographies of Europe: "Balkan as the dark other"

There were several historical events, such as the second Balkan war of 1913, or the assassination of the Austrian Archduke Franz Ferdinand in Sarajevo (which started the First World War), that helped to shape the image of the Balkans, and Serbia within, as a zone of violence, barbarism, and terrorism (Goldsworthy 1998: 74). These meanings stand as a peculiar marker for the position that Eastern Europe and the Balkans occupy on a symbolic cultural map of Europe. Several ground-breaking works have interrogated the symbolic distinction between the West and the Balkans that has been enacted through a deployment of negative representations and discourses about the Balkan region (Bakic-Hayden 1995; Todorova 1997; Wolff 1994). Identified with violence, incivility and barbarism, the Balkans represented the cultural and religious "Other" to Western Europe, and while during the Cold War the ideological Other, Communism, replaced the geographical Other, the symbolic imagery of Balkan inferiority was preserved (Bakic-Hayden and Hayden 1992: 1–4). Indeed, many scholars have pointed out how the discourse of Balkanism was created gradually and how, indeed, it is not an innocent or a historically neutral one. Thus, these authors in particular argued for the necessity of dismantling common-sense mental mappings (Todorova 1997; Goldsworthy 1998; Jezernik 2004).

However, ideas about "East" and "West" continue to create and shape perceptions of the places involved. The war in former Yugoslavia was seen as evidence for the idea that Eastern Europe is fundamentally different and more backward than Western Europe.[1] Thus, there are many examples of "Balkanist" popular and scholarly discourses. The way in which Huntington (1993; 1997) describes the new world order in his "clash of civilizations" is illustrative. His scheme, "the West versus the rest of the world," divides the globe into "order versus chaos," excluding non-Western countries from the modern civilized world. In the Balkans this line historically coincides with the Habsburg and Ottoman Empires, which today separates Croatia and Slovenia from the rest of the former Yugoslavia. On the Western side of the border is Western civilization, and Enlightenment stands as its marker. On the other side, Huntington claims, there is an Orthodox/Muslim civilization, with no respect for the individual or democracy.[2]

As Hammond (2005) writes, even though the dark image of the Balkans as the Other of the West has been replaced by al Qaeda, Western representational portrayals of the Balkans, and Serbia within, continue to be one-dimensional and politically crippling. The impact of this ill-informed Western discourse of the Balkan region is indeed irrevocable, and research efforts have been deployed recently to measure the intensity of that impact (see Ilic 2004; Todorova 1997). Less attention, however, has been directed to the appropriation of such and similar discourses within the Balkan region itself. There is a particular lack of research dealing with an appropriation of different Western (political) discourses since the collapse of Communism.[3] According to Skrbiš (1999), for example, the notion of the 'Southerner' continues to be employed in Slovenia to refer to people from other former Yugoslav republics, and the South "has been commonly perceived in a symbolic fashion as the personification of economic underdevelopment, hot-bloodedness and, most often, otherness" (Skrbiš 1999: 121).

Serbia, like all nations, has struggled to create a national identity[4], a struggle that has been complicated since the collapse of Yugoslavia in 1991. Particularly complex has been Serbia's relation to Europe and the West. During the former Yugoslav wars, the Milošević regime held that everything coming from the west was a conspiracy against Serbia and the entire Serb nation (Cosic in Zirojevic 2000). After the collapse of the Milošević regime in 2000, there were calls to "return to Europe." More recently, the Bush administration's "war on terror" discourse has been debated and sometimes appropriated.

With all the above in mind, we have decided to focus on Serbia as a case-study. We see it as symptomatic of a cultural-political shift we attempt to understand.

Serbia has had to renegotiate its global cultural and political position following the end of the former Yugoslav wars, the collapse of Milošević's regime, and the events of 9/11. After 9/11 the ensuing global political climate dictated a sudden attention to issues of influence and employment of "anti-terrorism discourse" everywhere in the world, including the former Yugoslav countries.

All of the above research points to how the choices of criteria used to define differences between regions such as Eastern and Western Europe, or Central Europe and the Balkans are never neutral. Rather they are guided by particular ideologies and supported by specific relationships of domination in the broader international political arena. Thus, we may ask, how have the 9/11 attacks on the World Trade Center and Pentagon affected and redefined Serbian discourses of identity? Has the relationship of Serbians towards the West been changed and reshaped yet again? Who, if anyone, is marked and framed as a terrorist in Serbia, and what kinds of characteristics are attributed to him/her? Has there been a new kind of rising phobia against Muslims not only in the USA, but also in Europe, and Serbia, in the aftermath of 9/11?[5] What kind of an image role do the Serbs – once themselves stereotypically shaped as "the Other" (Ilic 2004)[6] – employ today in the process of the restructuring of the global "anti-terrorism discourse"?

In seeking answers to these questions, we hope to contribute a much-needed empirical analysis of the role of the "anti-terrorism discourse." Our attempt is to investigate if and how young Serbian intellectuals adopt and use the Western discourse of "anti-terrorism" – characterized by a relatively uniform representation of a global situation after 9/11 that goes something like this: War has been proclaimed; the enemy is Islamic terrorism, personified by bin Laden; and the West has to unite in a war against terrorism (Bailey and Chermak 2003; Edwards 2004; Graham et al. 2004; Lazar and Lazar 2004; Chouliaraki 2005; Fairclough 2005; van Dijk 2005). In borrowing from and/or explicitly employing this discourse, our informants present themselves as those (misunderstood and betrayed) heroes that have been long fighting the terrorists in Kosovo and Bosnia, which are Muslim countries, in order to defend the Christian West. We explore the ideological use of "terrorism" and its reproduction in discourse of young intellectuals, when the concept of terrorism becomes a weapon to be exploited on the stage of global power. Thus, in its usage in contemporary Serbian discourse, expressions such as "war on terror" or "fighting Muslim terrorists" are turned into legitimate terms designating political wishes of belonging and even legitimizing the violent former-Yugoslav wars. Here the same dismissal of Islam and its anti-democratic ideals in global politics gets projected with very little reflection. Islam is suspected of being hostile to Serbia, and of being in continuity with the terrorists who call for radical Islam.

The former Yugoslav political-historical context

The historical idea for the formation of Yugoslavia was created on the perception that those Slavs who lived between the Adriatic Sea and the Black Sea were connected by their common language and culture. After the Second World War, different regional elites viewed the formation of a single Slav state as a politically and culturally desirable project. According to its "engineers," Yugoslavia promised to surpass the contradictions of nationalism and ethnic grouping. It was an obvious political engineering project and was symbolically based on the common memory of the struggle against Austrian, Hungarian and Turkish Empires at the beginning of the 20th century. Thus, the Socialist Federal Republic of Yugoslavia (SFRY) was created from six different nations or republics, and "Titoism" was founded on the assumption that economic and political homogenization would lead to the creation of a pure workers' state (Woodward 1995).

During the 1980s, after the death of its president Josip Broz Tito in 1980, the suppressed nationalisms conquered the social sphere. Two major ethnic groups, Serbs and Croats, claimed to have been the victims of a continued persecution by the other, who, they claimed, dominated the Yugoslav federation. In 1986, the Serbian Academy of Science and Art prepared a Memorandum – a long list of Serbian grievance against their position within the federation. Much of the document dealt with the "genocide" of Serbs in Kosovo, and articulated the need for Serbs throughout Yugoslavia to collectively assert and organize themselves. Milošević reproduced the so-called historical and "scientific" data for the construction of the nationalistic ideology of a "Greater Serbia." Its crucial vision was the idea that all ethnic Serbs needed to live in the same state (MacDonald 2002).

In 1991 began what was seemingly a fratricidal civil war. Specifically, the war began in Slovenia when the Yugoslav People's Army (JNA), which became a Serbian army under Milošević's direct command, attempted to forcibly prevent Slovenia's independence. In Croatia, Serbian irregulars instigated violent clashes with Croatian paramilitary forces, followed once more by an intervention of JNA. As the fighting spread from Croatian Eastern Slavonia to Krajina and later to Bosnia and Herzegovina, it was clear that Europe was witnessing its first major military conflict since the Second World War. Serbs and Croats alike were exploiting their own pasts (the nineteenth century, the First Yugoslavia, and especially the Second World War) in order to present themselves as the victims. However, political elites in both Croatia and Serbia agreed in their opposition to Bosnia, arguing over how to divide the Bosnian territory between their respective states. Importantly, both sides committed war crimes, which included "ethnic cleansing", establishment of concentration camps or "collective centers", destruction of physical property (including destruction of approximately 1,400 mosques), and numerous massacres of civilians (250,000 deaths; see more in Skjelsbaek and Smith 2001; Taylor and Kent 2000). In both countries, the mainstream representation positioned Bosnian Muslims as little more than an invented and artificial nation with no historical claims to the Bosnian territory. For Croats and Serbs alike, the Muslims were the harbingers of a dangerous Islamic conspiracy, poised to take over the Balkans and Western Europe. Such mainstream representation of Muslims continues after the wars (MacDonald 2002). On December 14 of 1995, following over three years of bloody conflict, the Dayton Peace Agreement brought an end to the Bosnian war. While claiming its objective to be reconciliation, democracy, and ethnic pluralism, the Agreement, in the eyes of its critics, legalized the ethnic partition between Bosnian Serbs, Bosnian Croats, and Bosnian Muslims. Bosnia-Herzegovina was divided into two entities: the Federation of Bosnia-Herzegovina (with 51% of the territory) inhabited mostly by Bosnian Muslims and Bosnian Croats, and the Republic of Serbia (with 49% of the territory) populated almost exclusively by Bosnian Serbs. Furthermore, the Agreement separated the Federation of Bosnia-Herzegovina into ten ethnically distinct cantons with very little intermixing between the two ethnic groups. Although fighting ceased in 1995, the conflict is not entirely resolved. Ethnic fragmentation and "uncertain transitions" from socialism to democracy (Verdery and Burawoy 1999) have contributed to the country's current situation of economic, social, and political suspension. Today, almost ten years after the last military struggles in Bosnia and Herzegovina, international military forces are still present and it is the international community which controls and negotiates the peace in Bosnia and Herzegovina. Furthermore, there are still conflicting visions of the Bosnian-Herzegovinian future.

The next crucial conflict area in the former Yugoslavia continues to be Kosovo, the province predominantly populated by Albanian Muslims within the union of Serbia and Montenegro.[7] For centuries, the Serbs have cultivated a myth about Kosovo as the cradle of Serbian Orthodox civilization that has to remain a part of Serbia. The Yugoslav constitution of 1974 established the status of Kosovo as an autonomous province; furthermore, the death of Yugoslav President Tito triggered Albanians' aspirations for the independence of Kosovo. However, in 1989, Kosovo lost its status as an independent region and became a part of Serbia. Albanians declared the Serbs to be colonizers, and Kosovo a colony. On the other hand, Serbian politicians represented Albanians as "colonizers" and "persecutors", pointing to the massive migration of Serbs from Kosovo in the 1980s that has been the cause and the consequence of the change in the ethnic structure and also in the quality of inter-ethnic relationships. However, according to Serbian voices, the Serbs in Kosovo had a "historical right" to continue their rule of Kosovo.

During the 1990s, the rights of Kosovo Albanian Muslims have been systematically violated, and a passive resistance movement failed to secure independence.

In the mid-1990s, an ethnic Albanian guerrilla movement, the Kosovo Liberation Army, intensified its attacks on Serbian targets. The attacks precipitated a brutal Serbian military crackdown. In November 1997, the first armed conflicts occurred between the Kosovo Liberation Army and the Serbian military. The war escalated and was ended with the NATO bombing of Serbia in 1999. Kosovo continues to be administered by the UN, and, even today, still occupies one of the central positions in the Serbian national imaginary.

In the light of the global "war on terror" discourse, the enthusiastic attempts of the Balkan countries themselves to borrow and exploit the global "war on terror" in order to remain in the center of global attention are significant and remarkable. In the Balkan region there have been many suspicions raised that Islamic extremists may have used Bosnia as a military base, but such accusations have never been confirmed. According to one established international think tank, the International Crisis Group (ICG), such accusations have proven especially insulting for the Albanians who are pro-American and, like most other Balkan peoples, consider their Balkan neighbors more backward than themselves and sustain a negative image of the East (ICG 2001: 3–8). Furthermore, there has been a continuous widespread moral panic in the region about the danger of the arrival of tens of thousands of foreigners who came from Arab countries between 1989 and 2002, and their supposed plans to create an Islamic Terrorist state in Bosnia-Herzegovina (Erjavec 2003). The anti-Islamic campaign in the Balkans has become part of the politics of self-representation. Yet, it is precisely this self-representation that ultimately reproduces and in turn reaffirms the dominant perceptions of the Balkans as a land of blood and eternal conflict. The accumulation and convergence of anti-Islamic reporting in Slovenia, for example, as Erjavec (2002) argues, further serves to position non-ethnic-Slovene cultures as threatening, criminal, foreign, and even barbaric. Such mainstream reporting frames Slovenia as civilized and Christian in opposition to the barbaric Balkans.

Methods

We make no pretense here of dealing with the whole discursive configuration of the West in Serbian history and culture. We will present, rather, an insight into the role of the global "anti-terrorism discourse" in re-shaping Serbian culture and social life at a specific moment in time. First, we provide some information about the data we have analyzed in this study, while following Morley (1996), when he calls for the anthropological ethnographer to explicitly acknowledge the unequal (textual) relations of power that position him or her as a privileged interpreter and arbiter of human social reality. The ethnographer should not, however, succumb to a dangerous relativism in which his or her account of a phenomena, relation, object, etc. becomes one of a million equally valid analyses.

The corpus included 16 problem-centered, qualitative interviews with Serbian intellectuals aged 23–40, in which a range of questions concerning the former Yugoslav wars, and the terrorist attacks in the USA were asked and responded to. Young intellectuals were drawn from a universe composed of journalists, writers, artists, and government/opposition politicians. The empirical data are based on in-depth, semi-structured individual interviews conducted in different regions in Serbia in 2002, with some follow-ups in 2003 and 2004. All the interviews were conducted in the Serbian language by both of the researchers. Although there were specific questions, the interviewees' responses sometimes called for improvisation. The interviews were transcribed verbatim by both researchers and analyzed in terms of recurring themes. We used this technique of research to gather data on our informants' perceptions beyond the official declaration of leaders, or as reported in the media, and thus to offer more in-depth information on perceptions that surveys generally show. To ensure the respondents' anonymity, we labeled our informants using letters.

The textually oriented Critical Discourse Analysis (CDA) is employed here for the analysis of empirical data. CDA is based upon the assumption that "language is an irreducible part of social life, dialectically interconnected with other elements of social life, so that social analysis and research always has to take account of language" (Fairclough 2003: 2). For CDA, "texts are sensitive barometers of social processes, movements and diversity, and textual analysis can provide particularly good indicators of social change" (Fairclough 1995: 209).

An analysis of the linguistic resources that characterize the representation of the events of 9/11 and the interdiscursive relations constructed through them provides a possible explanation of different interpretations and appropriations these events have had in order to serve particular ideological interests at the local level. At the same time, this analysis of the linguistic and discursive characteristics of the discursive formation of 9/11 allows us to describe the particular ways in which language reproduces and challenges naturalized social representations about Others.

The textual analysis is based on an analysis of the representation of social actors which provides some linguistic evidence as to how social actors are included in different forms (van Leeuwen 1996). The exploration of interdiscursivity (Fairclough 1992) allows for the analysis of the more dynamic aspects of discursive representation such as response to or evocation of other discourses. Furthermore, ideological aspects of discourse are explored in the use of discourse strategy and argumentative structures deployed in the construction of in- and out-groups (van Dijk 1995; Wodak 1996).

Serbian anti-terrorism discourse

The representation of social actors

In the transcripts analyzed, one of the main functions of social representation of the actors serves to affirm their ideology by contrasting it to an opposing ideology. It is precisely for these reasons that we consider Hall's "discourse of difference" as the most effective method to think through binary positions. Hall (1989) understands "discourses of difference" (913) as those that make a distinction between "us" and "them." Any group, to be identified as a group, must be differentiated from the Others – internal and external ones. Any kind of identity, as Hall further suggests, is primarily defined as a difference from the Other. That meanings of "we" and "they", implying identification with and differentiation from, are not ontologically given but ideologically constructed becomes clear through linguistic analysis. Still, because they appear so natural, this "we" and "they" dichotomy is rarely questioned. Yet, these are the concepts that have the greatest power as they "go without saying because they come without saying" (Bourdieu 1977: 167). The construction of identity is a process of differentiation, a description of one's own group and a differentiation from others (Wodak 1996). This means that the identities of social actors in the texts are mostly constructed and defined as members of groups when the emphasis is placed on representing the Other as different, deviant or as a threat.

All informants use the same discursive strategy of division into two groups, "us" versus "them", in order to construct a self-group identity and appropriate the situation after 9/11 in order to advance the in-group ideology. Hence, the informants construct the two groups by associating themselves with "the victims" (of the former Yugoslav wars). "The Other" is portrayed as a perpetrator and is embodied in a "non-Western/non-European/non-Christian" way, primarily by geographical, biological, religious and moral standards. This group includes: Muslims in general, Muslims in Kosovo and Bosnia, the Kosovo Liberation Army, Islamic fundamentalists, Islamic radicals and Osama bin Laden.

It is important to note that the quotations we analyze are an example of a type of discourse the informants use, not the entirety of this discourse. The following example shows how the informants construct a dichotomy between "us, the Serbs" and "them, the Bosnian Muslims":

> It seems to me that the logic in every nation is always a simple dichotomy of a victim and a perpetrator: we are the victims and the other one, the enemy, is a perpetrator. This also works like this in the Balkans... and we need to explain the situation in this region to the West through some examples of the connections between Bosnian Muslims and Islamic fundamentalists. (Informant V)

Furthermore, the next citation posits that the Muslim Kosovo Albanians are similarly framed as "the Balkan Other." The informants attempt to make an explicit linguistic-semantic connection between terrorists and Kosovo Albanians:

> You know that Islamic radicals have been supporting Muslim Albanian rebels fighting in the region, including members of the Kosovo Liberation Army... (Informant V)

In a similar way, the informants were attempting to establish a connection and ties between their (created) enemies and Osama bin Laden (cf. Bucholtz and Hall 2004; Hodges, chapter 4). The Bosnian Muslims were equated with bin Laden:

> Look at the Bosnian Serbs... I understand that they cannot live together with the Muslims and Croats in the internationally recognized state of Bosnia. Bosnia is sponsored, created by Saudi Arabia... and Osama bin Laden. (Informant Y)

In the process of inventing, shaping, defining, and presenting Muslims as "the Other", the informants stress and emphasize the religious difference and dichotomy that they understand as a crucial one: the one between the Christian Orthodox Serbs and the Balkans' Muslims, belonging to Eastern Islam. Our informants seem to be eager to jump on the "band-wagon" by identifying themselves as a part of the West:

> There is a huge religious difference between Serbs and Muslims. We are Christians as the others in the Western world; they belong to Eastern Islam ... (Informant J)

Representation of "the Muslim other"

Bailey and Chermak (2003) argue that the translation of the 9/11 attacks into the discursive terrain of terrorism enabled it to become globally perceived as a symbol of Islamic violence. As indicated in the discourse of our informants, the Muslims from the former Yugoslav countries become defined as the "Serbian Other." They become framed and represented as the enemies of the Serbs, and thus linked to Islamic fundamentalism. By denoting Bosnian and Kosovar Muslims as terrorists, Islamic fundamentalists, and Islamic radicals, the informants reduce all Muslims to a monolithic and irrationally violent "Other", and in that sense, recycle the Western stereotype about Muslims and Islam (Karim 1997; Said 1978, 1997).[8] Karim (1997) in particular argues that violence, lust, and barbarism seem to be the primary western image of "Islam" and he cautions against drawing hurried conclusions about the nature of Islam.

It is important to note here that our informants were indeed replicating the Western stereotype about Muslims. Muslims in these imaginaries are described in terms of a unified mass with a common subjectivity that is at odds with the rest of the democratic world.[9]

It seems that the "war on terror" now includes many essentialist stereotypes about Islam and violent Muslims. Similarly, most of our informants recycle these stereotypes of Muslims as terrorists. Overall, this stereotypical image is explained by global and regional political factors, yet it contains very essentialist and simplistic biological evidence: "terrorism is in Muslims' blood." In a sense, denied any type of a civilized behavior, the Muslim's difference was explained in explicitly biological and evolutionary terms (coded as primitive and violent by their nature). This so-called biological strategy of argument additionally means that the Muslims are defined to be Serbian/Christian eternal enemies who cannot be fought by rational and political means. One could argue that, with this strategy, our informants legitimize the Serbian use of violent means while fighting the Muslims in former Yugoslav wars. This language naturalizes the difference by making it appear to coincide, inevitably, with predetermined boundaries. The language used in this kind of argumentation is a very common-sense one, and uses common-sense slogans such as "everybody knows" or "we all know" to further naturalize this polarization:

> This situation here has a long historical background, and furthermore, global political and economic framework... but you should understand... everybody knows that the Muslims are terrorists... It is in their blood. (Informant A)

Thus, Islam was simplistically defined as a "terrorist religion." For example:

> Islam is a terrorist religion… Look at history and the Ottomans…history repeats itself… (Informant L)

Muslims as social actors also appear in extremely negative terms that emphasize violence in opposition to the positive terms that construct Serbs as having a "non-violent identity":

> I feel on the one hand that the whole world perceives all Serbs to be somehow aggressive and violent by nature... the brutal truth is that the Serbs are not violent by nature... as the Muslims are... (Informant D)

With representing all Muslims as "violent by nature" the informants tend to shape themselves as ones "not violent by nature," while denying and resisting the stereotypical image of the Serbs in the West (van de Port 1999).

The next case shows how the Muslims are framed as having a different way of life than the Serbs and other Europeans. The informants blame the Muslims for trying to transform and change "our European way of life." They use the words "terrorists" and "Muslims" synonymously, just as "Serbs" is interchangeable with "Europeans." There is a specific strategy of cultural differentiation noticeable here

– informants also seek to construct a meaning that exists as a homogeneous one, expressing a bounded and a unified European cultural way of life and at the same time again deny any structural discrepancies between them and other Europeans.

> Terrorists... Muslims... are backward... they came to this region and try to infiltrate their habits here, and change our European way of life... (Informant M).

> They do not share the European manners, they are not developed in such a way (Informant L).

> They do not share common European values (Informant P).

Thus, besides very essentialist geographical, biological, and religious differences between the Serbs/Europeans and Muslims/terrorists, the informants emphasize the cultural differences – grounded in the cultural Otherness of Muslims (including a way of life, habits, customs and manners). Many scholars (e.g. Barker 1981; Balibar and Wallerstein 1991; Miles 1994) define this kind of cultural differentiation as a kind of "differentialist racism", "cultural racism" or "culturalist racism." Furthermore, Rosaldo (1994) coins the phrase "cultural citizenship," using the term to explore the lines of exclusion that are implicated in imagining a one-language nation. And as Stolcke (1995) suggests, throughout the 1980s and up through the present, the rightist rhetoric of exclusion in Europe defined extracommunitarian immigration as an invasion of alien culture, as an attack that would destroy the homogeneity of the nation.

Interdiscursivity and the representation of the events of 9/11

The discursive constructions and appropriations of the 9/11 events attempt to establish some kind of a continuity with other historical events – all in order to explain the meaning of the 9/11 attacks. Fairclough defines the ways in which these other narratives are brought into the text. He adopts ideas from French discourse analysis and argues for intertextuality as the case where specific other texts are overtly drawn upon within a text (e.g. parts of other texts are incorporated into news reports with devices such as quotation marks and reporting clauses), whereas interdiscursivity or manifest intertextuality is a matter of how a discourse type is constituted through a combination of elements of orders of discourse (Fairclough 1992: 64). The concept of interdiscursivity focuses on discourse conventions rather than on other texts as constitutive. An example of interdiscursivity would be 'mixed genres', which combine elements of two or more genres, such as 'chat' in television chat shows, which is a part of entertainment and a part of performance (Fairclough 1992). This textual analysis explores some of the forms of interdiscursivity; that is, how specific other discourses are brought in to a discourse.

Interestingly, our informants used comparison as a form of argumentation and as a way of guiding us on how to interpret the events by connecting them to our available social mental models. Informants used comparison as a form of framing the events of 9/11 within a particular ideology – the one of power and/or the one of solidarity. The analogy, "Serbia is to Muslims as USA is to terrorists," starts to serve as a strategy of legitimizing the Serbian war against Muslims in the former Yugoslavia. In other words, for our informants the events of 9/11 were similar to events committed by Muslims in the Balkans. In this way, history is re-articulated and the war in former Yugoslavia is transformed and equated with the war against terrorists:

> It is very tragic, what has happened in the former Yugoslav republics … we were fighting the Osama terrorists by ourselves already then. (Informant M)

The "war on terror" is a vehicle to justify an array of policies involving wars in Bosnia and Kosovo. In this sense, the Serbs are defending themselves against the terrorists continuously from the 1980s onward.

> Just see what is going on around the world today... Some people in Serbia recognized the danger of fundamentalism and terrorism in the 1980s... those were the ones who warned us we need to defend ourselves in Bosnia, and Kosovo... (Informant N)

Thus, in this rhetoric, the Serbs are continuously fighting terrorism – they were fighting it long before the West recognized terrorism as a real danger:

> At the same time, I must say that during the past fifteen years, the West was trying to understand what was going on in the region of former Yugoslavia viewed only through the prism of their own interests. Now, for instance, it is crucial to explain to them that Serbia was always on the right, democratic side during the wars in this region... We need to develop the necessary political vocabulary and concepts to explain what those crimes in Bosnia actually represented – the Serbs were fighting terrorism, already when USA was still happily dreaming... (Informant C)

In these accounts, the "terrorism" suffered by the USA is equated with the "terrorism" perpetrated by the Muslims in the form of the war in the region of former Yugoslavia. The informants extended the meaning of the word "terrorism" to all the violent acts – historical and contemporary – committed against them, the Serbs. Terrorism has been defined as a violent act carried out by Muslims for political purposes. Indeed, the "terrorists" are now presented as Muslims, who continue to employ violence against the Serbs. For example:

> The Serbs know how terrorism works… These are Kosovo Liberation Army's attacks on us … (Informant G)

A relationship of identity and attributions is established through a comparison of events. This type of relation brings out the act of judgment and valuation of the events within a larger ideological frame. Thus, the terminology of the "war on terror" has been naturalized in a specific way. In this way, the informants are also (re)producing a hegemonic global order of discourse. In other words, an allegedly agentive act is at one and the same time the very act that (re)produces a hegemonic order which, arguably, created the "opportunity" for the informants to learn a dominant (political) language.

Discussion

The above analysis shows first, that the conduct of any identity is embedded in, and articulated through, the negotiation and articulation of sameness and difference (cf. Hodges' discussion in chapter 4 of Bucholtz and Hall's (2004) tactics of intersubjectivity). Categorizing others and positioning ourselves is what the struggle for power and resources is all about. As Harvey puts it, "[I]t is hard to discuss the politics of identity, multiculturalism, 'otherness' and 'difference' in abstraction from material circumstances and from political projects" (Harvey 1993: 41).

Yet, one faces a specific logic here which is slowly but surely replacing the old meanings of terrorism with new ones. As shown, terrorism as an idea is a very powerful one, and it gets appropriated and exploited in different ways. We end up with phrases like the "war on terror" that invite conceptual incoherence and cloud the ability of the public to think and act. And what one sees globally, not only in the former Yugoslav states, is a continuing attraction of specific belonging that reasserts the mythical dichotomy between the Christian and Islamic worlds. In a global context, the events of 9/11 have exercised a radically conservative influence. The Serbian discourse of a war against Muslims follows an American "war on terror" and evokes a Manichean theological mindset that divides the world into a battle of good and evil, and takes for granted that one's own side is good. This simplistic, moralizing, and absolutist doctrine is similar to the discourse of the Bush administration (Kellner 2002: 153; cf. Stochetti, chapter 12). It is absolutist to assume that one's enemy is evil and must be destroyed, and to privilege military action. It is also opportunistic, allowing one to determine that the enemy of the moment is a part of a matrix of evil that requires destruction.

Thus, the above informants' discourse was not original; they drew on contemporary images of terrorism and understandings of Serbia's place in the global world. After all, one needs to stress the role of larger political, economic and ideological forces in the appropriation and (re)production of a specific meaning. Also, the imagining of nations through the construction of discourses of belonging is also a place-based process. For example, different countries are often represented as Western in a process of democratization, and Europeanization, while attempting to emphasize their modern, liberal, democratic nature. Discourses of place in Serbia involve a rewritten version of global, national and local histories which reject or contest the former period. However, one needs to understand the current attempts to revise history in all parts of Europe – all these attempts coincide with a much more radical revisionism of the Second World War times. Clearly, the issue of dealing with the past is not peculiar to only Serbia, but to the political, social and cultural frustrations which accompanied, for example, German unification that have exacerbated the confrontation between German and non-German (foreigners) views of cultural identity and citizenship (see Habermas 1994).

Further, in a larger sense, the new global focus on terrorism made it possible for the Serbs to rearticulate the imagery of enemies and victims. In this reading, Serbian wars against the Muslims are now largely interpreted as the war against terrorism. Perhaps the anti-Muslim attitudes (claimed to be anti-terrorist ones) are to a considerable degree the result of a Serbian project to improve its international image. Thus, in the desire to resist and negotiate the country's compromised international image, Serbia has employed the antiterrorism discourse that is actually a reincarnated Kosovo discourse. Our informants seek to imply parallels between the war in Bosnia and the global war on terror. What our informants are retelling us, has perhaps been a deeply rooted, and a repeated myth about the Serbs as guardians of the Western spaces. Serbs seek to reposition and reassure their histories and continue to see themselves as the last line of defense of Christian Europe against the fundamentalist danger embodied in Muslims. They have deployed discourses of the past as truth claims centered around their role as the "defense walls of Christianity." This not only recalls past events or myths, but also becomes the contemporary site of contestation.

Thus, a discourse of "anti-terrorism" has been manipulated to justify violent political actions and past crimes. The respondents' accounts of the war in Bosnia and Kosovo paint Kosovar Albanians as terrorists, either by accusing them directly or through unquestioning reports of Serb accounts. The discourse links alleged Albanian terrorism to religious fanaticism and suggests a threat to democracy and civilization itself. The concept of terrorism, so depicted, is a part of the political undercurrent of any discussion of intervention in Kosovo.

The discourse of terrorism, with which popular consciousness is assailed, deflects attention away from a critical examination of the past. Yet, the employment of the "anti-terrorist discourse" is a rather contradictory one in its rewriting of the past. Overall, the interviews with our informants reflect the ambivalence of this relationship towards the violent 1990s. The discourse of "fighting terrorism" provides the respondents with an excuse for the wars in Bosnia and Kosovo. Some of

our informants, while discussing Serbian geographical, historical, cultural and political positions, would claim that in the Serbian perception, the battle in Kosovo
in 1389 is not seen as a Serbian defeat, but represents a Serbian sacrifice to prevent
the Turks from conquering Europe. The same myth reappears nowadays in a new
form: if once Serbia was protecting Europe from Turks, today Serbia is protecting
Europe from the terrorists. In light of the new global anti-terrorist discourse, there
are attempts in Serbia to employ and exploit the global anti-terrorist agenda to
reassure themselves and the world of their importance.

The discourse clustering around the memories of Serbian victimhood forms
an analytically connected cycle of Serbian national discourse. In this politics of
memory, the symbolic is firmly built upon a new kind of vision. From such discourse, it is clear that in the context of post 9/11 events, new kinds of rewriting of
the past are emerging as a synthesis of anti-terrorism discourse on the one hand
and scapegoat ideologies on the other. However, to conclude, we do not wish to
suggest here that the above processes of re-writing and re-imagining the mode of
society are taking place only in the former Yugoslav countries. In the USA, for
example, the processes of rewriting the past and present involve an identity transformation, the refashioning of an individual citizen that involves designing a particular type of a society (see more in Andrejevic 2004).

The Serbian discourse was by no means original. Because G.W. Bush's "war on
terror" discourse is simplistic, moralizing, and absolutist (Kellner 2002), it gets
appropriated and exploited in different ways by different global actors. What one
sees globally is the ongoing appropriation of this discourse into local contexts. The
Serbian informants' discourse is not the only case. Different nations are increasingly deploying the terms of a particular type of discursive exclusion – exclusion
based on belonging to the "war on terror." In Russia, for example, the discourse of
"the war on Chechen terrorists" was recontextualized in the context of the presidential election (Tishkov 2004). Research in Central and Eastern Europe similarly
shows how paranoid nationalistic discourses become part of more mainstream
discourses – and how they continue to be organized around similar binary oppositions. Milica Bakić-Hayden and Robert M. Hayden highlight several statements of
Slovenian and Croatian public figures to demonstrate how they were involved in
constructing a chain of "nesting Orientalisms", claiming "a privileged 'European'
status for some groups in the country while condemning others as 'Balkan' or
'Byzantine', hence non-European and Other" (Bakić Hayden and Hayden 1992: 5).
Furthermore, as Erjavec points out, Slovene elites also appropriated and deployed
the "war on terror" discourse during the process of EU and NATO integration –
(re)joining Europe – so as to re-imagine their own Slovene identity as belonging
to "the right", Western side of the European collective imagination (Erjavec 2002;
see also Volcic 2005). Similar strategies are enlisted by Croatian political elites

when they construct an image of their own European identity on the basis of differentiating it from the Serbs who are portrayed as unable to understand Western Catholic civilization, since they belong to the Orthodox collective spirit (Buden 2002; Žižek 1997). The Croatian attempt to differentiate itself from Serbs is reinforced by a call for the creation of "defense walls of Catholicity" (while the Serbs see themselves as "defense walls of Christianity.") Thus, all those elites use a discursive strategy of orientalism (Said 1978), which Bakić-Hayden (1995) defined as "a subjective practice by which all ethnic groups define the 'Other' as 'East' of them" (919). A struggle among Slovene, Croatian and Serb elites to define the prevailing meaning of 9/11 represents an ongoing attempt to shape a specific sense of belonging to a "civilized, European/Christian/Catholic" world, and to frame the meaning of being a "Slovenian", a "Croatian" or "Serb" and thus the boundaries of "acceptable" Slovene-ness, Croatian-ness, Serbian-ness. Namely, for any group to be identified as a group, it must be differentiated from all others, locking up identity and difference in a sort of dialectic. Importantly, these socially constructed entities create cohesion through discourses that invoke common cultural codes and experiences. So, at one level of analysis, the degree of internal differentiation of one entity (nation, culture) becomes insignificant compared to the degree of difference that exists in relation to another entity. Internal differences are glossed over in the face of a common enemy.

Notes

1.   It is important to note here that neither the West nor the East exist as absolute terms but are conceptualized in relation to each other. They are continually redefined by specific histories. In this sense, we need to get away from seeing the East and West (The Balkans/Western Europe) as fixed locations. The inside/outside discussions actually help to conceal the mutual dependency within the relationship, that is, that the "West" needs an "East" as other, in order to identify itself.

2.   In the year 1054, the Christian world was divided into Orthodox and Catholic. The Serbs adopted Orthodoxy, while the Croats and Slovenes stayed on the side of Rome, under Habsburg rule until the collapse of the Habsburg Monarchy in 1918. Serbia and the rest of the Balkans were under Turkish rule from the 16th century, until 1867.

3.   See Volcic (2006) for more on the public deployment of the concept "civil society."

4.   We accept the discursively based definition of national identity of Wodak et al (1999): "If a nation is an imagined community and at the same time a mental construct, an imaginary complex of ideas containing at least the defining elements of collective unity and equality; of boundaries and autonomy, then this image is real to the extent that one is convinced of it, one believes in it and identifies with it emotionally. The question of how this imaginary community reaches the minds of those who are convinced of it is easy to answer: it is constructed and conveyed in

discourse, predominately in narratives of national culture. National identity is thus the product of discourse" (44–45).

5.   See Hutcheson et al (2004) and Domke (2004) for discussions on rising patriotism and Muslim-phobia in the USA after 9/11.

6.   Ilic (2004) attempts to unveil why and how the majority of Western media shaped a stereotypical and biased image of the Serbs. Ilic offers an historical analysis of misinterpreting and misrepresenting Serbia in Western media. He claimed that Western media discourse created the "evil Serbs" in order to justify international (military) policies resolving the Yugoslav crisis. He writes, "the discourse, although implicitly, also served to arrange social and political spaces in countries [which] sought to stop the Yugoslav wars (p. 2)."

7.   Re-telling the story of Kosovo poses many serious problems for any researcher. It appears to be one of those stories that helps to constitute and reshape the society; and its status presently occupies historians of the conflict, politicians, and the public alike. It has to be emphasized that disputes over Kosovo do not remain isolated within the Academy, but instead entail broader political struggles over the meaning of the past, and the shaping of the future. The problem of Kosovo has generally been subjected to simplistic interpretations, fabrications, and mystifications by all sides involved.

8.   The Western media images we mostly see today of people like Osama bin Laden and his followers riding horses with turbans on their heads and rugged mountains or cave entrances in the background certainly validate the above arguments and render them more convincing. However, in the absence of a contextual understanding of Islam, Muslims and their religion are often posited as anti-modern. Another problem of this kind of stereotypical depiction lies in how some scholars simplify their explanation of Muslims by lumping them all into one homogeneous category whose beliefs are always predicted by their submission to Allah. It is the insistence to overlook the complex process in which Islam is interpreted, reinterpreted, and negotiated beyond the highly visible expressions of religious extremism which represents only a fraction of Muslims worldwide that is highly problematic, yet so powerful.

9.   However, important to note here is that it is Western academic works, such as Huntington's *Clash of Civilizations* (1997), or Barber's *Jihad vs. McWorld* (1995), that aggravate this image of Islam as completely removed from the world of democracy and modernity. Barber reduces the world to two extremes in which Islam is the antithesis of anything and everything related to the West. Muslims today live in the Middle East, parts of Asia, North and sub-Saharan Africa as well as in large concentration in non-Muslim countries in Europe, the United States, and Australia. This kind of cultural diversity is rarely invoked in the recent public debates that populate discussions of a unified Islamic civilization.

References

Andrejevic, M. 2004. *Reality TV: The Work of Being Watched*. Boulder: Rowman and Littlefield.

Bakic-Hayden M. 1995. "Nesting Orientalism: The case of former Yugoslavia." *Slavic Review* 54: 917–931.

Bakic-Hayden, M. and Hayden, R. 1992. "Orientalist variations on the theme 'Balkans': Symbolic geography in Yugoslav cultural politics since 1987." *Slavic Review* 51:1–15.

Bailey, Y.F. and Chermak, S. 2003. "Introduction." In *Media Representation of September 11*, S. Chermak, F.Y. Bailey and M. Brown (eds.), 1–14. Wesport: Praeger.

Balibar, E. and Wallerstein, I. 1991. *Race, Nation, Class. Les Identites Ambigues*. Paris: Editions La Decouverte.

Barber, B. 1995. *Jihad vs. McWorld*. New York: Ballantine.

Barker, M. 1981. *The New Racism*. London: Junction Books.

Bourdieu, P. 1977. *Outline of a Theory of Practice*. Cambridge: Cambridge University Press.

Bucholtz, M. and Hall, K. 2004. "Language and identity." In *A Companion to Linguistic Anthropology*, A. Duranti (ed.). Malden, MA: Blackwell.

Buden, B. 2000. "Europe is a whore." In *Media and War*, N. Skopljanac Brunner, S. Gredelj, A. Hodžić and B. Krištofić (eds.), 53–62. Zagreb: Centre for Transition and Civil Society Research.

Chouliaraki, L. 2005. "Introduction: The soft power of war: Legitimacy and community in Iraq war discourses." *Journal of Language and Politics* 4: 1–10.

Debeljak, A. 2002, June 8. "European forms of belonging: A view from Slovenia." *Eurozine*. Available: http://www.eurozine.com/article/2002–08–06-debeljak-en.html

Domke, D. 2004. *God Willing? Political Fundamentalism in the White House, the 'War on Terror' and the Echoing Press*. New York: Pluto Press.

Edwards, J. 2004. "After the fall." *Discourse and Society* 15: 155–184.

Erjavec, K. 2002. "September 11. Media Construction of Risk Discourse: Critical Discourse Analysis." *MediaJournal* 4: 19–31.

Erjavec, K. 2003. "Media construction of identity through moral panics: discourse of immigration in Slovenia." *Journal of Ethnic and Migration Studies* 1: 83–102.

Fairclough, N. 1992. *Discourse and Social Change*. Cambridge: Polity Press.

Fairlough, N. 1995. *Critical Discourse Analysis: The Critical Study of Language*. London: Longman.

Fairclough, N. 2003. *Analysing Discourse: Textual Analysis for Social Research*. London: Routledge.

Fairclough, N. 2005. "Blair's contribution to elaborating a new 'doctrine of international community'" *Journal of Language and Politics* 4: 41–63.

Geertz, C. 1973. *The Interpretation of Cultures*. New York: Basic Books.

Goldsworthy, V. 1998. *Inventing Ruritania: The Imperialism of the Imagination*. New Haven: Yale University Press.

Graham, P., Keenan, T. and Down, A. 2004. "A call to arms at the end of history: a discourse-historical analysis of George W. Bush's declaration of war on terror". *Discourse and Society* 15:199–222.

Habermas, J. 1994. *The Past as Future*. Cambridge: Polity Press.

Hall, S. 1989. *Ideologie, Kultur, Medien: Neue Rechte, Rassismus*. Hamburg: Argument.

Hammond, A. 2005. "The danger zone of Europe: Balkanism between the Cold War and 9/11." *European Journal of Cultural Studies* 8(2): 135–154.

Hannerz, U. 1996. *Transnational Connections*. London, Routledge.

Harvey, D. 1993. *The Condition of Postmodernity*. Oxford: Blackwell.

Huntington, S. 1993. "The Clash of Civilizations?" *Foreign Affairs* 72:3.

Huntington S. 1997. *The Clash of Civilizations and the Remaking of the World Order*. New York: Touchstone.

Hutcheson, J., Billeaudeaux, A., Domke, D. and Garland, P. 2004. "U.S. national identity, political elites, and a patriotic press following September 11." *Political Communication* 21: 27–51.

ICG. International Crisis Group. 2001, 9 November. "bin Laden and the Balkans". Report no. 119. Available: http://www.crisisweb.org.

Ilic, D. 2004. "Politics of identity as a threat". *Eurozine*: 1–12. Available: http://www.eurozine. com/article/2004–04–15-ilic-en.html.

IWPR, Institute for War and Peace Reporting. 2001, 28 September. "Macedonian Press 'Expose' Taleban Plot". *Balkan Crisis Report* 284.

Jezernik, B. 2004. *Wild Europe: The Balkans in the Gaze of Western Travellers*. London: SAQI (in association with the Bosnian Institute).

Karim, K.H. 1997. "The Historical Resilience of Primary Stereotypes: Core Images of the Muslim Other". In *The Language and Politics of Exclusion: Others in Discourse*, S. H. Riggins (ed.), 153–82. Thousand Oaks, CA: Sage.

Kaplan, R. 1993. *Balkan Ghosts: A Journey through History*. New York: St, Martin's Press.

Kellner, D. 2002. "September 11, Social Theory and Democratic Politics". *Theory, Culture and Society* 19: 147–159.

Lazar, A. and Lazar, M. 2004. "The discourse of the New World Order: 'Out-casting' the double face of threat." *Discourse and Society* 15: 223–242.

MacDonald, D. 2002. *Balkan Holocausts?* Manchaster: Manchaster University Press.

Malcolm, N. 1996. *Bosnia: A Short History*. London. Papermac.

Mihelj, S. 2004. "The Role of Mass Media in the (Re)Constitution of Nations: The (Re)Constitution of the Slovenian Nation through the Media Representations of the Plebiscite for an Independent Slovenia, Bosnian Refugees and Non-Registered Migration (1990–2001)." Ph.D. diss., Ljubljana Graduate School of the Humanities.

Miles, R. 1994. "Explaining Racism in Contemporary Europe". In *Racism, Modernity and Identity*, A. Rattansi and S. Westwood (eds.), 189–221. Cambridge: Polity Press.

Milosavljevic, O. 2000. "Yugoslavia as a Mistake". In *The Road to War in Serbia*, N. Popov (ed.), Budapest: CEU Press, 10–24.

Morley, D. 1996. "The geography of television: Ethnography, communications, and community". In *The Audience and Its Landscapes*, J. Hay, L. Grossberg, and E. Wartella (eds.), 317–342. Boulder: Westview Press.

Patterson, P. 2003. "On the Edge of Reason: The Boundaries of Balkanism in Slovenian, Austrian, and Italian Discourse." *Slavic Review* 62 (1): 110–141.

Rosaldo, R. 1994. "Cultural Citizenship and Educational Democracy." *Cultural Anthropology* 3: 402- 411.

Said, E. 1978. *Orientalism*. New York: Pantheon.

Said, E. 1997. *Covering Islam*. New York: Vintage Books.

Skrbiš, Z. 1999. *Long-distance Nationalism: Diasporas, Homelands and Identities*. Aldershot: Ashgate.

Stolcke, V. 1995. "Talking Culture: New Boundaries, New Rhetorics of Exclusion in Europe." *Current Anthropology* 1: 1–24.

Šabec, K. 2004. "Na dnu Evrope ali na vrhu Balkana". *Dialogi* 11–12: 49–64.

Skjelsbaek, I. and Smith, D. (eds.) 2001. *Gender, Peace and Conflict*. London: Sage Publications.

Taylor M. and Kent M.L. 2000. "Media Transitions in Bosnia. From Propagandistic Past to Uncertain Future." *Gazette*, 62(5): 355–378.

Tishkov V. 2004. *Chechnya: Life in a War-Torn Society*. San Francisco: University of California Press.

Todorova, M. 1997. *Imagining the Balkans*. New York/Oxford: Oxford University Press.

Van de Port, M. 1999, "It takes a Serb to know a Serb: uncovering the roots of obstinate otherness in Serbia". *Critique of Anthropology* 1: 7–30.

Van Dijk, T. 1995. "Ideological Discourse Analysis." *New Courant* 4: 135–136.

Van Dijk, T. 2005. "War rhetoric of a little ally: Political implicatures and Aznar's legitimation of the war in Iraq." *Journal of Language and Politics* 4: 65–91.

Van Leeuwen, T. 1996. "The presentation of social actors". In *Texts and Practice: Readings in Critical Discourse Analysis*, C.R. Caldas-Coulthard and M. Coulthard (eds.), 32–70. London: Routledge.

Verdery, K. and Burawoy, M. 1999. *Uncertain Transition: Ethnographies of Change in the Postsocialist World*. Lanham, MD: Rowman & Littlefield.

Volcic, Z. 2005. "The Machine that Creates Slovenes: The role of Slovene Public Broadcasting in re-affirming the Slovene national identity." *National Identities Journal* 7 (3), pp. 287–308.

Volcic, Z. 2006. "'They are all anti-war profiteers!' Contesting Civil Society Landscapes in Serbia." Paper presented at ICA, Dresden, June 1–23.

Wodak, R., de Cillia, R., Reisigl, M. and Liebhart, K. 1999. *The Discursive Construction of National Identity*. Edinburgh: Edinburgh University Press.

Wodak, R. 1996 "The Genesis of Racist Discourse in Austria". In *Texts and Practices: Readings in Critical Discourse Analysis*, C. R. Caldas-Coulthard and M. Caoulthard (eds.), 107–128. London: Routledge.

Wolff, L. 1994. *Inventing Eastern Europe: The Map of Civilization on the Mind of the Enlightenment*. Stanford: Stanford University Press.

Woodward, S. 1995. *Balkan Tragedy. Chaos and Dissolution After the Cold War*. Washington. D.C.: The Brookings Institution.

Zirojevic, O. 2000. "Kosovo in the Collective Memory". In *The Road to War in Serbia*, N. Popov (ed.), 189–211. Budapest: CEU Press.

Žižek, S. 1997. "The Enjoyment of Submission and Slavery". *Naša Borba* 5:1.

CHAPTER 11

"Fear of terror attack persists"

Constructing fear in reports on terrorism by international news agencies[1]

Maija Stenvall

Introduction

Major terrorist attacks like the one in Madrid in March 2004 tend to "fuel", "renew", "spark", "stoke" or "trigger" fears, just to mention some of the expressions that are widely used in news agency reports. It is not only new attacks that bring the issue of "heightened" fears into the news; an official warning of unspecified but "credible" threats or the anniversary of the September 11 attacks may call for extra security measures, too. Overall, the emotion of fear and other related emotions, such as worry and concern, have had a prominent role in terrorism discourse since the September 11 attacks in 2001 and the ensuing U.S. led 'War on Terror.'

My focus is on the construction of fear in the dispatches of two big international news agencies, the American AP and the British Reuters. The data are collected from their wires in 2002 and in 2004. Researchers of news media (see e.g. Hartley 1982; Fowler 1991; White 1998, 2003) have shown that although journalists strive for objectivity, factuality, and neutrality, and often themselves are convinced of their success in this, news reporting is, in White's (2003) words, "necessarily subjective ... conditioned by a complex set of ideologically-determined assumptions, beliefs and expectations about the nature of the social world" (61). The global news agencies AP and Reuters, as "leading news suppliers"(cf. Tunstall 1999: 191), share an extra burden of responsibility; and in their editorial policy statements, published on their websites, both stress the ideals of being "accurate" and "balanced." Further, AP sees as its "mission" to provide "distinctive news services of the highest quality, reliability and objectivity" (Associated Press 2004), and Reuters says that it is "committed to reporting the facts" (Reuters 2004).

Emotions are, basically, subjective experiences, something that is hidden in people's mind. Thus, while it is an uncontestable fact that many people fear terrorism, the actual reporting of that fear involves a great deal of interpretation on the part of the writing journalist. In this sense, we can see the media involved in the on-going process of constructing a press narrative around the fear of terrorism. Press narratives, according to Toolan (1988), "construe and reconstrue newsworthy facts and events" (237). Toolan also notes that "changes of emphasis, over time, are very likely" (237). The narrative of fear of terrorism in news agency reports indeed shows some – at least temporary – "changes of emphasis" when the reports of the first and the third anniversary of the September 11 attacks are compared. At the same time, as will be shown, the basic narrative of fear remains unchanged and very much alive, affecting the alleged factuality of news agency discourse.

Defining fear

While interest in the study of emotions before the 1970s was primarily limited to the fields of psychology and philosophy, today it attracts researchers from several other academic disciplines: linguistics, sociology, anthropology, political science and neuroscience (e.g. Abu-Lughod & Lutz 1990; Berezin 2002; Tudor 2003).

Given the vast literature on emotions, it is understandable that scholars have difficulties in agreeing on what an emotion is (cf. Berezin 2002: 37). Many of them have sought to identify the so-called 'basic', 'primary' or 'fundamental' emotions, with fear appearing on every such list (cf. Kövecses 2000: 4; Tudor 2003: 241). Psychologist Robert Plutchik (1980) defines emotions as "the end results of a complex cognitive process" (15). His table of "the complex, probabilistic sequence of events involved in the development of an emotion" (16) includes eight primary emotions. The following sequence is presented for the emotion of fear: "*stimulus event*: threat; *inferred cognition*: danger; *feeling*: fear, terror; *behavior*: running or flying away; *effect*: protection."

Plutchik's sequence of events, as such, presupposes that fear is aroused by a relatively *immediate* threat. In regard to terrorism fears, it could apply, for instance, to a hostage situation. But Plutchik's 'frame' for fear could also be widened to concern the public warnings of threats of terrorist attacks that are common in the media, and the seemingly natural "protection effect" of such a mediated danger: the increased security measures. Fear focuses always on the future, on the negative events that may take place; but, as Tudor (2003) points out, the flexibility of its "temporal dimension" is an important factor in that "fear experienced and articulated over an extended period is likely to be more open to socially patterned processes of reinforcement and routinisation" (241). This is a vital aspect in the study of terrorism fears, too.

The Appraisal framework, which is an extension of M.A.K. Halliday's Systemic Functional Grammar, offers a linguistic model for analyzing emotions.[2] Appraisal is divided into three interacting systems: attitude, engagement and graduation. One of the three sub-systems of attitude, called affect, deals with "resources construing emotion" (Martin 1997: 18). Table 1 below compares the emotions of fear, worry and concern according to variables outlined in the Appraisal framework (cf. Martin 1997: 20–23; 2000: 148–151).

Table 1. Evaluating fear, worry and concern

variable	fear	worry	concern
positive/negative	negative	negative	negative(+positive)
scale of intensity	high	'median'	low
realis/irrealis	irrealis	irrealis	irrealis

As Table 1 shows, these emotions would all belong to the affect group of "irrealis", which here means that these feelings refer to the future; the feared state has not yet been realized (or may not be realized at all, especially if the fear that is felt is irrational). Fear and worry are negative, while concern could have a positive streak in it. Concern could mean that the person in question has an interest in taking some positive action in order to remove the source of concern (cf. Coston 1998). Of these three emotions, fear has the highest intensity, worry has 'median', and concern has low intensity.

Data

My corpus consists of about 6,000 "pages" (over 2.7 million words), collected in several batches during 2002 and 2004 from the news wires of AP and Reuters. I have mostly used "terror" or "terrorist" as the search word. However, one file of about 500 pages has been gathered with "fear" as the search word, and another file of about 1,000 pages contains all incoming dispatches for 24 hours from both AP and Reuters (i.e. one hour each day on 24 consecutive days).

To get an overview of the words denoting the emotion of fear (*fear/fears, worry/worries, concern/concerns*), and of the context of these words in my data, I have made use of computerized concordance lines. Thus in the analysis below, I sometimes refer to (relative) frequencies of some word or expression, although my focus is on the qualitative analysis. I want to stress that the quantitative findings should be taken as merely suggestive.

In fact, the very nature of news agency reporting would pose difficulties for reliable quantitative analysis. First, the flow of reporting in the global news wires is continuous, and the total volume of the reports, even for one day, is huge. Second, unlike newspaper stories, news agency reports cannot be regarded as separate unities. A major event, such as a terrorist attack, generates several dispatches during one day. These can be, for example, short, successive messages, each giving new information; or longer summaries, repeating much of what has been reported earlier. The stories start with a keyword slug line[3], followed by a headline and a lead, but the beginning of a dispatch also contains a wealth of other information which does not belong to the story itself: "topic codes" (cf. Wood 1995), notes to the receiving media, and so on. This special feature of news agency reporting would have to be taken into account when counting words or pages.

In this paper I focus on the nouns denoting the emotion of fear: *fear, fears, worry, worries, concern,* and *concerns.* Table 2 shows the distribution of these six nouns in the data gathered with the search term "terror/terrorist" in 2002 and 2004 (about 4,500 pages; the corpus of AP being much larger than that of Reuters).[4] Table 3, for comparison, gives the number of the occurrences in the data collected by using the search term "fear" in 2004 (about 500 pages; the corpus of Reuters being now larger than that of AP).

Table 2. *Fear* words in "terror/terrorist" -files

	fear	fears	worry	worries	concern	concerns
AP	140	178	12	29	180	159
Reuters	60	137	5	19	76	91
Total	200	315	17	48	256	250

Table 3. *Fear* words in "fear"-files

	fear	fears	worry	worries	concern	concerns
AP	67	153	1	11	21	33
Reuters	62	353	14	56	51	70
Total	129	506	15	67	72	103

The tables suggest that *worry* is the least popular of these six words. It has to be noted, though, that contrary to the other words shown in the two tables, *worry* appears more often as a verb than as a noun. Nearly the whole "fear"-file was collected in March 2004, just after the major terrorist attacks in Madrid on March 11. Therefore, as could be expected, the *fear* words in Table 3, too, are almost exclusively connected to terrorism discourse. Especially in Reuters dispatches, a major part of those "fears" – and "worries" and "concerns" – come from financial and economic reports. The "markets" have naturally reacted to the attacks, and to the news that there could be an al Qaeda connection; there are also fears of new attacks that could affect the global economy or "could disrupt oil supplies" (Reuters, March 19, 2004, report), and so on.

Above all, the comparison between the two types of files shows evidence of the special characteristic of news agency discourse that was discussed above. A newsworthy event – such as the Madrid attacks – gives rise to an abundance of reports in which whole paragraphs from earlier dispatches tend to be repeated, and this may lead to an over-representation of some words or expressions.

Tools for analysis

In my analysis, I draw on three central concepts of M.A.K. Halliday's Systemic Functional Grammar: *nominalization*, *grammatical metaphor* and *transitivity*.

Following Halliday (cf. 1994: 352), I take the nouns *fear*, *worry* and *concern* to be nominalizations and, moreover, grammatical metaphors. The grammatical systems of nominalization, grammatical metaphor and transitivity are, in fact, intertwined. Nominalization, according to Halliday (1994) is "the single most powerful resource for creating grammatical metaphor" (352). In a grammatical metaphor, meaning is "construed in a different way by means of a different grammatical construction" (Hasselgård 2000). When we 'unpack' a nominalized grammatical metaphor, trying to reveal the 'original' construction, we often find a process with participants, which then can be analyzed by looking into transitivity.

Transitivity is a semantic concept belonging to the *ideational metafunction* of Functional Grammar. The meaning of the "clause as representation" is essential in the transitivity system, which "construes the world of experience into a manageable set of PROCESS TYPES" (Halliday 1994: 106). In our discourse, we choose between various options of transitivity, and "the choice we make – better, the choice made by the discourse – indicates our point of view, [and so] is ideologically significant" (Fowler 1991: 171).

The grammar of the clause consists of three elements of the process: the process itself (typically realized by a verbal group), participants in the process, and circumstances associated with the process. The main types of process are: *material processes: processes of doing; mental processes: processes of sensing;* and *relational processes: processes of being* (Halliday 1994: 107–138). The central participant in material processes – "the one that does the deed" (109) – is called an Actor, and the second (optional) participant is a Goal. Another term for the latter function is

Patient, "meaning one that 'suffers' or 'undergoes' the process" (110). The participant roles for relational processes are Token and Value (or Carrier and Attribute) (124–129), and for mental processes Senser and Phenomenon (117–119). My analysis also refers to a fourth type of process; verbal processes, where the main participants are Sayer, Receiver, Verbiage and Target (140–142).

Nominalization transforms processes (verbs) or properties (adjectives) into nouns after metaphorical rewording (352). The shift from 'process' or 'property' to 'entity' (a 'thing') also means that the nominalized word now can function as a participant in processes, or as a part of a prepositional phrase (cf. Halliday 1998: 197; Fairclough 1995: 112). From the point of view of news agency discourse and its alleged factuality, it is important to note that nominalization is "inherently, potentially mystificatory" (Fowler 1991: 82). In addition to obscuring the participant roles, it can leave open the tense of the verb (of the original process), the type of the process, etc.

Let us consider two nouns – nominalizations/grammatical metaphors – that have a central role in terrorism discourse (cf. Stenvall 2003): *attack* and *threat*. When a reporter writes, for example, that "the attack killed 100 persons," the original material process (of attacking) has become an Actor in a new material process (of killing), and the real perpetrators may remain hidden. The 'unpacking' of the nominalization "attack" would result in 'X attacked/has attacked.' But often, in terrorism discourse, journalists speak of "new" or "future" or "possible" attacks, i.e. of attacks that have not yet happened (or may never happen). The grammatical metaphor "an attack" would then be reworded differently: 'X may attack/will attack.' When the verb *threaten* is nominalized into *threat*, even the type of the process can become ambiguous. For example, *terrorist threat* (see Stenvall 2003: 376) could – depending on the context – mean either 'terrorists are/pose a threat' or 'terrorists make (utter) threats.' In other words, the original process could be either relational or verbal.

Since the major part of my analysis focuses on the strategies news agency journalists use for blurring their own 'voice' and the responsibility of the news actors, I have also chosen one tool from Toolan's "basic toolkit" for analyzing political discourse (Toolan 1988: 238). In addition to the aspects of nominalization/grammatical metaphor and transitivity, I look into a linguistic feature which Toolan calls "[s]uppletion of agentless passives by intransitive clauses" (239). This feature refers to "clauses with the semantic pattern of an affected participant followed by the process that participant has experienced" (239), i.e. the process expressed by an intransitive verb. We can say, for example, that "a bomb went off," instead of saying "a bomb was detonated;" or that "the prize went to X," instead of stating that "the prize was awarded to X," and so on. A common feature to the "important lexicogrammatical systems" included in Toolan's "toolkit" (which also includes nominalization and transitivity), is that all of them are systems "where choice of formulation, or 'slant' is possible" (238).

Constructing collective fear on september 11 anniversaries

Emotions are fundamentally individual experiences. Therefore, speaking of a group emotion, according to Kemper (2002), only means that "some aggregate of individuals is feeling something that is sufficiently alike to be identified as the common emotion of that aggregate" (62). Commemorations, like those that have been held on September 11 every year since 2001, can be seen as ritual action generating collective emotions, or as what sociologists call *communities of feeling* (see e.g. Berezin 2002: 44–45). However, such solemn ceremonies are likely to foreground other emotions than fear: feelings of common sorrow, solidarity, maybe anger. Furthermore, the physiological signs of fear are not for everybody to see (unless the fear is extreme, for example panic), in the way tears could stand for sadness, and holding hands for solidarity.

Given the immense effects of the September 11 attacks, it is not surprising that September 11 anniversaries differ from other commemorations in the magnitude of the ceremonies. The events marking the first anniversary of the attacks in 2002 were extensively covered by both AP and Reuters, and in addition to the commemorations in the United States, the reports focus on reactions all over the world, and on threats and security. The solemnity and the emotionally charged atmosphere of the day are reflected in the writing style, as examples (1) and (2) from AP show.

(1)   A cascade of memorial events marked a moment whose echoes still resound from New York to Afghanistan, and everywhere in between -- a moment that even a year later left many transfixed by the horror, burdened by sadness, plagued by fears.
It was a day of jitters and heightened security. Officials issued a "code orange" – the second-highest level of alert -- and warned that terrorists might strike again. (AP, Sept 11, 2002, report)

(2)   And overshadowing memorials was a now familiar fear. Citing "credible and specific" threats, some U.S. embassies in Asia, Africa and the Middle East were closed, and U.S. military bases and embassies in Europe enforced tightened security. (AP, Sept 11, 2002, report)

The emotion of fear in these examples can be conceptualized as being collective. Example (2) reports on world reaction, especially on the feelings of Americans working abroad, but it does not specify whose fear has led to tightened security measures. Neither does the reporter in example (1) define to whom the word 'many' refers. In contrast to these abstract fears, the grief of the ordinary people participating in the U.S. memorials is usually described in a more concrete manner; as Reuters says in one of its reports in 2002, "many wept seemingly inconsolably" (Sept 11, 2002, report).

Two years later, on September 11, 2004, ceremonies were smaller and "more subdued" (Reuters, Sept 11, 2004, report) than on the two preceding anniversaries. The emotion of sadness still prevailed among the family members of the attack victims in New York, who, according to an AP report (Sept 11, 2004, report), "descended a long ramp into ground zero, sobbing, embracing each other." The mourning is presented as "worldwide", but due to the U.S.-led Iraq war, anger, especially among Muslims, also "runs high" (AP, Sept 11, 2004, report).

The emphasis in the narrative of fear had, at least temporarily, shifted from the US – and the Americans at home and abroad – to other areas, due to the recent school tragedy in Beslan, North Ossetia, and the suicide car bombing outside the Australian Embassy in Jakarta. This was reflected in the keyword slug lines containing two central concepts of the fear frame: threat and security. In September 2002, the following slug lines appear frequently: "ATTACK-ANNIVERSARY-SE-CURITY", "ATTACK-THREAT", "ATTACK-ANNIVERSARY-THREATS" (Reuters) and "SEPT 11-WORLD SECURITY", "SEPT 11-US-ATTACKS-THREATS" (AP). Two years later, in September 2004, no slug lines with THREAT can be found, while SECURITY is still common, especially in Reuters slug lines. The word SECURITY in Reuters reports is included in a variety of combinations. Mostly, though, it is followed by the word INDONESIA, whereas AP has many reports slugged as "RUSSIA-SECURITY."

As we have seen, collective fears in news agency dispatches are mostly presented rather vaguely or they are left implicit so that the reports just speak about "threats" and "security measures" without mentioning the word *fear*. Even if fear as a negative emotion is, undoubtedly, newsworthy,[5] ordinary people's subjective fear is rather seldom described. However, especially in connection with the September 11 anniversaries, people's feelings are often explored through interviews for polls, the results of which then get into the news. In 2002, both AP and Reuters reported on such surveys. Based on the results of four different polls, AP (Sept 11, 2002, report headline) states in a headline: "Poll: Public optimism, patriotism high despite continuing fear of attacks," while in the Reuters headline one day earlier (Sept 10, 2002, report headline), the focus is on the fear: "9/11 – Poll shows Americans fear more attacks." Two years later, in September 2004, AP had made a poll of its own. The headline of an AP report (Sept 9, 2004, report headline) summarizes its results as follows: "Fear of terror attack persists; Sept. 11 memories almost universal."

Polls rely on precise figures, and figures can certainly be regarded as being 'factual.' But as these three headline examples show, the results of polls leave space for interpretation, and the journalist is in a position to choose one particular focus. In September 2004, by making a poll of its own, AP could bring up two newsworthy aspects that otherwise could not be expected to be as visible during this anniversary as one year after the September 11 attacks: the emotions of solidarity and fear. People interviewed for the poll were asked where they were when they learned about the attacks. Collective memory, thus awakened, is likely to produce "a feeling of solidarity," that "we were all there together" (cf. Berezin 2002: 45). In addition, the narrative of the "persisting" fear among the Americans surfaced again, even if major threats at that time were felt to be in other parts of the world.

Blurring responsibility

When analyzing political *news* reports, we have to keep in mind that they are examples of a special kind of political discourse, and as such are affected by values and conventions typical of news writing. For example, the – often unconscious – choices of formulation that news journalists make when they write 'hard news' reports aim at backgrounding their own voice. For that purpose they adopt "a tactic of impersonalisation" (White 1998: 267). As part of this "tactic" they often tend to blur the role of the human agents, as will be shown below.

The first part of this section examines the options of transitivity that news agency journalists have selected in their reports on the fear of terrorism. The second part gives evidence of two linguistic features that also help to obscure the responsibility of news actors in news agency stories, namely, agentless passives and intransitive clauses.

Fear and the options of transitivity

The Reuters headline from Sept 10, 2002, quoted above, gives an example of fear as a mental process:

> (3) **9/11 – Poll shows Americans fear more attacks**

'Fearing' is clearly a process of feeling, and thus "mental" (cf. Halliday 1994: 117); "Americans" who fear are Sensers, and "attacks" are what they fear, i.e. the Phenomenon. It is notable, though, how this simple assertion, in accordance with the impersonal style of 'hard news' reports (White 1998), is attributed to the results of the "poll", and not to the writing journalist.

In examples (4) and (5), fear has been nominalized:

(4) But the police chief in charge of securing the northern city [Ayodhya, India] said his biggest fear was a terrorist attack. (Reuters, March 11, 2002, report)

(5) "…The bombs are our biggest fear. If I want to go to the market [in Baghdad], I get scared." (Reuters, March 18, 2004, report)

The noun *fear* has become a Value, a participant in an identifying relational process. In other words, "a terrorist attack" and "the bombs" (Tokens in the process) are identified as (his, our) "biggest fear." If the grammatical metaphors – "his/our biggest fear" – in the clauses were 'unpacked' into a mental process, we could say, for instance: 'a terrorist attack is what he fears most'/'The bombs are what we fear most.' Despite the nominalization of fear, the Sensers and the Phenomenon of the original mental processes are easily recognized in these examples. But just as in example (3), the word "fear" here occurs in an attributed clause: in an indirect and a direct quote, respectively.

In unattributed statements, it is typical of news journalists to present emotions as "affectual states" or "as simply reflecting reality" (White 1998: 271, 272) so that the connection between the emotion itself and the one who feels it is blurred. News agency journalists, in my data, speak more frequently of (indefinite) *fears* than of *fear* in the singular. These fears – or fear – are mostly participants in material processes. The events that are reported on sometimes take place "amid", "on" or "over" fears; in other words, fear has become a part of the "circumstantial element" of a material process (Halliday 1994: 149–161), only loosely tied to the Actor of the process in question. Similarly, when reporters write that terrorist attacks, threats, or warnings, etc., "stoke", "spark", "heighten", "raise", "renew" or "revive" fears, putting the emotion in the role of a Goal, it is not always clear whose fears are referred to; at the same time, the existence of fears is presupposed, taken for granted.

The following example, which shows "fears" as a Goal, includes as many as seven nominalizations altogether (nominalizations are marked in italics):

(6) Any *indication* that al-Qaida or other Islamic terrorist groups were behind the *bombings* stokes renewed *fears* about the *sophistication* of international *terrorism* and potentially intensifies the *fallout* on global markets from the Madrid *attacks*. (AP, March 11, 2004, report).

The nominalizations in this sentence make the language extremely imprecise. If we look at the nominalizations as grammatical metaphors and try to 'unpack' them, we find several processes 'hidden' underneath. The participant roles in these processes, accordingly, become obscure. The Actor of the material process is a rather vague nominalization "indication", which is said to be responsible for potentially intensifying "the fallout on global markets," and not only for stoking the fears. Finally, who are the Sensers of the original mental process of fearing? Since the reporter speaks about the possible negative effects that the "indication" could have on global markets, we can deduce that those who fear are primarily the investors acting on those markets. What is feared – the Phenomenon of the original mental process – is not very clear, either. Instead of simply referring to "terrorism", the journalist speaks about its "sophistication." And if we give the role of Sensers to investors, we can further presume that they ultimately fear losing their money because of "the sophistication of international terrorism."

From the point of view of the 'factuality' of news agency reports, the most significant process choice, arguably, is the one illustrated by the following two examples:

(7) LONDON, Jan 2 (Reuters) –Europe's biggest airline, British Airways, cancelled a London-Washington flight on Friday as security fears grounded a U.S.-bound plane for the seventh time in just over a week. (Reuters, Jan 2, 2004, report lead)

(8) **British Airways flight to Washington delayed, after security concerns stop service two days in a row** (AP, Jan 3, 2004, report headline)

Emotions have become Actors in material processes. In these examples, fears and concerns are premodified by *security*, which is a central concept in the anti-terrorism discourse; in my data it is, by a huge margin, the most popular pre-modifier of these two emotive words. "Security fears" refer to the possibility of 'losing security', but "security concerns" could also mean – more positively – concerns of the authorities for *maintaining* security. As consumers of the present day news media we can figure out that these nominalized fears and concerns do not refer to flight security in general, but, more specifically, to the possibility of terrorist attacks.

The material processes in examples (7) and (8) have, besides an Actor, also an affected participant, a Goal ("a U.S.-bound plane" and "service", respectively). The verbs "grounded" and "stop" are 'transitive' in traditional grammar. In Halliday's words (1994), "some entity 'does' something…'to' some other entity" (110). When the emotions – "fears" and "concerns" – in this way are presented as Actors, the human agents, and their responsibility, remain hidden in the important introductory parts of these news reports: the lead in example (7), and the headline in example (8).

This kind of reporting can be argued to rely on the conventions of news writing (cf. Stenvall forthcoming). The traditional structure of a news report has two main features. Van Dijk (1988: 43) speaks of "relevance organisation in news," and of the *installment* character of topic realization. In other words, the most important – or at least the most newsworthy – piece of information is presented at the beginning of a news story, and the information is delivered discontinuously, in installments, proceeding from general to more specific details. Fears as Actors appear in all parts of news stories, but given these two general principles of news

writing, it is hardly surprising that this kind of material process is popular, especially in the headlines and leads. First, fear as a negative emotion is certainly a
newsworthy 'actor'; and second, it is a general, abstract term, which then can be
specified later. The lead in example (7) gives – besides "fears" – another Actor for
cancellations: British Airways. The specifying details in the reports, from which
examples (7) and (8) have been taken, reveal that the airline has acted on the "advice" of the U.K. government and U.S. authorities.

Nominalization leaves the role of the Senser of the original mental process (of
fearing) unspecified. Who is the one who 'fears' or is 'concerned'? Is it British Airways; or is it those who have given advice to the airlines, the U.K. government and
U.S. authorities? In either case, these officials do not fear for their own security but
for that of the potential flight passengers, which further adds to the ambiguity of
these expressions.

Threats and security – agentless passives and intransitive clauses

As discussed above, the narrative of fear tends to surface in the media on September 11 anniversaries. Even if no fresh attacks are made, there are always new
"warnings" and "threats", causing fear and calling for "stricter security." The warnings and alerts may come from "the U.S. government" or just from "officials", but
often – at the beginning of the news reports in particular – journalists resort to the
use of agentless passives or to intransitive clauses, which obscure the role of human agents. Things just 'happen' or 'are made', as example (9) shows (agentless
passive and semantically intransitive clauses marked in italics):

(9)   *Security boosted* across the world on anniversary of Sept. 11 attacks
      ---
      KUALA LUMPUR, Malaysia (AP) -- *The world went on terror alert* Wednes-
      day, as memories of the Sept. 11 attacks last year intensified fears surrounding
      numerous new but unconfirmed threats.
      U.S. embassies and those of America's closest allies closed in nine countries.
      Police and troops wielding automatic rifles, sometimes backed by armored
      vehicles, patrolled outside diplomatic compounds.
      Jitters about new terrorist attacks also translated into stricter security at airports,
      government and private offices, American social clubs, tourist spots and other
      key *sites that could become targets*. (AP, Sept 11, 2002, report opening)

In this extract, the only human agents are "police and troops," who are "wielding
rifles" and "patrolling." Other Actors that are 'doing' something "'to' some other
entity" (Halliday 1994: 110) in material processes are mental states, "memories"
and "fears", which 'intensify' and 'surround', respectively. Human agents are, of

course, needed for giving a terror alert, and for closing the embassies. The humans could be, for instance, "U.S. authorities", but here the use of constructions with intransitive verbs serves to hide their role. The Actors (grammatical subjects) of these two intransitive clauses – the "world" and the "embassies" – are, semantically, 'affected participants' (cf. Toolan 1988: 239): the world has been alerted, and the embassies have been closed.

At the beginning of the last sentence in example (9), the Actor ("jitters") has undergone the process of being "translated into stricter security." In addition to the intransitive verb, the two nominalizations – "jitters" and "security" – contribute to blurring the identity of the real actors, as well as the cause-effect relationship. Who – which authorities – have been nervous and feared "new terrorist attacks", and who, as a result, have ordered stricter security measures? The hidden 'actors' in the final part of that sentence are easier to retrieve. According to the AP dispatch, security is increased at certain key sites "that could become targets", i.e. *terrorists might attack them.*

Weaker than fear: the emotions of worry and concern

The nouns *fear*, *worry* and *concern* can, broadly speaking, be taken as synonyms. As Tables 2 and 3 suggest, *fear/fears* appears in my data more often than *worry/ worries* or *concern/concerns*. One reason for the popularity of using expressions referring to fear is presumably the fact that as an emotion fear has the highest intensity of the three (cf. Table 1). Thus it is associated with a high degree of *negativity* and, according to Galtung's and Ruge's *news values*, it can be regarded as being more newsworthy than concern or worry.

At the same time, especially in the figures for the files given in Table 2, *concern* and *concerns*, too, have relatively high frequencies, despite their lower intensity. Concern, as mentioned above, differs from fear and worry in being potentially less negative than the other two emotions. But, as Coston (1998) – speaking of the fear of crime – points out, even if 'concern' means that a person is interested in the matter that engages her/his attention, that "does not automatically result in action on the part of the one who is effected [sic]." In example (8), *security concerns* had stopped the flights; the concerns (of authorities?) had resulted in action. In addition to appearing in the (popular) noun phrase *security concerns, concern* is often preceded by the verb *express*, i.e. it functions as a Verbiage in a verbal process. The Sayers in these processes – those who are construed as showing interest in a positive action – are usually politicians, officials, governments, nations, etc.

In example (10) below, "concern" seems to have led to "scattered protests," although the vague language tends to blur the participant roles and the causal relations. This Reuters dispatch is about the commemoration of the first September 11 anniversary in Asia (nominalizations are marked in italics):

(10)   *Fears* mingle with *prayers* on Sept 11 anniversary

SINGAPORE, Sept 11 (Reuters) – Flags flew at half mast, churches offered *prayers* and choirs sang requiems in Asia on Wednesday as a *wave* of memorial ceremonies for the September 11 dead swept round the world amid *fears* of further *violence*. But *concern* about Washington's international role one year after the deadly suicide *hijackings* intruded on the collective *remembrance*, with scattered *protests* in a handful of Asian cities by opponents of a new war on Iraq. (Reuters, Sept 11, 2002, report opening)

In September 2002, the United States and its allies were looking for proof of weapons of mass-destruction in Iraq, and the threat of a possible U.S. attack generated hard feelings and protests in Asia. Both AP and Reuters took note of this discord in the otherwise worldwide sympathy towards Americans on the September 11 anniversary. It is notable, though, how the Reuters journalist resorts to several nominalizations and noun phrases to hide the criticism of the possible U.S. plans to attack Iraq, which the reporter calls "Washington's international role." The only 'actor' in the second paragraph is the (weak) emotion of concern, which is presented as "intruding" on another mental state (remembrance). The stronger – and thus more negative – emotion of fear appears in the headline and the lead of the report. Despite the imprecise language, we can deduce that "concern" and "fears" here refer to two different potential causes of 'fearing.' "Fears" are construed as collective emotions, haunting the memorial ceremonies "round the world;" what is feared is "further violence," i.e. new terrorist attacks. At the same time, "concern" of a possible war on Iraq touches only "a handful of Asian cities."

All the three emotions of 'fear' are, in my data, often connected to financial matters, but this feature is especially conspicuous in the case of the word *worries*, which as a noun can seldom be found outside the financial or economic reports. I have chosen one example from each news agency:

(11)   Tokyo stocks closed lower, with tech stocks hit by concerns that security worries would hurt leading economies. Retail and property shares rose as investors bet on Japanese recovery. (Reuters, March 16, 2004, report)

(12)   Investors shop for bargains despite worries about Sept. 11 anniversary

---

NEW YORK (AP) -- Investors smarting from last week's sharp Wall Street decline shopped for bargains Monday, sending stocks higher despite concerns about the upcoming anniversary of the terrorist attacks. (AP, Sept 9, 2002, report opening)

Although worries in examples (11) and (12) are said to be about "security" or the "Sept. 11 anniversary", respectively, they primarily concern the investors' finances. Concerns – whether on "security worries" or "about the upcoming anniversary" – also focus on the looming financial loss. However, the interplay between the words "concerns" and "worries" can be argued to affect the news *rhetoric*. In example (11), the reporter underlines the vulnerability of the economic situation by presenting two negative emotions – concerns and worries – as powerful actors, who "hit" and could "hurt." In example (12), the two words are, in fact, interchangeable; it seems that the journalist has just wanted to avoid tautology with her/his word choice.

Some examples in my data do show clear evidence of the "positive streak" in *concern* (see the section on "Defining fear" above). At the same time, examples of terrorism *fears* and *worries* in news agency reports do not support the common view of worry being some kind of unspecified anxiety and fear being a "response to an *immediate* situation" (Stout 2004; Coston 1998).

Concluding remarks

Furedi (2002) claims that "Western societies are increasingly dominated by a culture of fear" (vii). Fear, according to Furedi, has long been "a big thing", since before the September 11 attacks, and one important consequence of "society's disposition to panic" (45) is its "worship of safety" (8). In terrorism discourse, as news agency reports on terrorism show, fears (or worries or concerns) are often combined with the concept of security. As Tudor (2003) notes, we know from history how "whole regimes of domination" have been based on citizens' fear (244). In the United States, people's fear and the ensuing quest for security could help the authorities to win the citizens' acceptance for stricter security measures. In fact, the result of a Gallup poll in 2002, according to AP (June 11, 2002, report lead), showed that as many as "four in five Americans would give up some freedoms to gain security." Towards the end of that dispatch, AP has an indirect quote from a psychiatry professor, who argues that "talk of the war in Afghanistan, airline security and terrorist threats is propelling fear."

Terrorism fears, at least in news agency reports, are often construed as some kind of powerful, free-floating entities with little or no visible connection to those who fear. At the same time, the almost continuous warnings from authorities and threats relayed in the reports certainly are apt to create fear even in people who have no personal experience of terrorist attacks. The 'sequence of events' of these fears differs considerably from the model presented by Plutchik (see the section on "Defining fear" above). First, the "stimulus event" (threat) comes from the authorities via the media. Second, flight as "behavior" is of no use; and third, "protection" (security measures) is also mostly left to the authorities. In other words, individuals with "cognition of danger" and "feelings of fear" cannot do much to overcome their fear.

Paradoxically, the events do not always have to be 'unexpected', i.e. 'new', to get into the news. In their famous study on newsworthiness, Galtung and Ruge (1970: 264) have included *consonance* and *continuity* in the list of twelve factors, generally known as *news values*. They argue that the threshold of reporting is lower when the event in question fits "a pattern of expectation" (287), and when something has once been accepted as 'news', it continues to be reported (264). In news agency reports, the frequent occurrences of warnings and "unconfirmed" threats repeat a well-known pattern, and so, in regard to terrorism threats and fears, a seemingly never-ending narrative of fear has been established. The examples from AP and Reuters news reports have shown how abstract "fears" and "concerns" and "worries", together with other nominalizations, have become 'actors'. The use of this kind of vague language hides the role of the real actors. At the same time, it undermines the 'factuality' of news agency discourse.

Notes

1.   The research presented here was supported in part by the Academy of Finland Centre of Excellence funding for the Research Unit for Variation, Contacts and Change in English at the Department of English, University of Helsinki. I am grateful to Jan-Ola Ostman for his valuable comments on an earlier version of this study.

2.   The Appraisal Website (http://www.grammatics.com/appraisal/index.html) presents the Appraisal framework in rich detail.

3.   Before the actual headline, on the first line of a news agency report, there is a "slug line" consisting of at least one word, but usually two or three words. This "slug," as Reuters says, "uniquely identifies that story."

4.   The differences between the two news agencies regarding the size of their corpora are simply due to the fact that during a given time period one of them sent more reports than the other containing the search word in question ("terrorist", "terror" or "fear.") The size of the "pages" in news agency reports may vary a little, depending on the breadth of the columns. In view of the number of pages, the font size is relevant, too; in my files it is (Arial) 10.

5.   *Negativity* is probably the best known of the factors generally known as *news values*. In their influential study on newsworthiness (published in the *Journal of International Peace Research* in 1965, reprinted in 1970), Galtung and Ruge presented twelve factors, which could be claimed to

affect both the selection and the presentation of news. Besides *negativity*, the list of news values includes, for instance, *eliteness, personification, unexpectedness, consonance* and *continuity.*

References

Abu-Lughod, L. and Lutz, C.A. 1990. "Introduction: Emotion, discourse, and the politics of everyday life." In *Language and the politics of emotion,* C.A. Lutz and L.Abu-Lughod (eds.), 1–23. Cambridge: Cambridge University Press.

Associated Press. 2004. "About AP, facts & figures." Available: www.ap.org/pages/about/about. html.

Berezin, M. 2002. "Secure states: Towards a political sociology of emotion." In *Emotions and Sociology,* J. Barbalet (ed.), 33–52. Oxford: Blackwell Publishing/The Sociological Review.

Coston, C.T.M. 1998. "Methodological shortcomings in the measurement of the concept of 'fear' in criminal justice tesearch." Available: www.worldsocietyofvictimology.org/wsv/index.aspx.

Fairclough, N. 1995. *Media Discourse.* London: Edward Arnold.

Fowler, R. 1991. *Language in the News: Discourse and Ideology in the Press.* London: Routledge.

Furedi, F. 2002. *Culture of Fear: Risk-taking and the Morality of Low Expectation.* London: Continuum.

Galtung, J. and Ruge, M.H. 1970. "The structure of foreign news." In *Media Sociology,* J. Tunstall (ed.), 259–298. Urbana, IL: University of Illinois Press.

Halliday, M.A.K. 1994. *An Introduction to Functional Grammar* (2nd edition). London: Edward Arnold.

Halliday, M.A.K. 1998. "Things and relations. Regrammaticising experience as technical knowledge." In *Reading Science: Critical and Functional Perspectives on Discourses of Science,* J.R. Martin and R.Veel (eds.), 184–235. London and New York: Routledge.

Hartley, J. 1982. *Understanding News.* London: Methuen.

Hasselgård, H. 2000. "Grammatical metaphor." University of Oslo Functional Grammar Course Homepage. Available: folk.uio.no/hhasselg/systemic/phr.metaphor.halde.htm.

Kemper, T.D. 2002. "Predicting emotions in groups: Some lessons from September 11." In *Emotions and Sociology,* J. Barbalet (ed.), 53-68. Oxford: Blackwell Publishing/The Sociological Review.

Kövecses, Z. 2000. *Metaphor and Emotion: Language, Culture, and Body in Human Feeling.* Cambridge: Cambridge University Press.

Martin, J.R. 1997. "Analysing genre: Functional parameters." In *Genre and Institutions: Social Processes in the Workplace and School,* F. Christie and J.R. Martin (eds.), 3–39. London: Cassell.

Martin, J.R. 2000. "Beyond exchange: Appraisal systems in English." In *Evaluation in Text,* S. Hunston and G.Thompson (eds.), 142–175. Oxford: Oxford University Press.

Plutchik, R. 1980. "A general psychoevolutionary theory of emotion." In *Emotion: Theory, Research, and Experience,* R. Plutchik and H. Kellerman (eds.), 3–33. San Diego: Academic Press.

Reuters. 2004. "Reuters: About us." Available: about.reuters.com/aboutus/editorial/.

Stenvall, M. 2003. "An actor or an undefined threat? The role of 'terrorist' in the discourse of international news agencies." *Journal of Language and Politics* 2: 361–404.

Stenvall, M. Forthcoming. "Setting the agenda – responsibility and the conventions of news agency discourse." In *Responsibility in Discourse and the Discourse of Responsibility,* J.O. Östman and A. Solin (eds.). Berlin: Mouton de Gruyter.

Stout, J.H. 2004. "Worry." Available: stout.bravepages.com/h/worry.htm.

Toolan, M.J. 1988. *Narrative: A critical linguistic introduction.* London: Routledge.

Tudor, A. 2003. "A (macro) sociology of fear?" *The Sociological Review* 51: 238–256.

Tunstall, J. 1999. "World news duopoly." In *News: A Reader*, H. Tumber (ed.), 191–200. New York: Oxford University Press.

Van Dijk, T.A. 1988. *News as Discourse.* Hillsdale N.J.: Erlbaum.

White, P.R.R. 1998. *Telling Media Tales: The News Story as Rhetoric.* Unpublished Ph.D. Dissertation, University of Sydney. Available: www.grammatics.com/appraisal/AppraisalKeyReferences.html.

White, P.R.R. 2003. "News as history: Your daily gossip." In *Re/reading the Past: Critical and Functional Perspectives on Time and Value*, J.R. **Martin** and R.**Wodak** (eds.), 61–89. Amsterdam and Philadelphia: John Benjamins.

Wood, M. 1995. "Reuters style guide, the second edition." Unpublished internal memorandum.

CHAPTER 12

The politics of fear

A critical inquiry into the role of violence in 21st century politics

Matteo Stocchetti

Introduction

This chapter is an inquiry into the communicative dimension of the politics of fear. With this concept I mean a specific type of social activity that has indiscriminate violence as its main resource and the compliance of masses as its main objective. As a form of politically relevant behavior, it is deliberately performed by identifiable elites but involves virtually every individual and group in society. Here I propose a rather conventional political analysis of the politics of fear – as a public policy, with actors, having interests, resources and the ability to use them, etc. – in an effort to rationalize the analysis of violence that appears essentially irrational. The goal is not to accept or even less so to legitimize but rather to establish a standing point where political manipulation through the exploitation and reproduction of fear can be resisted.

The idea that fear is politically relevant is not new (e.g. Lasswell 1941, 1962, Wolfers 1952, Waever 1995, Corey 2003). What I believe is novel is the scope and the intensity of the current threat posed by illiberal elites, their ideologies and practices to key democratic values and to the lives of millions of people. The discussion in this chapter is by no means adequate to tackle the magnitude of this threat. It is rather a first step designed primarily to identify suitable conceptual categories for further and more systematic inquiry. The focus is here on the communicative dimension of the politics of fear; and in particular, on the narratives and metaphors that provide discursive support for this distinctive form of organized violence. I am holding to the assumption, common to critical approaches, that communicative practices are necessary to the reproduction of the practices and conditions constituting the politics of fear and the unequal set of costs and benefits, advantages and disadvantages implied by this type of relationship.

The chapter is divided into three sections. The first one interprets the practices of terrorism outside the conceptual constraints of mainstream interpretations. In the second part I look at the role of the crusade metaphor and its influence on the narrative patterns that support the politics of fear. In the concluding section I propose that efforts to oppose the politics of fear must involve breaking out of the circularity of these narratives.

The politics of fear

For the sake of simplicity and understanding I would start with a classic and essential notion of politics:

> The study of politics is the study of influence and the influential... The influential are those who get most of what there is to get. Available values may be classified as *deference, income, safety*. Those who get the most are *elite*; the rest are *mass*. (Lasswell, 1950: 3. Emphasis in the original)

Along with this definition of politics, I would define politics of fear as the competition for the control of conditions that make safety of paramount value. The study of the politics of fear is the study of the practices entertained by the elite to control the distribution of fear and exploit its effects upon the population. The main argument is that terrorist and anti-terrorist elite, despite having different goals, share a common interest in preserving the conditions that support the politics of fear as a means by which deference, income, safety and other values are distributed in society.

International order and clash of civilizations

The mainstream views on terrorism – which for sake of simplicity I shall refer to here as the "international order" and the "clash of civilizations" respectively – reflect identifiable political ideologies and serve as interpretative and prescriptive conceptual frameworks.

The first view expresses universalism's illusion that, with the "defeat" of Communism, liberal ideology can authoritatively perform as the bedrock for world economic, political and social order. In this view terrorist violence is perceived as organized crime within a "global" society, while its religious, ethnic or political connotations are of secondary importance. The "international community", through its representative bodies such as the UN, is supposed to be an actual governing body in international politics, capable of expressing a legal "order" assisted by legitimate force – i.e. within the legal framework of international law upheld by the UN. The second interpretation reflects the idea that institutions such as individual (economic) freedom and democracy are distinctively Western and that their spread to the rest of the world produces hostility by different "civilizations." While the first view establishes a universal order apparently deprived of cultural connotations, the second one is overtly cultural. Rather than mere organized crime, Islamic terrorism is seen as a cultural expression of hatred, and a direct and lethal threat to core values of the "West." The roots of violence are to be found in irreducible cultural differences enhanced, rather than reduced, by the increased interdependence of the international economy. The response against this type of threat is a "war" that cannot be constrained by legal or normative principles – principles that would only make Western "civilization" more vulnerable against an Enemy that does not acknowledge them.

Both of these images – the international order and the clash of civilizations – perform as influential interpretative frameworks in explaining the causes of terrorism and, most importantly, in orienting the search for solutions. Both of them, however, are unable, for different reasons, to oppose the social effects of terrorist strategy and unable to resist the detrimental changes that the terrorist challenge is bringing about in Western societies and virtually everywhere in the world. The main problem with the first interpretation is that it overestimates the universal acceptability of Western liberalism, its authority in non-Western societies, and consequently, its suitability as a global governing principle. The main problem with the second interpretation is that it assumes an idea of the "West" which is far from shared even among "Westerners." It holds up the false belief that cultures are discrete and homogeneous entities whose traits are relatively independent from each other. It suggests that the people of some nations, namely the US and United Kingdom, are more "Western" than others – e.g. the Greeks, the Spanish or the Italians whose contaminations with Byzantine, Arab and other Mediterranean influences make their cultures somehow "spurious." It portrays the Arab as a single and undifferentiated entity and Islam as a threatening force *per se*. Ironically, this view supports the Islamic fundamentalists' claim that their interpretation is the only "true" interpretation of Islam. But the most serious problem with these mainstream images is that, by taking the differences between terror and anti-terror at face value, they hide the common stake of radical elites in both the West and the Middle East in the use of fear as a tool to gain political leverage and to preserve a position of influence they would not be able to maintain otherwise in their respective societies and abroad.

Terrorist challenge should and can be effectively resisted; but the formulation of a more pragmatic interpretation of the role of violence in 21st century politics is a necessary and preliminary step in this direction. Terrorist and anti-terrorist are surely engaged in a deadly confrontation. Their practices unquestionably differ but their rationale appears very much the same: to induce compliance through the threat of destruction. This strategy has already been at least partially successful in undermining certain ideas and values distinctively Western in their historical matrix but whose appeal spreads worldwide. These ideas and values however are far from shared even among the West. Their potential for social change threatens reactionary forces both inside and outside the West.

Dreams for some, nightmares for others: freedom of communication

An alternative and more effective interpretation of terrorism should preliminarily acknowledge that the threat of violence afflicts both people in the West and in the Middle East. My argument is that the current strife is better understood as a response of radical conservative elites in both political systems against the opportunities (risks, from their perspective) of uncontrolled social change. From the perspective adopted in this chapter – that of the communicative processes – these opportunities result from the spread of one particular form of freedom: the freedom of communication.[1] It is exactly this type of freedom, as I shall argue shortly, that carries with it, for the societies experiencing it, the risk of legitimation crisis as expected by Jürgen Habermas:

> A legitimation crisis can be predicted only if expectations that cannot be fulfilled either with the available quantity of value or, generally, with rewards conforming to the system are systematically produced. (Habermas 1975: 75)

Freedom of communication is a source of expectations and can be thought of as one of the "faces" or dimensions of secularization. Its scope and nature reflects material and immaterial conditions affecting an individual's access to other individuals. Here I will discuss two of these conditions: the impact of innovation in information and communication technology (ICT) and the nature of individual needs supporting the social demand for this technology

An important and preliminary point too often forgotten in the discussion about the alleged "revolutionary" impact of new ICT is that the spread of these technologies and their seemingly destabilizing impact is not promoted by some subversive political doctrine but by the mere working of the capitalist mode of production, distribution and consumption. On the one hand, consumerism is the attitude or lifestyle required for the effective functioning of modern economies. On the other hand, consumerism is also associated with frustration; and frustration activates the search for alternatives to the existing state of affairs. While surely creating and preserving economic disparities, capitalism makes people equal worldwide in at least one sense: individuals are transformed into frustrated consumers no matter how diverse their social status, education, personal history, etc. might be. It is precisely this ambiguous attitude of frustration coupled with desire for novelty that, in my opinion, supports the growing need to access communication technology, the inclination to explore remote social worlds and, if possible, the establishment of contact with individuals in distant communities. A common idea among critical thinkers is that technological innovation eventually preserves the unequal distribution of values in the society (Winston 1986). We might however look at it somewhat differently. Instances of technological evolution, e.g. the use of the computer as a functional communicative "extension" (Hall 1990: 4), create favorable conditions for an aggregation of individuals beyond the constraints of physical and cultural spaces. People can identify with a variety of individuals, leaders or groups beyond those available at close range. This dramatic increase in the quantity and quality of communicative opportunities has brought *diversity* into the lives of a great number of people beyond ethnic, linguistic or spatial barriers.

In addition to offering the technological possibility to access diversity, perceived as novelty, and to exchange considerable volumes of information, data, experience, etc., capitalism has another important macro-effect. While supporting the individualization of society it also creates a residual need for new types of bonding. While challenging individuals' entitlements by birth it creates strong pressures on the search for new and voluntary, or elective, social identities – new settings for individuals' histories once the history of the community is not available any longer for that purpose. The forces of the market, and the requirements of surplus-value creation, demand the individual to be "freed" from all types of bonds that cannot be expressed in material value and/or made available on the market. Since individuals need more durable social identities than that offered by the market but cannot escape this mechanism, the response involves using available alternatives to construct new forms of communities and new types of identity.

Once diversity is transformed into an accessible good within the broader conditions of unsatisfied sociality, the chaotic implications of this type of freedom become rather clear. The key issue here is not only about the range of opportunities available to individuals for exchanging information with other individuals but, most importantly, about the implications that this communicative exchange have on the construction and reproduction of communities – or more precisely, the bonding between the individual and the community.[2] In situations where communication is hampered by material or immaterial constraints – e.g. lack of suitable telephone lines and distance, censorship or illiteracy – a minority of individuals can exchange a relatively small amount of information through institutionalized rituals. Therefore, the control of the potential for social change is in the hands of a few elites. In these types of societies, innovation and change are relatively uncommon and slow processes selectively affecting the members of communities. Within these communities most of the individuals lack the tools and the capacity to establish meaningful connection with members of other communities, and stereotyped representations of the other can survive unchallenged. In societies with a high degree of communicative freedom, not only large quantities of information circulate in every direction but the opportunities for unpredictable social change are very high since changes in "relationality" (Condit 2006) and the experience of the other (Shepherd 2006) establish and support original connections between conventional and new or "mediated" communities. A variety of media rituals and other forms of identity building practices and symbolic exchange (Couldry 2003, Rothenbuhler 2006) may eventually prolong the existence of these new mediated communities beyond ephemeral life and provide for their institutionalization in the social, cultural and political domains.

My suggestion is that freedom of communication *per se* does not trigger a process of change toward a more liberal and democratic society: it only triggers change and complexity. More radically, it is not a "solution" but rather a "condition": the dynamic element simultaneously associated with the "liquid modern" as both cause and effect. The "liquid modern", as described by Zygmunt Bauman, is "a society in which the conditions under which its members act change faster than it takes the ways of acting to consolidate into habits and routines" (Bauman 2005: 1). Rather predictably, the spread of technologies and habits of technological consumption that foster this type of freedom present formidable challenges to the legitimation (Habermas 1979: 182–183) of any political order. In this respect, and far from being a tool for more equitable social order, information and communication technologies are effectively just powerful sources of change; and therefore, they are consequently challenges to existing orders regardless of their nature. The nature of this challenge eludes the "civilization" discipline implied in Huntington's vision, but it also undermines the very assumptions at the core of liberal universalism à la Fukuyama (1989). It rather suggests the need for a new form of political rationality: a "cosmopolitan vision", in the words of Ulrich Beck (2006), based on "the affirmation of the other as both different and the same" (58).

Since Eric Fromm's unsurpassed account of this process, including its causes and risks, in "The Fear of Freedom" (2002 [1942]), Ulrich Beck (1992) and Zygmunt Baumann (2001, 2005 :15–38) have reintroduced these themes in mainstream reflection on contemporary society, adding beneficial insights on living the crisis of the modernist ideology. From a different perspective, the promise contained in the technological developments of the last twenty years and the evolution of individual needs and ability in the same period seems to promote the kind of participatory politics that Habermas (1992) envisaged as the only effective solution to the problems of mature capitalist societies (Heng and Moor 2003). Finally, and from a completely different epistemological ground, an influential tradition in French sociology acknowledges that the media hold the key capacity for creating "imaginal" communities (Maffesoli 1996: 69–70): communities held together exclusively by the common access to visual narratives. Like Anderson's (1991 [1983]) "imagined communities", these new forms of association are influential as "cultural artefacts of a particular kind" (4).

Different theoretical perspectives indicate a common and very important point here. These "new" and mediated – i.e. technology dependent – communities, together with the "cosmopolitan" ideologies and visions associated with them, are easily perceived as a formidable threat by elites whose power relies on traditional and non-mediated relationships. Their attitude is well described by the words Bauman uses to illustrate the beginning of the individualized society era:

> "Tearing up the old local/communal bonds, declaring war on habitual ways and customary laws, shredding *les pouvoirs intermediaires*: the overall result of all that was the intoxicating delirium of the 'new beginning'" (Bauman 2001: 20)

The elites that may feel threatened by the spread of communicative freedom are many, but not all elites feel equally threatened by an exponential increase in the possibility of uncontrolled social change. While elites with fundamentalist ideologies, rigid orthodoxies, and dogmatic sets of beliefs are particularly vulnerable, the difference in their response reflects an ideological inclination to resort to violence and an access to the material and immaterial resources necessary for organized coercion.

The transformative power of fear

For fundamentalist elites all over the world, fear is an effective antidote against the secularizing effects of communicative freedom. Violence is a crucial political resource because fear produces observable effects on individual and group behavior. The key goal of both actual violence and narratives of fear is to induce the changes in attitude and behavior in large numbers of people that Philip G. Zimbardo (2003) calls "the transformative power of fear." He summarizes these attitudes and behavior as follows:

– Vulnerability, uncertainty
– Loss of control
– Learned helplessness
– Paralysis of action, communal apathy
– Child-like regression
– Simplified perceptions / narrow thinking
– Obedience to powerful authority
– Conservatism, avoidance of risks / change / novelty
– Maintenance of status quo
– Paranoid ideas, conspiracy theories
– Revenge motives, pre-emptive counter attacks

- Punitive attitudes, punishing scapegoats
- Cumulative, enduring, delayed effects

Important effects follow. First, the changes experienced in individual attitude and behavior as a consequence of a prolonged exposure to fear – as a result of actual violence or effective narratives – promote authoritarian leadership and conservative ideologies. Second, the politics of fear support the mass inclination to give up freedom in exchange for security (Fromm 2002). Third, masses become too weak, too vulnerable and too scared to perform as *demos* in democracy and to be a credible repository of political authority. Expected consequences of this development are, for example, the tendency to shift the balance of power from representative to executive bodies and from participation to decision-making – a process justified in terms of organizational responsiveness which makes governments and military actors even more independent from parliamentary or other forms of democratic control. All this leads to the obvious conclusion that *in the politics of fear the masses are the net loser*. People remain vulnerable to violence, while the public control over organized violence diminishes. Moreover, the organizational short-term interest of conservative governments to engage militarily with terrorists rests unchallenged, and the politics of fear reproduces itself as the final outcome.

Fear and social change

By targeting public transportation – New York 2001, London 2005, Mumbai 2006 – and tourist resorts – Bali 2002, Sharm el Sheikh 2005 – terrorist military strategy has been rational insofar as it inhibits communication, exchange, and promiscuity with all the opportunities that mass movement and cultural "dislocation" imply. The response, in the West and elsewhere, so far has been more effective in taking advantage of the terrorist military strategy to restrict freedom of communication rather than in removing the terrorist threat.

In the US, the Patriot Act and the *de facto* institutionalization of military tribunals with virtually unlimited jurisdiction and territorial competence have been contested but are still perceived as acceptable initiatives in the "war on terror" by large sectors of the public.[3] In Europe on May 28th 2004, the EU Commission bowed to US pressures to set up airline "passenger name records" – a system designed to eventually provide a number of US agencies with a wide range of information on individual travelers – despite a no-vote of the EU Parliament on this issue.

Where freedom is a possibility rather than an actual practice, the politics of fear supports reactionary elites. One such example comes from Iran, an Islamic republic. In the year 2000, national elections resulted in a landslide victory for the Reformists. Yet five years later, in April 2005, Conservatives won the presidency of the state. The 2005 elections took place against the backdrop of threats of military action by the US, which played into the hands of the Conservatives (De Luce and Burke 2003). However, the same threats have failed, so far, in discontinuing Iran's nuclear program.

Finally, there are two more specific consequences on communication that should raise concern and that I would like to mention here. First, the pressures exerted by the security and the business communities to achieve control of the World Wide Web are producing detrimental structural changes in the potential for this type of technology to support the freedom of communication (Deibert 2003: 502). The principle leading this logic is in itself a by-product of the politics of fear: every individual is a potential terrorist *until proved otherwise*. In this type of regime, compliance is solicited by dissuasion. Being subject to suspicion is even dangerous since it can lead to arrest or detention without charges or legal assistance, or even to deportation and torture in countries – amazingly enough – suspected of supporting terrorists (Jehl and Johnston 2005). The second development, which reinforces the social effects of the surveillance regime, is an important change in the narrative connotation of organized violence.

The narratives of fear

In the previous section I sketched the political rationale for the politics of fear. In this section I will focus on the concept of crusade and its influence on the narrative patterns that support the politics of fear. Politics is very much about communication, and the politics of fear depends on narratives to establish a particular state of affairs. As Harold D. Lasswell put it many years ago:

> Successful violence depends upon coordinating such other salient aspects of the total act as organization, propaganda, information (Lasswell 1950: 62).

Elsewhere, Lars Lundsten and I have argued that the crusade metaphor has been greatly influential in the narratives associated with the Iraq war and the "war on terror" more broadly (Lundsten and Stocchetti 2005, 2006). My point here is that identifiable elites from opposite camps have a common interest in the polarization and moralization effects of the narrative of violence as framed by the crusade metaphor.

The "power" of metaphor

The communicative and social importance of metaphors extends beyond rhetoric and dwells well into the domain of human cognition and cultural behavior. As George Lakoff and Mark Johnson (1980) wrote, "The essence of metaphor is under-

standing and experiencing one kind of thing in terms of another" (5). The implications of this definition are well described in the ARGUMENT IS WAR metaphor:

> ... we don't just *talk* about arguments in terms of war. We can actually win or lose
> arguments. We see the person we are arguing with as an opponent. We attack his
> positions and we defend our own. We gain and lose ground. We plan and use
> strategies ... Many of the things we *do* in arguing are partially structured by the
> concept of war... It is in this sense that the ARGUMENT IS WAR metaphor is one
> that we live by in this culture; it structures the actions we perform in arguing. Try
> to imagine a culture where arguments are not viewed in terms of war ... a culture
> where an argument is viewed as a dance, the participants are seen as performers,
> and the goal is to perform in a balanced and aesthetically pleasing way. In such a
> culture, people would view arguments differently, experience them differently,
> carry them out differently and talk about them differently. (Lakoff and Johnson
> 1980: 4–5; emphasis in the original)

The key point here is that metaphors have to do not only with *understanding* but
also with *experiencing*. In practice this means that metaphors are communicative
devices that, while allowing communication and understanding, are also capable
of transferring the attitudes and the behavioral patterns associated with one domain to another (Chilton 1985, 1988, 1996; Chilton and Ilyin 1993, Musolff 2006).
The description of a problem in metaphorical terms contains within it opinions on
essential aspects of the problem itself. The use of metaphors creates inter-subjec-
tivity and solicits consensus about value judgments that are not, however, discussed and on which criticism is evaded. For political metaphors these effects are
common in both political-theoretical and political-practical discourses (Rigotti
1992). As particular forms of knowledge, political theories are grounded on more
or less explicit metaphors such as those of the *body politic*, the state as *rational actor*, the political system as *black box*, etc. (Chilton and Lakoff 1995). These and
other metaphors are based upon an inter-subjective and culture-specific understanding of some basic aspects of political reality, which is reproduced through
their use. The same understanding influences the way political problems are addressed; but this is not the focus of theoretical debate and criticism.

The crusade metaphor

I would now like to take a closer look at some of the practical effects produced by
the crusade metaphor on political communication and describe their relationships
with the politics of fear.

When George W. Bush described his commitment against terrorism as a "crusade" on Sunday, September 16, 2001, he used a metaphor that was soon to be
picked up by those against whom his action was directed.

> "This is a new kind of --- a new kind of evil. And we understand. And the American people are beginning to understand. This *crusade*, this war on terrorism is going to take a while. And the American people must be patient. I'm going to be patient" (Bush 2001a).

In fact, the crusade metaphor is a meaningful and influential one for both Western and Arab audiences.[4] It might be observed that Bush only voiced what many people, including neo-conservatives and others, already thought. In many respects, Bush's crusade is only the logical follow up, the next step, of Samuel P. Huntington's (1993) representation of world conflict in the post-cold war era along "civilization" lines.[5]

> It is my hypothesis that the fundamental source of conflict in this new world will not be primarily ideological or primarily economic. The great divisions among humankind and the dominating source of conflict will be cultural. Nation states will remain the most powerful actors in world affairs, but the principal conflicts of global politics will occur between nations and groups of different civilizations. The clash of civilizations will dominate global politics. The fault lines between civilizations will be the battle lines of the future. (Huntington 1993: 22).

Not by chance, then, but rather interestingly, the concept of crusade has been quickly taken up also by Islamic terrorists. Despite different cultural connotations in the Middle East and the West, the crusade metaphor does have some important – and politically advantageous – common meanings for both parties. More precisely, the idea of a violent confrontation with the traits of a crusade implies:
– a total conflict;
– which is stretched indefinitely in time and space,
– and involves all levels of society,
– where whatever costs – including suffering by the domestic society and cruelty against the enemy – are justified;
– and where the leadership is positioned beyond the reach of rational criticism – since the nature of the struggle is defined in terms of spiritual commitment rather than practical goals.

The meanings attached to the conceptual metaphor of "crusade" establish a *cognitive framework that functions in the legitimization of both terrorist and anti-terrorist violence*. In practical terms, this means that whenever bin Laden preaches his jihad against "Christian crusaders" his narratives support the practices of those who preach the "crusade against terror." Meanwhile, Bush's call for unity in the "world's fight" (Bush 2001b) for freedom legitimizes bin Laden's call for a "jihad." More precisely, this metaphor polarizes and moralizes the narrative of violence: it identifies only two relevant identities in the terror vs. anti-terror binary and it establishes a moral ground for the legitimization of violence based on a socio-political *identity* ascribed to the victimizer rather than his *behavior*.[6]

These effects induced in the narrative of violence by the crusade metaphor are important for the practices they facilitate or hamper. Framed within the "clash of civilizations" conceptual framework, the crusade metaphor conveys the idea of a complete saturation of the world social space by the requirements of the struggle. No individual, group, government, nation, race, class or gender is immune from the need to take sides. Intrinsic in the crusade metaphor is the idea that the magnitude of the struggle does not allow any actor to be neutral or indifferent. As Bush himself made explicit, "either you're with us or against us" (Bush 2002).

The most visible effects of polarization are a dismissal of criticism and disagreement as hostile behavior and the treatment of critics as enemies. In doing this, polarization creates artificial identities – forcing actors' positions into the roles of friends or foes (either-or) – which dramatically constrain the possibilities for accurate information, reporting and debate, and enhance, by contrast, the influence of prejudices and stereotypes. In sum, polarization brings exclusionary effects that further undermine the efforts to effectively extinguish terrorism but effectively reproduce the politics of fear. Politically speaking, this means that the adoption of the crusade metaphor by opposite fundamentalisms is synergic. Moreover, it has detrimental effects on support for more moderate and liberal interpretations of Western and Arab values. Finally, it should be added that the communicative effects of this metaphor are supportive of political polarization in a broader sense, as Charles Tilly has put it:

> Polarization generally promotes collective violence because it makes the us-them boundary more salient, hollows out the uncommitted middle, intensifies conflict across the boundary, raises the stakes of winning or losing, and enhances opportunities for leaders to initiate action against their enemies. (Tilly 2003: 22–23).

But the crusade metaphor also has moralizing effects. By moralization, I mean the attribution of a moral stand – good or bad – to an actor, depending on his stereotyped identity rather than his actual behavior. Normally, people are considered good or bad depending on what they do. In the politics of fear the enemy is not bad for what it *does* but for what it *is* – an Islamic fundamentalist or a Western crusader. Moralization idealizes the fighters as holy warriors, independently of the brutality of their practices and legitimizes whatever suffering is imposed on civilian populations, whatever cruelty is performed against the enemy, and the most blatant violations of human rights and other forms of freedom (e.g. minority rights, civic rights, etc.).

The polarization and moralization of political discourse produced by the crusade metaphor puts the actions of the leadership above criticism, legitimizes brutality and undermines the position of moderate political actors. Additional effects that ultimately support and reproduce the spiral of violence – and the politics of fear – can be summarized as follows:

- **De-rationalization of the enemy.** In the narratives of the "war on terror" the enemy is elusive, deadly and fanatic. In the overt rhetoric of public communication, there seems to be no interest in a rational assessment of the enemy's goals, strategy and capabilities. Secrecy spreads to cover whatever information might provide clues for an informed debate aimed at establishing the limits or the constraints of the terrorist threat. Depicting the enemy as a group of fanatics rather than an organization moved by identifiable goals makes the rational assessment of anti-terrorist initiatives virtually impossible. If initiatives cannot be rationally assessed, the leadership that promotes them cannot be criticized. The de-rationalization of the enemy and its strategic behavior ultimately works toward the preservation of decision-making elites engaged in the politics of fear.

- **Passivization of the *demos*.** Civilians are the victims of both terrorist and anti-terrorist violence. The practice of disregarding civilian casualties as "collateral damage" is insulting if perceived from the standpoint of those values – democracy and freedom – that the US and its allies allegedly want to uphold in the fight against terror. That practice, however, functions to subjugate civilian populations with the fear of indiscriminate retaliation should their leaders behave in ways that might provoke US resentment. Beyond this short-term function, this practice has far reaching political implications. The narrative of "innocent victims" supports the idea that the *demos* is too vulnerable to be a credible source of authority. In the form of hostages, civilian members of national communities become a source of vulnerability for governments committed to the "war on terror." Entire populations subjugated to imperatives dictated by fear cannot credibly perform as a repository of political sovereignty. They are rather the object to be protected through decisions and practices taken in their name by the national executives.

- **Undermining sovereignty.** The narrative effects described above have additional macro implications on the principle of state sovereignty and on the structure of international politics. The proclaimed will of the US government to prosecute and preemptively strike suspected terrorists wherever and whenever appropriate obliterates the inside/outside distinction (Walker 1993): the separation between domestic and foreign policy, between the space of legal order and that of anarchy. It asserts in practice and in principle[7] the claim of a monopoly of legal violence that acknowledges no other authority – not even a legitimate representative body of the international community such as the UN – while commanding compliance from other states and governments. In the rhetoric of the "crusade", the legitimacy of a state depends on its stand on a polarized and moralized interpretation of the terrorist problem (White House 2003: 17–18).

But the main reason why the crusade metaphor plays an important function in the politics of fear is that it effectively creates conditions for the maintenance of high expectations of indiscriminate violence in domestic and foreign politics. Its effectiveness results from cognitive simplicity: it brings a complex issue down to very easy social categorizations – "with us or against us", "they are bad, we are good" – whose roots lie in an individual's need to organize experience and reduce the complexity of social reality (Tajfel 1981). It changes the nature of the stakes in the conflict – from interests to a principle – and the scope and intensity of the confrontation – from limited and rational to total and potentially irrational. It mobilizes societies to the saturation point, legitimizing the extraction of material and immaterial resources and the control of virtually every aspect of private and public life by the "security" elites. It undermines the authority of representative bodies, such as national parliaments, to the advantage of the executive bodies. Finally, it puts the leadership on both sides above criticism, undermines moderate elites and creates favorable conditions for conservative and authoritarian styles of governance, or "strict father" type leaders (Lakoff 2003). And these conditions of the politics of fear apply equally well when waged by both terrorist and anti-terrorist.

Concluding remarks

The tendency to consider terrorism as irrational and terrorists as fanatics is not only misleading but also risky. On strategic grounds it leads to a "dangerous underestimation of the capabilities of extremists groups" (Crenshaw 1990: 24). In broader social terms, however, it produces that "paralysis of criticism" Marcuse described about forty years ago. And what was said of the nuclear threat during the Cold War might also be said of the terrorist threat:

> ... causes remain unidentified, unexposed, unattacked by the public because they recede before the all too obvious threat from without – to the West from the East, to the East from the West. Equally obvious is the need for being prepared, for living on the brink, for facing the challenge (Marcuse 2002: xxxix).

In this chapter I have proposed an unconventional reading of terrorism as part of the politics of fear – a specific form of political behavior whose main rationale is, in our times, to oppose communicative freedom. My argument is that radical elites in both the West and the Arab world feel threatened by the evolution of the communicative behavior of the masses and by the potential ideological, cultural, religious and ethnic contamination that this implies. Elites, whose ideologies are too dogmatic to adapt and too repressive to attract consensus, engage in the politics of fear because they are still influential enough to have a certain control on organized violence at their disposal. Their strategic goal is to change the very meaning of politics as a social practice for the allocation of values in society: to thwart the value of communication, knowledge and information and to foster the value of coercion as a political resource.

In the perspective adopted in this chapter, the politics of fear is primarily a practice for the repression of the radical potential intrinsic in the material and immaterial communicative conditions of our times. From the same perspective, the practical possibility of resistance depends on the general awareness of the communicative dangers implicit in the crusade metaphor and in the intrinsic ambiguity of its narratives. This metaphor and concomitant narratives establish a *circle of violence* in which the identities of the victimizers are (a) mutually constitutive and (b) self-reproducing.

By *mutually constitutive* identities I mean that each of the antagonists depends on the other for the legitimacy of its own actions.[8] The most obvious example of this kind of dynamic is the appearance of bin Laden only four days before the presidential election in the USA which brought media attention away from issues potentially detrimental to Bush and back to terrorism – Bush's preferred terrain. Since the competitors are presumably aware of this dependency, each side has a somehow paradoxical stake in preserving the other side – at least as an icon, as a representation of something else or as a fetish, a visible object connected to a much broader, frightening and partially invisible reality. Furthermore, the narratives establishing the communicative conditions for the actions of both parties have *synergic* effects. First, they polarize cultural differences, construing functional identities that draw on arbitrary representations of history and religion for the effective mobilization of the masses in the fight against opponents. Second, they deliberately aim at eliminating dissent within their own societies. In these narratives, the appeal to unity and cohesion become arguments for, and give informal legitimacy to, the repression of opinions, ideas, values, standpoints, etc. that are critical or non-supportive of the militant attitude exhibited in the leaders' rhetoric. Third, and consequently, these narratives undermine moderate political elites on both sides, therefore weakening the practical possibility for alternative values and narratives to be included in political communication. Fourth, common narratives inspired by equivalent attitudes toward the political use of violence lay the ground for the socio-cultural acceptance of actions with very similar effects. Judging from these effects, rather than from their alleged goals, terrorist and anti-terrorist seem inspired by the common purpose of destroying very basic and common values in both Western and Arab societies, such as tolerance, multiculturalism, political participation, diversity, freedom of expression and movement, respect for human civil and political rights, and international legality, among others. Beyond the propaganda distinction between "innocent victims" and "collateral damage", the human costs of this confrontation and the atrocities committed on both sides present a synergic threat to human rights and human dignity – in themselves very fragile values.

By *self-reproducing* I mean that once the circle of violence is established every "effect" for one is a "cause" for the other. This is so because the rationale for each party's brutality and power is established upon the brutality of the other party's action/power. Once in place, this process is virtually endless since the conditions of restraints that normally determine the end of a conflict – lack of resources or defeat of the enemy – do not apply here. The "enemy" will always be there since, as seen above, his identity is constitutive of and constituted by the practices of the other side. In this sense, every "crusade", while creating its own "kingdom of Heaven" also establishes and preserves its own "empire of Evil." In practical terms this means that the narratives of the "war on terror" presumably strengthen Islamic fundamentalism in the Arab world and elsewhere, at least as much as bin Laden's threats and attacks support anti-Islamic and reactionary forces in the West. From both sides of this "crusade" the enemy is described as irreducible and elusive – more an abstract entity than a concrete competitor. The more elusive the enemy is, the wider and deeper the concentration of power in the hands of a few and the longer the duration of "extraordinary" measures. Innocent Americans, Afghans, Iraqis, Spanish and Britons – among many others – have died or had to suffer at the hand of assassins who legitimize their actions on the higher moral ground of a "crusade." Unscrupulous behavior by the US and their allies at Guantanamo, in Afghanistan, in Iraq at Abu Ghraib or elsewhere is not only morally highly despicable but – what is more important in relation to the topic addressed here – *also detrimental for effective anti-terrorist action* since it greatly facilitates terrorists' recruitment campaigns (IISS 2004). "Terror" might have triggered "anti-terror", but "anti-terror" supports, in practice, though not in principle, the practices of "terror." The opportunity for resistance, from this perspective, depends on the possibility of breaking this circle of violence.

Notes

1.   Habermas (2002) uses the notion of communicative freedom in ways that are compatible and presumably useful to the topic discussed in this paper. Habermas's concept, however, is far more complex; and its effective use would require a digression that would exceed the limits of this discussion.

2. In this sense the effects of enhanced freedom of communication are relevant from both the transmissive and the ritualistic views of communication. See Carey (1988:14–22).

3. According to a CNN/USA Today/Gallup Poll conducted June 16–19, 2005, 57% of the people in the US believe the Patriot Act is a "good thing." The interesting aspect is that, according to Gallup Poll statistics, the public is in general not familiar with the actual content of that text. See www.pollingreport.com/terror.htm for data.

4. On the notion of jihad and "dialogization" of this word in Arab societies see the chapter by Becky Schulthies and Aomar Boum in this volume.

5. It should be noted, however, that Bush explicitly recalled Huntington's views when he described the confrontation as "civilization's fight" (Bush 2001b).

6. An important point here is that the identities of political actors are constructed by the discursive practice referring to them and by their relative symbolic power (Bourdieu 1991).

7. This claim has been consistently reiterated in a number of documents since 2001. See for example the "National Security Strategy of the United States" (United States National Security Council 2002), the "National Military Strategy" (United States Joint Chief of Staff 2005), and the "National Defense Strategy" (United States Department of Defense 2005). For a closer look to the National Security Strategy document see the chapter by Patricia Dunmire in this volume.

8. For another analysis of the narrative processes involved in the construction of the Enemy identity see Adam Hodges in this volume.

References

Anderson, B. 1991 [1983]. *Imagined Communities*. London: Verso.

Bauman, Z. 2001. *The Individualized Society*. Polity Press: Cambridge.

Bauman, Z. 2005. *Liquid Life*. London: Polity.

Beck, U. 1992. *Risk Society: Towards a New Modernity*. London: Sage.

Beck, U. 2006. *Cosmopolitan Vision*. London: Polity.

Bourdieu, P. 1991. *Language and Symbolic Power*, G. Raymond and M. Adamson (trans). Cambridge, MA: Harvard University Press.

Bush, G.W. 2001a, September 16. Remarks by the President to the press on the South Lawn of the White House. Available: http://www.whitehouse.gov/news/releases/2001/09/20010916–2.html.

Bush, G.W. 2001b, September 20. Address to a Joint Session of Congress and American People. Available: http://www.whitehouse.gov/news/releases/2001/09/20010920–8.html.

Bush, G.W. 2002, June 12. Remarks by the President at Meeting of Homeland Security Advisory Council, The Indian Treaty Room. Available: http://www.whitehouse.gov/news/releases/2002/06/20020612–3.html.

Chilton, P. 1985. "Words, discourse and metaphors: The meaning of deterrent and deterrence." In *Language and the Nuclear Arms Debate: Nukespeak Today*, P. Chilton (ed.), 103–27. Pinter: London.

Chilton, P. 1988. *Orwellian Language and the Media*. London: Pluto Press.

Chilton, P. 1996. *Security Metaphors: Cold War Discourse from Containment to Common House*. New York: Peter Lang.

Chilton, P. and Ilyin, M. 1993. "Metaphor in political discourse: The Case of the 'common European house.'" *Discourse and Society* 4(1): 7–31.

Chilton, P. and Lakoff, G. 1995. "Foreign policy by metaphor." In *Language and Peace*, C. Schäffner and A.L. Wenden (eds.), 37–59. Aldershot: Dartmouth.

Carey J.W. 1988. *Communication as Culture: Essays on Media and Society.* Boston: Unwin Hyman.

Condit, C.M. 2006. "Relationality." In *Communication as—: Perspective on Theory*, G.J. Shepherd, J. St. John and T. Striphas (eds.), 3–12. London: Sage.

Corey, R. 2003. *Fear: A Biography of a Political Idea.* Oxford: Oxford University Press.

Couldry, N. 2003. *Media Rituals: A Critical Approach.* London: Routledge.

Crenshaw, M. 1990. "The logic of terrorism: Terrorist behavior as a product of strategic choice." In *Origins of Terrorism. Psychologies, Ideologies, Theologies, States of Mind*, W. Reich (ed.), 7–24. New York: Cambridge University Press.

Deibert, R.J. 2003. "Black code: Censorship, surveillance, and the militarization of cyberspace." *Millennium: Journal of International Studies* 32: 501–530.

De Luce, D. and Burke, J. 2003, June 1. "Iran Hawks feed on US anger." *The Guardian.* Available: http://observer.guardian.co.uk/international/story/0,,967975,00.html.

Fromm, E. 2002 [1942]. *The Fear of Freedom.* London: Routledge.

Fukuyama, F. 1989. "The End of History?" *The National Interest* 16: 3–18.

Hall, E.T. 1990 [1966]. *The Hidden Dimension.* New York: Anchor Book.

Habermas, J. 1975. *Legitimation Crisis.* Boston: Beacon Press.

Habermas, J. 1979. *Communication and the Evolution of Society.* London: Heinemann.

Habermas, J. 1992. *Moral Consciousness and Communicative Action.* Oxford: Blackwell.

Habermas, J. 2002. "Communicative freedom and negative theology: Question for Michael Theunissen." In *Religion and Rationality: Essays on Reason, God, and Modernity*, E. Mendieta (ed.), 110–128. Cambridge: Polity Press.

Heng, M.S.H. and de Moor, A. 2003. "From Habermas's communicative theory to practice on the internet." *Information System Journal* 13: 331–352.

Huntington, S.P. 1993. "The Clash of Civilizations." *Foreign Affairs* 72(3): 22–28.

IISS – International Institute for Strategic Studies. 2004. "Strategic survey 2003/04. Remarks by Dr. John Chipman, IISS director." Available: http://www.iiss.org/showdocument. php?docID=364.

Jehl, D. and Johnston, D. 2005, March 6. "Rule change lets C.I.A. freely send suspects abroad to jails." *New York Times.* Available: http://www.commondreams.org/cgi-bin/print.cgi?file=/headlines05/0306-01.htm.

Lakoff, G. and Johnson, M. 1980. *Metaphors We Live By.* Chicago: University of Chicago Press.

Lakoff, G. 2003. "Political nomenclature: Framing the Dems." Available: http://george.loper. org/%7Egeorge/archives/2003/Sep/970.html.

Lasswell, H.D. 1941. "The Garrison State." *American Journal of Sociology* 46: 455–68.

Lasswell, H.D. 1950. *Politics. Who Get What, When, How.* New York: Peter Smith.

Lasswell, H.D. 1962. "The garrison state hypothesis today." In *Changing Patterns of Military Politics*, S. P. Huntington (ed.), 51–70. New York: The Free Press.

Lundsten, L. and Stocchetti, M. 2005. "The war against Iraq in transnational broadcasting." In *Global War - Local Views. Media images of the Iraq War*, S.A. Nohrstedt and R. Ottosen, (eds.), 25–46. Göteborg: Nordicom.

Lundsten, L. and Stocchetti, M. 2006. "Dangerous Metaphors. The Media Coverage of the American Crusade " In *Implications of the Sacred in (Post) modern Media*, J.Sumiala-Seppanen, K.Lundby and R.Salokangas (eds.),139–158. Göteborg: Nordicom.

Maffesoli, M. 1996. *The Contemplation of the World: Figures of Community Style.* Minneapolis: Minnesota University Press.

Marcuse, H. 2002 [1964]. *One-Dimensional Man: Studies in the Ideology of Advanced Industrial Society.* London: Routledge.

Musolff, A. 2006. "Metaphor scenarios in public discourse." *Metaphor and Symbol* 21: 23–38.

Rigotti, F. 1992. *Il Potere e le sue Metafore.* Milano: Feltrinelli.

Rothenbuhler, E.W. 2006. "Communication as ritual." In *Communication as—: Perspective on Theory,* G.J. Shepherd, J. St. John and T. Striphas (eds.), 13–21. London: Sage

Shepherd, G.J. 2006. "Communication as transcendence." In *Communication as—: Perspective on Theory,* G.J. Shepherd, J. St. John and T. Striphas (eds.), 22–30. London: Sage.

Tajfel, H. 1981. *Human Groups and Social Categories.* Studies in Social Psychology. Cambridge: Cambridge University Press.

Tilly, C. 2003. *The Politics of Collective Violence.* Cambridge: Cambridge University Press.

United States Department of Defense. 2005. *National Defense Strategy of the United States of America.* Available: http://www.globalsecurity.org/military/library/policy/dod/d20050318 nds1.pdf.

United States Joint Chiefs of Staff. 2005. *The National Military Strategy of the United States. A Strategy for Today; A Vision for Tomorrow.* Available: http://www.defenselink.mil/news/Mar2005/d20050318nms.pdf.

United States National Security Council. 2002. The *National Security Strategy of the United States of America.* Available: www.whitehouse.gov/nsc/nss.html.

Waever, O. 1995. "Securitization and desecuritization." In *On Security,* R. Lipschutz (ed.), 46–86. New York: Columbia University Press.

Walker, R.B.J. 1993. *Inside/Outside: International Relations as Political Theory.* Cambridge: Cambridge University Press.

White House. 2003. *National Strategy for Combating Terrorism.* Available: http://www.whitehouse.gov/news/releases/2003/02/counter_terrorism/counter_terrorism_strategy.pdf.

Winston, B. 1986. *Misunderstanding Media.* London: Routledge and Kegan Paul.

Wolfers, A. 1952. "Security as an ambiguous symbol." *Political Science Quarterly* 67 (4): 481–502.

Zimbardo, P.G. 2003, November 15. Presentation at the Smithsonian Resident Associate Programme. Available: http://www.vodium.com/MediapodLibrary/library/stanford_psychology/index.asp.

Index

In the series *Discourse Approaches to Politics, Society and Culture* the following titles have been published thus far or are scheduled for publication:

CL

006.
312
024
658
8
BER